A Woman of *Chayil*

Far Above Rubies

(pronounced khah'-yil)

"At His Feet" Series

Book 1

Jane Carole Anderson

A Woman of *Chayil:* Far Above Rubies
At His Feet Series—Book 1

by Jane Carole Anderson
editing by John R. D. Anderson
illustrations, including cover, by Jane Carole Anderson

Bible abbreviations used:

AKJV, American King James Version

ASV, American Standard Version

AMPC, Amplified Bible, Classic Edition

BBE, Bible in Basic English

BSB, Berean Study Bible

GWT, God's Word Translation

HCSB, Holman Christian Standard Bible

ISV, International Standard Version

KJV, King James Version

NASB, New American Standard Bible

NET, New English Translation

NIV, New International Version

NKJV, New King James Version

NLT, New Living Translation

WNT, Weymouth New Testament

YLT, Young's Literal Translation

ISBN 978-0-9769835-4-5

Typographical changes have been made to some Bible verses to fit with the style of this publication.

Protus
Publications
www.TheThreadOfGold.com

DEDICATION

This book is dedicated to my six granddaughters: Sarah, Hannah, Abigail, Claire, Madison, and Naomi. It is my hope and prayer that what they will learn from these pages about their freedom in Christ will be written in their hearts by the Spirit of God, and that each one will become the godly woman she has been called to be. I pray that all of them will be among the great host of women who at the close of the age receive the word God gives and publish it boldly (Psa. 68:11, ASV)—to the shame of God's enemy and to the glory of our Lord and Savior, Jesus Christ.

TABLE OF CONTENTS

MY HEARTFELT THANKS TO ...

My husband, John, for his loving support, his invaluable help in authoring, and his faithful editing.

Lanell Allen, Karen Johnson, and Kay Leatherman for their wonderful friendship and for their combined many years of fellowship and prayer about matters covered in this book. I also thank them for their invaluable content reviews and helpful editing.

Other faithful Christian women I have been privileged to know over the years, for their inspirational stories and testimonies about how God has strengthened them and helped them become women of *chayil*.

My two sons and their wives for six wonderful granddaughters that have been a source of constant inspiration and motivation in the writing of this book.

The Author and Finisher of our faith, Who, by causing all things to work together for good, is the One who is ultimately responsible for this publication and the One I thank most of all.

AT HIS FEET

This book is one in a series entitled, "At His Feet," by Jane Carole Anderson. The series contains some of what Jane has learned sitting at the feet of Jesus with the Bible.

When she was twenty-five years old, Jane had her first experience of God teaching her from His Word. A few years later, she was openly denounced by a Christian leader and told that a woman could not get revelation from the Bible. As a result, she was confused and stopped reading the Bible for a long period of time. After Jesus healed her heart, she began to spend time again—at His feet. What she has learned from His Word is in accord with the following stanza from a hymn:

We limit not the truth of God
To our poor reach of mind,
By notions of our day and sect,
Crude, partial and confined.
Now let a new and better hope
Within our hearts be stirred:
The Lord hath yet more light and truth
To break forth from His word.

— George Rawson (1807–1889)

Readers can, of course, make up their own minds about Jane's inspiration. I think that the insights from the Holy Word of God that Jane has passed on to us in this writing speak well of both her and her teacher.

— John R. D. Anderson

WHAT OTHERS THINK

Jane and I met when we were both young coeds adjusting to university life. My first impression of her was one of amazement—she was actually reading one of the course books she had just purchased from the bookstore, even though classes had not yet begun! In the two years following, I learned what a fun-loving, creative person Jane was. Whether she was writing entertaining skits for her pledge class of our women's service club or supervising the construction of a homecoming parade float, Jane was full of enthusiasm and total focus on the task at hand. She participated in such projects while maintaining grades to earn her a place on the Dean's List. Over the years, I have grown to appreciate how God has blessed Jane with remarkable gifts of perception and application. In turn, her willingness to be transparent and share her experiences has been, and continues to be, a blessing to many people.

In the years that followed the publication of her book, *The Thread of Gold: God's Purpose, the Cross, and Me*, our friendship deepened as we both had life experiences that only the hand of God could have carried us through. Jane continues to be an inspiration as she consistently seeks the Lord and reflects His light to others. I thank her for introducing me to Katharine Bushnell's *God's Word to Women* and allowing me the privilege of seeing firsthand how Jane has gleaned the truths shared in it and the Bible to craft this book, *A Woman of Chayil*, and provide more insight regarding true freedom in Christ for women as well as men.

— Karen Johnson

In *A Woman of Chayil*, Jane has exposed Christian women's sin of staying silent and derelict in their duty in not holding Christian men accountable for ungodly actions. She explains, in biblical terms, that when both men and women are free to willingly submit to each other, they are then able to fully serve God. Anderson has, over the years as a believer in Christ, been tested relentlessly, yet not found wanting. This book contains revelation.

— Catherine B. Carter

I first met Jane in the 1970's when we both were meeting with the church that she wrote about in *The Thread of Gold*. Some years after leaving it, I cautiously reconnected with Jane when I realized she and John had also left that church. Through our growing friendship, I began to recover from those difficult years. Through many hours of fellowship and tears, one thing I learned about Jane: She is a lover of truth. At one time, we had unknowingly abandoned truth—and we got in trouble. Through Jane, I learned that the truth does indeed set us free; that sometimes, the truth hurts; that truth has a "ring"; and that, without truth, our spiritual walk is on shifting sand. I observed in Jane's life that truth doesn't just come our way by accident. We must make a conscious decision to choose truth regardless of the cost—and there is a cost. I'm thankful to the Lord for the blessing Jane has been to me in my life. Together, we have seen God working in unmistakable ways, as only He can, and have on occasion said to one another in awe of Him, "What kind of God is this we have?"

— Lanell Allen

Determined not to waste life's hard lessons, Jane possesses a strong commitment to share the insights she has learned while sitting at her Savior's feet. The revealing of these truths has brought her to a point of unwavering courage, and this truth will drive her legacy. When you meet her, it is evident that she has staked her entire life on the Gospel of Jesus Christ.

— Andi Smith

I've known Jane Anderson for over forty years. We first met in a non-denominational church in Houston, Texas, when our children were young and played together in our apartment complex. What drew me to Jane was her strong love for God and His Word. She has had a great influence on my life over the years by her strong determination to know the Truth and not to compromise with it, and her desire to help others to do the same. Her willingness to persevere to know Christ more deeply in the face of much persecution has been an inspiration to me and a beacon of light for many women facing the darkness of discrimination. I'm grateful to have known her, a pioneer of faith in a time when Christianity has been so terribly compromised. She continues to be a blessing to both men and women who want to know Christ and have a deeper walk with Him.

— Kay Leatherman

Jane Carole Anderson was like a breath of fresh air when we met at a Bible study group in our neighborhood. She clarified some of my thinking and extended some of my knowledge of the Lord and the Bible, both assets from which my subsequent life has benefited. She shared wisdom in the written word as well as her verbal gifts, and we became friends instantly. During the ensuing years, Jane continued to grow as her publication experiences continued. As an author, she shares of herself in much the same manner as I have described. Her warmth draws the reader to her topic while her knowledge of well researched material provides the foundation of her current project which clarifies for us God's intended role for woman as He created her to be. All that is required of us, her readers, is to turn the pages of this text to reveal its contents and to learn about *A Woman of* Chayil. Enjoy your journey.

— Barbara A. Hanner

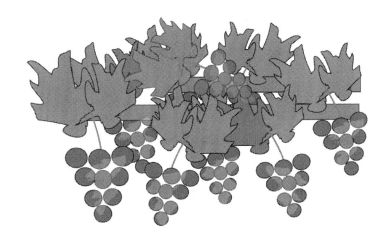

PART ONE:
WOMAN'S DILEMMA

Introduction: The Beginning

> And she had a sister called Mary, who also sat at Jesus' feet, and heard His word. But Martha was distracted with much serving, and she approached him and said, Lord, do you not care that my sister hath left me to serve alone? Therefore, tell her to help me. And Jesus answered and said unto her, Martha, Martha, you are worried and troubled about many things: But one thing is needed: and Mary hath chosen that good part, which will not be taken away from her.
> (Luke 10:39–42, NKJV)

IN MARY'S DAY, WOMEN WERE NOT TAUGHT the Word of God. The Oral Law taught by the Jewish leaders said,

"Let the words of the Law be burned rather than committed to women.... If a man teaches his daughter the Law, it is as though he taught her lewdness" (Sotah 3:4) (Hyatt, *In the Spirit,* 13–14).

Jesus' words and actions made perfectly clear His position concerning such corrupted traditional teaching. Not only did He allow Mary to sit at His feet and hear His words (I suspect He invited her), but He openly commended her for doing so by announcing that she had chosen the good part that would not be taken away from her. He gave her serving sister, Martha, a rebuke—a gentle one—but, nonetheless, a rebuke: "Martha, Martha, you are careful and troubled about many things: but one thing is needed...."

In discussions about this passage in the Bible, I have heard women proclaim that they believed they were "Marthas," not Marys, because God had made them Marthas. They declared that they were best at serving people practically and, therefore, believed that this—not sitting at the feet of Jesus—was their primary calling. I suspect that Jesus gave Martha the same opportunity to sit at His feet as He gave Mary, and that Martha's choice to forego time with Jesus for her domestic acts of service was not due to how God had made her but to her cultural comfort zone.

I have also heard women come to Martha's defense by saying, "Well, someone has to prepare the food!" Martha may well have said something similar. If so, all she needed was a few moments of serious reflection about just who this man was that she had invited into her home, and she might have realized that she could have made it her first choice to sit right alongside Mary and learn at the feet of Jesus. This man was quite capable of handling any food preparation needed, as He demonstrated when he fed thousands from the contents of a little boy's lunch basket.

Most likely, questioning eyes of the opposite gender were watching Mary as she entered the room. It was not an easy thing for her to bypass the kitchen and go and sit down at the feet of Jesus, thus taking the traditional posture of a rabbi's student. She was likely in fear of what her Jewish brothers might think or say about her—and, most of all, what the Jewish leaders would do to correct such a brazen action if they learned about it. She hesitated. Then, she turned and looked into the eyes of Jesus; and, at that moment, she made a bold decision. She walked across the room and took her place at His feet. What tipped her scale from fear to boldness? It was His love for her and hers for Him. He was talking, and she wanted to hear Him. This was an opportunity she would not pass up, no matter what anyone had to say about it, or about her. She sat before Him eagerly attending to every word that came out of His mouth. She would not let one of them slip from her memory. As Jesus said, one thing was needed.

I remember the first time that Jesus invited me to sit at His feet and learn from Him. In the pre-dawn hours of that day, I woke up and felt drawn to get up and go to some place private to read my Bible. I had never done this before. When I looked at the clock and realized that I had only been asleep for about three hours, I hesitated. I had been afflicted for many years with insomnia; and, on this particular night, I had been awake much of the night. Whenever I heard admonishment by others to rise early and spend time with Jesus, I always excused myself, knowing that if I tried to get up early, I would be so tired that I would not be able to make it through the day caring for two small children.

That morning's invitation from Jesus turned out to be a gift from Him that has never stopped giving. His grace, or as Paul described it, "His power resting upon me" (2 Cor. 12:9), somehow helped me up out of my bed that day, before my ever-present excuse got the better of me. An hour or so later, after a two-way conversation with Jesus as I read His Word, I rose up and walked into my day with a new outlook and hope. I felt strong and refreshed. God was with me! The things I read that morning had come alive off the pages. Jesus had talked with me. A short time later, I was greeted by a look of wonder on my husband's face when he entered the kitchen and found me there. He was surprised, first of all, because I was not in bed, and second of all, because I was holding a plate of eggs and toast cooked by me, just for him. Like Paul, I was experiencing the power of Christ resting upon me! As more mornings followed, the things I was hearing and learning from Jesus as I read the Bible were beginning to change me. Most amazingly, my long-term insomnia departed, never to return.

Over the years, many such mornings (or middle of the nights, or whenever He called me) have taken place, and my husband has had more eggs and toast, so to speak. Lest you misunderstand me, let me state plainly that I don't have a perfect sitting-at-the-feet of Jesus record or, for that matter, a perfect eggs-and-toast record either. But, as all who have once sat at His feet know, if you've been there and heard Him speak His words to you, you can never forget it, and you will be back! You will hear Him inviting you to that blessed place time and time again! And, when you don't hear Him calling, you learn to stir yourself up to go look for Him (Isa. 64:7).

The Message of this Book

This book contains some of what I have learned sitting at the feet of Jesus over the years. Foundational to its message is a biblical truth that He has fine tuned for me through many experiences, so I am bringing that truth to the forefront before continuing: *God requires us to do our part in having and maintaining right relationships with others, especially with fellow members in the body of Christ.* His Word requires that believers—whether victims, perpetrators, or witnesses—take biblical steps to remove sins in our relationships (Matt. 5:21–26, 18:15–17). If through disobedience, we allow them to remain, they will hinder God's blessing on the church and also hinder His answers to our prayers (Isa. 59, 1 Pet. 3:7, 12). Such unaddressed sins silently grow and spread like a cancer, interfering with the normal function of the body of Christ and producing spiritual death.

A Woman of Chayil [khah'-yil] takes an in-depth look at a huge, long-term sin in the body of Christ. This hidden spiritual cancer in the church has been growing for almost two millennia in the wrong relationships that exist between Christian women and Christian men. From the early beginnings of the church to the present, the devil has used deceived Christian men to carry out his ancient hatred against women. Christian women have perpetuated their own mistreatment by silently enabling it. Thus, both genders are responsible for grieving the Holy Spirit and frustrating His work on the earth.

Today in many Christian circles, women cannot speak about the topic covered in this book without facing criticism, opposition, and even shaming from those who have historically played a major role in silencing them. For Christian women to break silence and question the validity of their traditionally-defined place in the family of God is, in itself, an act outside the boundaries which have been established for them over many centuries. This sad situation is made even sadder by the fact that many God-fearing Christian women don't even venture to think about the topic, much less pose questions about it, lest they be found guilty by God of questioning what the Bible appears to spell out plainly. I was such a woman until God set me on an unexpected and unsought-after path that, to my great surprise and joy, led me into the discovery in God's Word of the wonderful freedom I, as a woman, had in Christ—freedom that I had no idea was mine.

Let me be clear that I do not consider myself to be a feminist. Rather, I am a free woman in Christ. I have written this book from my perspective as a Christian woman who spent many years in enabling silence, having been subdued and suppressed by numerous Christian men who believed their wrong treatment of me was according to God and His Word. They believed that the Bible they held in their hands supported and even mandated their dominating behavior. Now, with a firm biblical footing in the true freedom I have been given in Christ, I have overcome, to a large degree, my enabling of such men, and I see enabling for what it is: sin. It is fitting that I do my part to help other women recognize this sin and learn how to end their silence and stop enabling the Christian men who sin against them. In this way, they will begin to do their part—that which God requires of them—towards the removal of this deadly spiritual cancer from the body of Christ.

I hope that women who hear the message of this book will come to understand how important it is that they educate themselves and begin, with strength and humility, to speak the truth about God's view of women. As more women wake up and walk in the truth of their freedom in Christ, more men will be blessed and benefit.

An Important Topic for Men Also

I also hope that God will call and anoint more men to study and present the truth about women as it stands in the unadulterated Word of God. (Yes, there are some men who have been awakened to the truth about women— through some efforts of pioneering women. These men have studied it for themselves and given voice to the problem, but their number is relatively small.)

In general, Christian men lack awareness of the fundamental problem that Christian women face. Men cannot relate easily because they have not been overtly hindered and prevented (as Christian women have for centuries) from knowing and experiencing their freedom to follow Christ directly. I have written primarily with a female audience in mind; however, this book's contents are of equal importance for men. I hope that any who read it will keep this one fact in mind: Twenty centuries of history—in which men have not been motivated or inclined to take the initiative to delve into the truth about woman in the Bible—testify that their passive pattern will continue. Without help, men are not going to discover that women's freedom in Christ is no different than their own. With these thoughts in mind, it is not unreasonable to ask that men do their best to give an honest hearing to women who have taken on the task of speaking the truth about what they have discovered in God's Word concerning God's view of woman.

When Christian men and women can begin to acknowledge and correct the part they each play in the perpetuation of this great offense in the body of Christ, the church and the earth will begin to experience a fresh outpouring of spiritual life. There may be a spiritual revival of a magnitude never yet seen. Such a revival is certainly needed in the times in which we live.

May God bless this writing and use it to convict both men and women to repent to God and to one another. May it help Christians find the way to full freedom in Christ in their relationships with each other. May it also help readers consider their deeply entrenched traditional beliefs about women and allow them to be challenged and, hopefully, changed.

Chapter 1
The Bound: Women in Invisible Chains

The Spirit of the Lord GOD [is] upon Me; because the LORD has
anointed Me to preach good tidings unto the poor; He has sent Me
to heal the brokenhearted, to proclaim liberty to the captives, and
the opening of the prison to [those who are] bound;
(Isa. 61:1, NKJV)

God Gets My Attention

IN 2007, ABOUT TWO YEARS AFTER the publication of my
story in the book, *The Thread of Gold: God's Purpose,
the Cross, and Me,* while visiting with my son and his
wife in Washington D. C., a Christian man who was a
friend of my son's and who had just read my book,
approached me with a request. He asked me if I would
read a small book entitled, *The Magna Charta of Woman,*
by Jesse Penn-Lewis. He handed me a copy of the book
and told me he would like very much to hear my thoughts
about it before I returned to Texas. When I handed the
book back to him a few days later, he asked me, "So what
did you think?" I said, "If it were true, it would be
wonderful." He asked me to explain. I said, "In my heart, I
know what she has written is true, but I just don't see in
her book the solid scriptural support that I would need in
order to embrace it as truth." He then pointed out to me
that Penn-Lewis's book was a synopsis of a book by a
nineteenth century woman named Katharine Bushnell
(1847–1956) and encouraged me to get her book and read
it.

At that time, with regards to a Christian woman's
proper place in God's scheme of things, I had not allowed
myself to think about the validity of the generally
accepted norms for Christian women. I was not really
interested in the topic. The truth was that I had found a
way to live and walk with God within boundaries set by
the status quo for fundamental, evangelical, Christian
women, even though I had suffered long-term abusive,
authoritative handling by zealous Christian men. These
men had harshly applied woman-subduing Bible

teachings to me and had deeply wounded me both spiritually and psychologically. Still, I hadn't been moved to the place that I would ask questions. After all, how could I, a good Christian woman, ask such questions? That would be tantamount to questioning God and the Bible. I had learned by experience that, as a Christian woman walking with Jesus, I could bear up under anything by His grace—even the unjust treatment that came my way because I was a woman. I had no thought of rebelling or taking up some kind of feminist banner to right the wrongs I could see or had experienced. In my view, any attempt to right such wrongs would be wrong in itself. If this was a problem that needed solving, it was God's job, not mine. He was certainly infinitely more qualified than I to undertake such a task.

Another period of time passed, and then something else brought the question of women's biblical status to my attention again. I had some further thought about reading Katharine Bushnell's book, but I let it pass. The third time Bushnell's book was brought to my attention, I asked, "Is this You, Lord? Do You want me to read this book?" I had an instant answer in my heart, "Yes." Even though I was not interested in pursuing the topic, God seemed to be interested in my being interested in it.

That day, I found on the Internet *God's Word to Women* in the unabridged version. It took me many months to read it, because I quickly discovered that Ms. Bushnell had an intellect and vocabulary that far surpassed mine. She wasn't a spoon-feeding author. If she referred to a verse (and she referred to many), she typically did not quote it. She expected that the reader knew it or would look it up. The book consisted of one hundred lessons. I put it beside my bed, and each night I read one lesson. I spent time thinking about it and sometimes looked up the Scriptures she referenced.

A Pivotal Moment

A pivotal moment came for me, one which began a transformation of my thought and belief about God's view of woman, on the day I came to the lesson about the meaning and usage of the Hebrew word, *"chayil,"* in the

King James translation of the Old Testament. Bushnell wrote:

> Next we will consider the Hebrew word *cha-yil*, which occurs 242 times in the Old Testament. It is translated "army" and "war" 8 times; "host" and "forces" 43 times; "might" or "power" 16 times; "foods," "riches," "substance" and "wealth" in all 31 times; "band of soldiers," "band of men," "company," and "train" once each; "activity" once; "valour" 28 times; "strength" 11 times: these are all noun forms. The word is often translated as an adjective or adverb. It is translated "valiant" and "valiantly" 35 times: "strong" 6 times; "able" 4 times; "worthily" once and "worthy" once. We have now given you the complete list of the various renderings of this word excepting four instances in which the word is used in describing a woman. Please review the list, and get the usage of the word clearly in mind before proceeding further.

She proceeded to explain the four renderings related to women. In summary, she wrote,

> This Hebrew word, *cha-yil*, used over 200 times in the Hebrew Bible, signifies "force," "strength," "ability." But in every instance where it relates to women, and nowhere else, is it translated "virtue,"—i.e. "chastity." (Bushnell, para. 633)

This was a stunning piece of information to me. Bushnell asserted that the context of these four places made it a stretch to come up with the meaning "virtue" as a translation for the word *chayil*. She could only attribute such a stretch to the gender bias of the translators. The first time she had encountered cultural biases affecting Bible translations was when she was in China working as a medical doctor (Hyatt, *In the Spirit,* 175–176). Regarding the translation of *chayil,* she realized that male translators had simply not been able to bring themselves to use its obvious meanings (force, strength, ability) when this word was used in the Bible to refer to women (Bushnell, paras. 625–633).

Bushnell was able to clearly demonstrate the presence of gender bias in all four of these woman passages by comparing the King James Bible translations of the four passages to their much earlier translations in the Septuagint (the Old Testament in Greek):

Instance #1: Ruth 3:11

- Thou art a virtuous *[chayil]* woman (KJV)

- Thou art a woman of power *[chayil]* (Septuagint)

Instance #2: Proverbs 31:10

- Who can find a virtuous *[chayil]* woman? for her price is far above rubies (KJV)

- A masculine *[chayil]* woman ... more valuable is she than very costly stones (Septuagint)

Instance #3: Proverbs 31:29

- Many daughters have done virtuously [adverb for *chayil*], but thou excellest them all (KJV)

- Many daughters have obtained wealth, many have wrought valiantly; but thou hast exceeded, thou hast surpassed all (Septuagint)

Instance #4: Proverbs 12:4

- A virtuous *[chayil]* woman is a crown to her husband (KJV)

- A masculine *[chayil]* woman is a crown to her husband (Septuagint) (Bushnell, paras. 625–631)

The Septuagint translation of Proverbs 31:29, "many daughters have obtained wealth, many have wrought valiantly," is striking when compared with the King James Version which says "many daughters have done virtuously." The King James translators could easily have used one of the stronger meanings of *chayil*. Boaz described Ruth as a woman of *chayil* (Ruth 3:11) right after she proposed to him! She boldly did what a near male kinsman should have done for Naomi, and God greatly blessed her for it. She not only obtained wealth for herself and Naomi, she even became a great, great, great ... grandmother of Jesus. The Septuagint reflects this by the translation, a "woman of power." The King James' use of "virtuously," does not convey this meaning (Bushnell, para. 625).

I soon learned that Bushnell's discovery about the translation of the word, *"chayil,"* in passages about women, was only one of her numerous research findings. Her studies uncovered the role that innate male bias had played in the translations of a number of verses that pertain to women. She also showed how such mistranslations were at the root of the errant biblical beliefs about women that have existed in the minds of men and women alike for many centuries. She pointed out that, just as these beliefs have had a long-term, detrimental impact on women in the body of Christ, freedom from them would bring great healing in the body of Christ to both women and men and their families. It would also remove a massive hindrance to the mighty working of the Spirit of God on the earth.

Not a Second-class Citizen

It took me approximately one hundred days to read all of Bushnell's lessons. Not long after finishing, while resting one afternoon and thinking about all I had learned, I realized that something had happened to me: I had been set free. I felt an incredible peace and joy and thankfulness to God for continuing to point me to her writing. I thanked Him tearfully for not giving up on me and for leading me by the light of His Word to a place where I was free from a psychological bondage that I had lived in for many years without even knowing it. It was plain to me that God had wanted me to know and be able to experience the full freedom that I have as a female believer in Christ. I am not a second-class citizen in the kingdom of heaven. I am a bona fide child of the king, a new creation in Christ, in the same way as my Christian brothers.

God put Katharine Bushnell's book in my hand at a perfect moment in time—in the latter years of my life. The stage had been set with several decades of experiences as a Christian woman that prepared me to read and understand it. He used her book to set me free from invisible chains that were as much a part of me as my flesh and bones. Not only was I free, I understood that I was called to be a woman of *chayil*.

On the day I realized that my invisible chains were gone, I heard God's still, small voice in my heart saying with respect to Katharine's book, "Read it again." So, I began again my bedtime reading habit. This time, as I read through her book, the heavens seemed to swing open to me. Parts of the book were so enlightening and helpful that I determined I needed to carefully study the Scriptures and learn to articulate the truth about them myself. In particular, I needed to study the truth about the few biblical passages (one in the Old Testament and seven in the New Testament) that are the main sources of confusion about this topic. Also, as I studied some passages in depth, such as Genesis chapter three, God began to show me their applicability to our most basic human relationships: husbands and wives, parents and children, fathers and sons, God and man.

In the years that followed, I became convinced that God's concept of woman was strikingly different from mine, and also from that of most evangelical Christian women that I knew. I told a number of other evangelical women about Katharine Bushnell's book. I hoped that they, too, would walk through the Bible with her help and learn for themselves the truth about God's view of women. I soon discovered, however, that although most women to whom I talked were interested in the topic, few of them were successful in reading all of Bushnell's scholarly presentation.

A Woman of Chayil was born out of my desire to present, in an easier to read form, the inspirational essence of Bushnell's work along with some of the basic biblical support she gave for her findings. In the process, I wrote about some further realizations that God had given me which built upon her labors. Any who are helped by my presentation and want to find more biblical support for Bushnell's findings should read or refer to her book, *God's Word to Women*. (Although there is an abridged version available on the Internet, I recommend the original work. Both can be found at www.godswordtowomen.org).

I believe that God introduced me to Katharine Bushnell and her final life's work because He wanted me to be free to follow Him where He wanted to lead me, and He wanted me to be able to choose to do so without fear. He wanted me to go forward with boldness on the path He had planned for me. He knew I would be hard pressed to do so if I was not able to understand, resolve, and speak about what is true concerning His view of women and their role in His redemptive plan. Through God's love, faithfulness, and longsuffering with me, my thought about how God sees woman has been transformed. Not only that, I have had a corresponding transformation in my thought about how God sees men. Redeemed men and women together, according to the Bible, are the bride of Christ, a woman who is nothing less than a woman of *chayil.*

Others Who Are Like Me

There are many other women today who are, as I was—yielded and voiceless. Like me, they have never heard the topic of woman's biblical status mentioned as a matter worthy of inquiry, discussion, and biblical study. Ironically, those who have the greatest need for a fresh examination of the topic and its roots—Christian women—sit bound in silence by centuries-old traditions resulting from translations of the Bible by Christian men. Thus, many women are held in their "proper place" of secondary status to their male counterparts by chains they cannot see. Widely held, deeply-rooted cultural and religious beliefs regarding the role and place of Christian women make it virtually impossible for women to raise the topic for discussion with their male brethren. Just to ask questions, they must find the courage to go against traditions that prohibit them from asking questions! Not many Christian women are willing to move this far outside their comfort zones.

Woman's dilemma is not a simple one. In general, there are two primary views held in Christendom about women: complementarian and egalitarian. I will comment a little on these views in this book; however, I mainly share what I have learned as a greatly-blessed Christian woman who has been led by God safely through many difficult life experiences. At times, I felt like I was walking through a field of land mines that were planted by the devil to stop my forward progress. My observations are limited to that with which I am familiar—the status of evangelical, fundamental, Christian women. I find most of these to be wearing invisible chains, just as I was. The religious culture in which such women seek to serve Christ hinders them from being the persons that Christ has called and gifted them to be. It frustrates them from walking in all the good works that Christ planned for them (Eph. 2:10). They are bound by their inculcated beliefs. If any of them begin to believe that God is calling them to venture outside the typical roles afforded them in evangelical circles, and do so, they will find themselves with a problem: On one hand, they will find God's full acceptance and fellowship; on the other, they may find themselves under attack by fellow believers who evaluate them in the light of the traditional beliefs about women. They will have to wrestle with unwarranted doubt, anger, fear, shame, and guilt as a result.

A Curiosity

If I ask a group of evangelical women to raise their hands if they feel hindered as women by their Christian beliefs, few, if any, hands will go up. My question might even anger some. Why? Because, as I was, they are blind to the chains they are wearing. After all, they are born-again; and, they believe, as they have been told, that they are free in Christ. However, we should remember that Paul warned the Galatians that it was possible, as a believer, to be entangled in a yoke of bondage. It is not easy to see psychological chains that have been put in place by religious culture.

As the book of Galatians shows us, Judaizers of the apostle Paul's day—Jewish Christians with an agenda to preserve Judaism—were quick to carry their religious cultural chains into the early church and to work diligently to put the chains back on the Jewish believers in Christ, ones who had believed in and been set free by Christ's death and resurrection. The Galatians didn't realize what was happening to them, so Paul had to give them a strong warning to stand fast in the freedom to which Christ had called them. What the devil began to sow through the Judaizers in the early days of the church has sprouted and grown throughout Christian history. For most of my life, I wore psychological chains that resulted from ancient teachings sown by these Judaizers. The chains fell off when Christ came and opened the eyes of this captive woman, showed me in the Bible the liberty that He had already given me, and strengthened me to stand up and walk in it.

If I ask this same group of evangelical women if they can study the Bible and present a message to others from what they read, most will say no, with the exception that a few will say they can do so with children in Sunday school classes or possibly with some other Christian women. They might respond that preparing and giving messages from the Bible is not their job. They may explain how they consider themselves to be unqualified because they are female. They may say that God would not approve of such behavior; and, on top of all this, they might confide in me that they really do not want to do so.

If I ask them if God has ever revealed something new directly to them from their reading of the Bible, something that had a life-changing effect on them and others around them, again many will say no. If I ask them if they love the Bible and read or study it every day, some will say yes, and some will tell me that they still must be careful to learn about the Bible from persons who have the proper seminary degrees and really know the Bible, such as their preacher, a well-known evangelist, or a recognized and sanctioned Christian author. They will clarify that it is not their place to try to understand the Bible by themselves. They might express their fear of becoming deceived, saying that, after all, when Eve, a woman, repeated the words of God to the serpent, she got them wrong, and, furthermore, when she believed what he told her, she took a step that led the human race down a path of destruction.

I am sure there are some evangelical, fundamental, Christian women who are exceptions to the categories I am describing. Nevertheless, I believe such questions as these might benefit the remaining majority if they were asked to answer them. Maybe they would cause some women's mental wheels to begin turning, evaluating just where they *do* fit as women. This kind of thought-cart doesn't begin to move without some think-about-a-taboo-topic grease being put on its rusted axles.

If I ask for those in the same group of women to raise their hands if their husbands are Christians, many hands will go up. If I ask them to keep their hands up if they are godly, self-sacrificing men whose norm is to show their wives great honor, put them before themselves, always give up what they want for their wives' benefit, care for others before themselves, and show respect for their wives' insights from the Bible, I will be fanned by the breeze created as hands go quickly down. If I ask them to raise their hands if they believe that they have played any role in their ungodly Christian husbands' conditions, most hands will stay down.

Then finally, if I ask them if they know what to do to help their husbands become godly men, as previously described, other than pray for them and behave as good Christians should, there will probably be no hands. If I ask them if they believe their husbands could ever be truly godly men, most hands will rest in their laps, folded together, thus casting their votes with my mother, whose words and way of living with her husband, my father, taught me that you cannot do anything to help a man change—you just have to learn to suffer and live with him. Many times she admonished me, "You cannot do anything to change your father, so don't try."

Also, among this group of women, there would be divorced women and single women. I have not presented hypothetical questions to them, but if I did, their situation would also be exposed as one of confusion and silent suffering. A friend who is a single Christian woman expressed to me her feeling of almost being a non-person in the Christian world because she never married. This stigma followed her everywhere, even into the secular world. Husbands were so much a part of the definition of a Christian woman's role that she found herself basically undefined as a female believer. Where did she fit? She was not going to be saved by childbearing, as one verse in the Bible seems to indicate. Was she to submit to every male in her life because of their gender? To whom was she to ask her questions at home, as another verse indicates that women should do? (I reminded my friend that Katharine Bushnell was a single woman whom God used greatly, and that if she had been a married woman, she might have been hindered from writing her groundbreaking book!)

I suspect that if I actually carried out this kind of questioning, I would hear the kind of hypothetical responses I have just described. They would expose invisible chains, chains that God never intended for woman or for man. Satan has forged these chains in darkness, put them on his human victims, and used them to weaken individuals, marriages, and families. He has used them to isolate and afflict unmarried women and to pull marriages and families apart and destroy them. As the family crumbles, so does society. If society is to survive the works of the devil, then the understanding about God's view of gender roles and responsibilities needs a major overhaul—one that removes the chains.

Jesus said, "You shall know the truth and the truth shall set you free" (John 8:32). People need to see and embrace the truth about what the Bible has to say about women, about men, and about their relationships in marriage and family. This truth needs to be clearly articulated today, by all means—from pulpit preaching to Internet posting. The message itself needs to be so clear and compelling that it will become a broad cultural topic. Only such a truth-overhaul has the power to halt the destructive societal forces that have been set in motion by false beliefs and teachings rooted in the poor translations and interpretations of a very small number of Bible verses. Only such a truth-overhaul has the power to produce functional, flourishing, and society-building families.

Recently, I had a long visit with a childhood friend, whom I had not seen in twenty-five years, and two of her adult daughters. As I listened to my friend talk about her husband, I realized she had been blessed with what I call an Ephesians 5 husband. He was a godly Christian man who loved his wife with the self-sacrificing love of Christ and, likewise, cared for his children. He was definitely not a lording-it-over Christian husband. As I listened to both the daughters tell the story of how God led them to their husbands, the role that their father had played in his daughters' choice of husbands was evident. They both had wanted, expected, waited for, and had found godly husbands like their father. What he had modeled for them, as their father and as their mother's husband, had served as a strong deterrent to their making bad choices for mates. The very good news that this conveys is that, just as dysfunctional families tend to replicate, so do truly godly families.

Some Chain-rattling Truth

The biblical case for woman's freedom is not precariously balanced on a few toothpick Scriptures. It rests solidly on a biblical foundation made up of strong pillar verses. The Bible shows that when God made woman, He made her free, just as he made man free. He gave both Adam and Eve the freedom and power to make choices. He wanted them to believe His words and willingly obey Him and walk with Him, but He did not bind or coerce them into an obedient, subservient relationship to Him. Rather, He told them the truth, and He offered them the opportunity to choose to live and walk with Him in that truth—or not. Such is the character of God. Adam and Eve, under the temptation of the devil, exercised their God-given freedom and made their well-known, fatal choices—Eve first, and then Adam. The consequence was that they and their progeny became the devil's slaves. Such is the dominating character of the devil.

Immediately after their fall, God extended hope to Adam and Eve with the promise that the seed of woman would bruise the head of the serpent. The whole Bible tells the story of the fulfillment of that promise. The Bible also reveals that ultimately, Christ came through a free woman, Mary. She gave her willing assent to carry the child Jesus in her womb when she responded, "Be it unto me according to thy word" (Luke 1:38). Paul pointed to the absolute necessity of woman's freedom in the fulfillment of God's promise when he wrote, "Now we, brethren, as Isaac was, are the children of promise" and "... brethren, we are not children of the bondwoman, but of the free" (Gal. 4:28, 31). He was referring to Sarah, a free woman who was the mother of the promised seed, Isaac, and to Hagar, a bondwoman, who was the mother of Ishmael. Isaac was the son who was acceptable to God, the one who was born of a free woman.

After hearing God's pronouncement in the Garden of Eden, the serpent hated the woman and feared the promised seed who was to come from her. Knowing that God's way was to interact with beings who were free to choose, Satan began his further deceptive work behind the scenes to bring women into a state of bondage so they could not bring forth the promised seed. Over the centuries, he has used male human beings, whom he has brought into bondage, to misuse Scripture in such a way as to bring about the oppression of women. His first attack, in the Garden of Eden, was by recasting God's words, and so he has continued. His goal was, and still is, to frustrate the fulfillment of God's promise that the seed of woman would bruise his head.

The following statements bring into focus the false belief system that the devil has succeeded in producing through his subtle misuse of Scripture. I am giving these statements in summary fashion at the outset of this book, so as to not leave you wondering what I have come to believe about the Bible's view of woman. These statements may rattle the chains of male and female alike. So, if any statement stumbles you, please right yourself and read on. You will find biblical support for all of these statements in the coming chapters. If you began your reading of this book wearing invisible chains, I pray that when you finish it, you will find yourself as I did after reading Bushnell's book—chainless. Here is a summary of the biblically supportable truth I am going to present in the rest of this book:

1. The Bible does not hold Eve (or womankind) responsible for the entry of sin into the world and the Fall of mankind. Rather, it holds Adam responsible for the entry of sin and the Fall of mankind.

2. The Bible does not teach that, in the Garden of Eden after the Fall, in order to punish her for her sin, God cursed woman with pain in childbearing and put her under the rule of her husband. The truth is that God blessed woman in the Garden of Eden, promising that, even though it would be through great suffering, woman would bring forth the seed who would defeat the devil. (God only cursed two things: the ground and the serpent.)

3. God did not ordain that woman would be ruled over by her husband, but warned her that if she decided to turn away from God to her husband and look to him as the one to meet her needs, her decision would result in her putting herself in a position that her husband would rule over her.

4. The Old Testament law does not require the silence of women. Nowhere in the Old Testament law are women forbidden to speak. On the contrary, there were women prophetesses in the Old Testament who were greatly respected by men as people who spoke for God.

5. Paul allowed women to speak in church. The Judaizers of his day were upset about this because they practiced the traditional Oral Law (today's Talmud), which came into being during the four hundred years between the Old and New Testament periods. When the Judaizers opposed the idea of women speaking in the church, Paul stood up to them strongly in order to correct them. Paul himself ministered with women, and there is record in the New Testament of women teaching men.

6. Church leaders, who were involved in the canonization of Scripture (second and third centuries), came under the strong influence of the Talmudic beliefs when they asked Jewish rabbis for help with the Hebrew language. (The rabbis' help was sought because, by that time, Hebrew had become almost a dead language.) Poor translations and subsequent misinterpretations of Paul's words about women were a byproduct of the interaction between the Talmudic rabbis and the canonizers of the Bible.

7. The Bible does not prohibit women from teaching men. Paul's warning about women teaching was not intended to be a dictate for all women in all times, but was written in a private letter to Timothy advising him about the state of affairs in the church in Ephesus. If the interpretation methodology that has been used concerning what Paul wrote to Timothy about women was applied to some things that Paul wrote about men in other letters, then men might find themselves being told that they should not marry, because Paul said he would that all men were as he was, that is, single.

8. The Bible does not teach that man is the head of woman (her lord, authority, or dominating ruler) and that she is mandated to submit to him without question. The only supposed Old Testament support for this belief is Genesis 3:16; however, the phrase, "shall rule over her," in that verse is not imperative but indicative. This means that it is not a command but, rather, a statement of fact of what would happen to woman if she chose to look to her husband instead of God to meet all her needs. There are only two passages in the New Testament that appear to teach that man has authority over woman, and both can be shown to be mistranslations or misinterpretations.

9. The word in the King James Version (KJV) that is translated "power" in 1st Corinthians 11:10 means "authority" in Greek. This word has been translated in different ways, but the proper understanding is that a woman's head is under her own authority. Her ultimate submission is to Christ alone, and it is given willingly. Her willing submission is also to her husband and to other believers in general. Christ teaches willing and mutual submission among all God's children, as long as such submission does not require violation of God's word. She is free to choose to submit, just as Christ was free to choose to submit to His Father's will in the Garden of Gethsemane. The Bible does not teach that women are spiritually and psychologically inferior to men but, rather, that they are only weaker physically. Nor does it teach that women's duty and purpose is only domestic and not

spiritual. Spiritual and intellectual capability is not a matter of gender but of God's gifting. Jesus said that Mary had chosen the good part, to sit at His feet (along with men) and be taught directly by Him. He said this would not be taken away from her. This action was in sharp contrast to the Jewish custom of the day which did not allow women to be taught God's Word at all.

10. The Bible does not teach that women are saved by the suffering that takes place at the time of physical childbirth, as 1st Timothy 2:15 appears to say. If so, then women who do not have children could not be saved! It does teach that they are delivered from the devil by bringing forth godly male seed, according to the promise in the Garden of Eden after the Fall.

11. The Bible does not teach that women are responsible for men's lusting after them and that, therefore, they should be covered or veiled as the Talmud says. It does, however, encourage women to dress modestly. Men are responsible for their own lust. The Bible states that if your eye causes you to sin that you should pluck it out.

12. The New Testament shows that Jesus held women in high regard. He gave the first gospel message to a woman and sent her to proclaim it to men. He also had female disciples who traveled with Him. (Luke 8:1–3 dispels the notion that Jesus had only male disciples.) It also shows that Paul held women in similar high regard.

This list is not all-inclusive, but it is sufficient for the time being. In summary, by His death and resurrection, Christ has set women free from oppressive, devil-produced cultural norms. He has set them free to obey Him and follow Him, just as he has set men free to do likewise. Each woman is accountable directly to Christ and has not been put in a position of forced submission to an authoritarian male intermediary. The devil hates and fears woman because of God's promise concerning her seed.

The truth is that women can experience a fresh anointing and revelation when reading or meditating on the words of the Bible, the same as men can. They can make their own decision to follow and obey Christ. The prayer of the psalmist, "Order my steps in thy word ..." (Psa. 119:133), can be prayed by women as well as men. When John wrote, "the same anointing teaches you of all things and is truth ..." (1 John 2:27), he was writing to women as well as men.

Whenever men and women turn their hearts to the Lord and seek to know the truth concerning God's view of woman, He will set them free by removing dark veils of wrong teaching and thinking. He will lead them to true repentance from wrong and unhealthy gender-based beliefs and practices. Wherever a situation of mutual freedom, respect, and willing submission to God and to one another is found among Christian men and women, *there will be a fresh, ongoing, outpouring of the Spirit and undeniable evidence of God's manifest blessing. Devil-binding and people-releasing prayers will be answered!*

God's Woman of Chayil

What did God have in mind when He portrayed His redeemed ones as a woman, the bride of Christ? Christians today are familiar with the concept of the "bride of Christ," but do they realize that the bride of Christ is no ordinary woman, that she does not fit the mold of what we typically consider to be female?

We know that she is composed of all those who are redeemed by faith in Christ, both male and female, but what will she look like? Will she be reticent, quiet, plainly appareled, and purposefully inconspicuous? Will she have no idea or thought of her own? Will she never venture to interpret God's Word for herself? Will she make no decision? Will she stand in the shadows watching for the slightest beckoning of her husband, ready to meet His every need and bow in absolute, unthinking submission to His every request? Will she fade into the background while He stands front and center receiving glory and praise from all around Him? Will she work behind the scenes doing menial tasks with a joyful, song-filled heart so that He can carry out God's kingdom business? Will she rejoice to have no personhood of her own, having abandoned herself so completely that she functions only as a faded backdrop for the glory of her husband?

Some of these characteristics are worthy ones that should belong to God's redeemed people when in proper relationship to Christ; but, is there anything about God's idea of woman that we have missed or misunderstood? Do the characteristics of the bride of Christ differ from, or go beyond, those we commonly consider as belonging to the female? I believe they do. I believe that her characteristics are different and that they go far beyond what we typically understand as female!

Paul says, "Therefore, if any man is in Christ, he is a new creature, old things are passed away, behold all things are become new" (2 Cor. 5:17). He also says that in Christ "there is neither male nor female" (Gal. 3:28). Interestingly, even though this verse plainly says there is *neither* "male nor female," because of what I observed and experienced as a woman in Christian community, I always understood it to mean "in Christ there is no female, only male." In the church, males were in the forefront, and females were in the background, mostly serving silently, learning from men and never teaching them, obeying them and never questioning them. Females were only the help staff of males, and males made sure that females maintained their subservient place and did not open the door to the devil as Eve had done.

But, Galatians 3:28 does not only say that there is no female; it also says there is no male. There is *neither male nor female*. It says that in Christ there is a new creation; and, even more interestingly, the Bible does not view or portray this new creation, the church, as a male but, rather, as a female! God sees the church as a woman, an extraordinary woman—the bride of Christ who, as this book will show, is a woman of *chayil*. She is made up of extraordinary believers who look just like her, all of whom, male and female, are new-creation beings free in Christ. Together, they are God's woman, the bride of Christ—God's woman of *chayil*.

Chapter 2

The Bunch: "Lemons" in a Vineyard of "Grapes"

I N THE BIBLE, THERE ARE A SMALL NUMBER of familiar passages that are at the root of wrong beliefs about women and authority. These few verses exist like one bunch of "lemons" hanging on a grapevine in a Biblical vineyard laden with many "grapes."

Satan is behind the production of these lemon translations, translations which have adulterated and corrupted the real meanings of God's words. It is time for men and women alike to stand up and speak the truth as Paul did when he said:

1 Therefore, since we have this ministry, as we received mercy, we do not lose heart, 2 but we have renounced the things hidden because of shame, not walking in craftiness or adulterating the word of God, but by the manifestation of truth commending ourselves to every man's conscience in the sight of God. (2 Cor. 4:1–2, NASB)

There is one big lemon translation in the Old Testament: Genesis 3:16. There are seven lemon translations in the New Testament: 1st Corinthians 11:2–16; 1st Corinthians 14:29–40, Ephesians 5:22–24, Colossians 3:18, 1st Timothy 2:8–15, Titus 2:3–5, and 1st Peter 3:1–2.

There were no female members on early Bible translation committees, so it was easy for Satan to use innate male bias to influence the translations of verses that pertained to women's roles. Historically, females have not been afforded the same access to education as males; so, even if men had desired the presence and input of women on their translation committees, at the time the Bible was being translated, there was no pool of women Bible scholars from which to select. Regardless of the reason why women were absent from translation committees, the simple fact remains: The female voice and perspective were not present in Bible translation efforts. Females would have been able to recognize and challenge any translations pertaining to women that displayed male bias. The absence of female input provides a rational explanation for why seven somewhat difficult to translate and interpret Bible passages in the New Testament stand out as anomalies among the more numerous grape passages.[1]

---

[1] Numerous other verses are sprinkled throughout the Bible which reference women, and Bushnell proves that these have been influenced by gender bias in translation. Bushnell says, referring to such verses showing male bias, "These instances are trivial, when taken one by one, but many straws floating in one direction prove that the current runs that way strongly" (p. 277). The overall effect of such translations was the cumulative development of wrong thinking and teaching about women.

The message of the seven lemon translations is diametrically opposed to the message of the grape passages. Unfortunately, the lemon translations have become the best known Bible passages about women, and their wrong message is dominant in the church. The lemon translations bear responsibility for much of the demeaning psychological, and even physical, abuse of women throughout the centuries. They have been used by people who claim to love and serve Christ and by non-Christians alike to justify the suppression of women. They have been used to sanction and even to mandate hierarchical control of some believers by other believers. As a result, some members of the body of Christ are in bondage to other members, and Christian wives are held in bondage to the dominating control of their husbands. The kind of control exercised in such cases is not true authority. It does not correspond with God's nature and His ways but with the devil's nature and his ways. The bad fruit that is produced reveals the source of the lemon translations.

But Lemons Are Prescriptive

Some may argue that the seven New Testament lemon translations are, and should be, dominant because they are prescriptive passages, not descriptive like most of the grape passages. A general principle of Bible teaching is to teach what the Bible teaches or prescribes about behavior, and not to teach authoritatively about what can only be observed about behaviors of people in the Bible. I will not argue this point, but will say strongly that whatever is taught prescriptively should produce what is seen descriptively in the Bible. If a teaching produces something different than what the Bible illustrates or describes as proper behavior, it is unhealthy teaching and should be questioned and re-examined.

The seven lemon translations in question have not produced behavior that matches the grape passages in the Bible. They have produced the contrary. This one fact tells us that there is something seriously wrong with the understanding and use of the lemon passages. They are misfits in the overall picture, and they produce very bad fruit (by their fruits you shall know them [Matt. 7:20]). They are responsible for a huge sin-wound in the body of Christ which has rendered the church weak and ineffective in prayer. Many born-again believers think they are serving God; but, as they live and practice the errant message of the lemon translations, they are behaving in a way that is not at all in line with the nature and character of God. The Bible says that as a man thinks in his heart, so he is (Prov. 23:7, KJV). Satan has masterfully made use of wrong translations to construct a belief system that has fueled and supported women's dilemma, men's dilemma, and society's dilemma. The fact that these passages exist as they do today is testament to the success of the devil's long-term plan of deception. We are in a time in which truth must prevail and bring a much needed wave of repentance that will catapult the church into a strong position of righteousness from which to engage in devil-stopping spiritual warfare!

Fertilizer for Feminism

The lemon translations played a significant role in germinating the nineteenth century's feminist movement. The ideas set forth in these passages provided fertile soil in which feminism grew. If the truth of the freedom given to women in Christ had not become obscured by the misunderstanding, misuse, and dominance of the lemon translations, the destructive effects of ungodly feminism would probably not be twining everywhere in society today like kudzu vines.

In the beginning of the 19th century's feminist movement, some intelligent, truth-seeking Christian women began to question a God whose word appeared to support and promote the suffering and subjugation of women. Susan B. Anthony, a Quaker, was molded by the Quaker's atypical belief that men and women were equal. Her Quaker upbringing was responsible for propelling her into her lifelong quest to obtain equal rights for women.[2] She began a movement of women who sought equal rights for women in a society that was built on the premise that all men were created equal by God.

Unfortunately, these women found their chief opponents to be the clergy of the day.

_____

[2] Quakers let women preach equally with men. This was unheard of elsewhere during the 1800s. When Anthony tried to speak in public at a temperance meeting, she was told she was a sister and was there to listen and learn only. This lit a fire in her that never went out as she spent her whole life seeking to gain equal rights for women. She also believed, as a Quaker, that girls should be educated equally with boys. She wanted to learn math in her school, but the instructor said there was no reason for this. She was despised by many in the early years of her struggle for women and wrote about how painful this was, but she had strong faith and pressed on throughout her life, joining with Elizabeth Cady Stanton, who wrote Anthony's speeches. She became one of the most well known people of her day. She had tea with the queen of England and was invited to the White House regularly. Near the end of her life, she met with Theodore Roosevelt, who was famous for saying "a square deal for all," but he had been quiet on the matter of women's rights. Anthony asked him to take action about women's rights and leave it as part of his legacy. He gave a polite but vague answer and did nothing (Bio).

_____

Some women during that time, one of whom was Elizabeth Cady Stanton, found that they could not reconcile their belief in the freedom of individuals with the state of woman (bondage) that was produced by the teachings of the Bible and the church. Thus, they concluded that the Bible's suppressive teachings about woman disqualified it from being the inspired word of God. Therefore, the oppression of women in society and women's reaction to it is directly tied to the lemon translations. Stanton and others blamed this state of affairs on men. Unfortunately, aided by the serpent, they reached the wrong conclusion. Stanton and others worked together to write a highly controversial book in their day, *The Woman's Bible,* which, without a solid basis in scholarly research, appears to distort some of the contents of the Bible.

Women in the feminist movement were eventually able to obtain a measure of secular freedom for women, but unfortunately, the movement that they birthed also set women on a long-term path that was free from the governance of God—the only One who offered them true freedom. Waves of the feminist movement in the twentieth century became openly anti-God and paved the way for other ungodly gender-based movements. Such movements have produced unanticipated and undesirable consequences for the family unit and society at large, creating a situation of ever-increasing bondage to the enemy of God, who thrives wherever the Word of God is rejected.

The lemon translations continue to give reason for many modern-day women to line up with the causes of secular feminists and other gender-based movements that are clamoring for equality—while practicing intolerance. The lemon translations are also responsible for hiding from Christian men the message about women found in the grape passages. That message shows how men should treat women, and vice versa, and it lines up perfectly with the example observable in both Christ's life and death.

Translators' Responsibility: To Turn Lemons into Grapes

The time has come for translators to turn lemons into grapes! How can this happen? Biblical scholars involved in translating the Bible need to recognize the seriousness of the problem caused by questionable translations and subsequent faulty interpretations of a few verses. Bible translators need to devote adequate time and effort to re-evaluate what the Bible says about God's view of women, and also what it says about men with respect to women.

The purpose of this book is to turn a bright light on the small number of misfit lemon translations in the Bible, which are nothing less than devil-influenced translations. These simply cannot be allowed to remain, especially when they already have been successfully challenged, tested, and found faulty by educated women who began serious language investigations in the mid-nineteenth century and also now by an increasing number of men and women who have done likewise.

Some argue that current translations of these verses are sanctioned by God because He would not have allowed the devil to misrepresent His words. A Christian man once told me that he had the assurance that the Bible translation that he used daily was the one translation that was the very Word of God, because God would not have put a Bible translation in his hand that was not perfectly accurate! I have heard others say it is dangerous to question Bible translations because this is to question God's sovereignty; and, if the translation of one verse is questioned, the door will be opened for all verses to be questioned.

These arguments may sound reasonable to some; however, some things in the Bible show that such reasoning is faulty. For one, when the devil spoke to Eve, he re-interpreted the words that God had spoken in order to give them another meaning (Gen. 3:4–5). God did not prevent him from doing this. For another, Jeremiah wrote:

> 7b But My people do not know
> The ordinance of the LORD.
>
> 8 "How can you say, 'We are wise,
> And the law of the LORD is with us'?
> But behold, the lying pen of the scribes
> Has made [it] into a lie. (Jer. 8:7b–8, NASB)

Jeremiah realized that some scribes had changed the meaning of some Scriptures so that they were not true to God's meaning but were a lie. God did not prevent the scribes from doing this, but He did show Jeremiah that this had happened. Since the devil is the father of lies, we can see his handiwork in the lying pen of the scribes. As the father of lies, he is a master at misusing and misrepresenting truth. In the wilderness temptation, Satan misapplied the meaning of God's words from Psalm 91 by using a quote from it to tempt Christ. Christ rebuffed his misuse with another Scripture (Matt. 4:5–7). Christian men and women today must be able to do likewise.

When the validity of a translation is called into question, it is important to carefully study the Word of God using its original languages (Hebrew, Aramaic, and Greek) to resolve the question. The Word of God is infallible, but because of the devil's subtle workings, translations and translators are not. Translations of the Bible were necessary because they brought God's word into the hands of people who spoke different languages. However, at the same time, they afforded the devil opportunity to use men to introduce wrong ideas into the Bible in such a way that they appeared to be God's thoughts, when they were not.

Bushnell says concerning the validity of re-examining translations:

> We have called attention to some of these misinterpretations, as well as mistranslations of the Bible, as to women. But a certain type of mind is sure to reason: "What am I to believe, then? And *whom* am I to believe?"—as though it were ever intended that our faith should rest in human beings,—uninspired, as these translators are, as well! Let us hope, however, that the majority of those who will read these Lessons will rather say, "We must never rest until we have seen to it that a sufficiently large number of young women are kept in training in the sacred languages, so that women can always command a hearing, as to the precise meaning of such passages in the Bible as relate to the interests of women specially. Thus only will women's temporal and spiritual interests receive their due consideration." Better, *far better,* that we should doubt every translator of the Bible than to doubt the inspiration of St. Paul's utterances about women; and the justice of God towards women: or, above all, to doubt that "Christ hath redeemed us" (women) "from the curse of the law" (Galatians 3:13). (Bushnell, para. 371)

Rational, objective, and careful readers of the Bible would agree that, at the very least, Bible translators should openly acknowledge this fact: The lemon translations carry a message about women that is the antithesis of the message conveyed by the grape passages. It is incumbent upon translators to carefully study this problem and do their best to explain the contradictions. When they discover that it is next to impossible to justify the lemon translations in the context of the whole Bible, they should completely re-evaluate them with the help of educated women and men who already have studied these passages in their original languages.

The co-existence of contradictory messages about women in the Bible is completely unacceptable. God is not the author of such confusion. The antithetical state of affairs caused by the simultaneous existence of both lemon and grape passages casts aspersions on God and offers reasons to doubt the validity of the Bible.

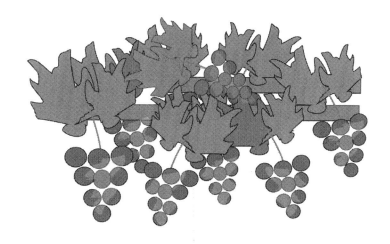

PART TWO:
THE OLD TESTAMENT ERA

Chapter 3
The Big Lemon: Genesis 3:16

THE BIG LEMON IN THE OLD TESTAMENT is the translation of Genesis 3:16 as it appears in current Bibles. This mistranslated and, therefore, misunderstood verse exists as a foundational building block in Satan's strategy against mankind and, in particular, in his strategy against women. It is the Old Testament base upon which the lemon translations in the New Testament rest. In order to comprehend the seriousness of its mistranslation, we first need to take a look at a conflict that began many eons ago between Satan and God. Understanding the fundamentals of this conflict will give us the key to understanding the devil's reason for the subtle mistranslation of Genesis 3:16 and why it is critical that the translation of this verse be corrected.

The Bible gives us a glimpse of what happened in the universe before God created man. It also gives us clues to the reason for Satan's covert warfare against mankind. Long, long, long before man was created, Lucifer, the supreme archangel, rebelled and tried to usurp God's throne (Ezek. 28). After this, he became known as the devil or Satan. He is also referred to as the prince of the power of the air (Eph. 2:2), the prince of devils (Matt. 9:34, 12:24; Mark 3:22), and the prince of this world (John 12:31, 14:30, 16:11).

In the following verse, the Bible alludes to a background problem on earth at the time God created mankind:

> Then God blessed them, and God said to them, "Be fruitful and multiply; fill the earth and subdue it; have dominion over the fish of the sea, over the birds of the air, and over every living thing that moves on the earth." (Gen. 1:28, NKJV).

The word, "subdue," in this verse tells us that something on the earth was not right. One can deduce from what happened to Adam and Eve in the Garden of Eden that Satan was at the root of the un-subdued situation on earth. His sneaky entrance into the Garden of Eden and his subtle trickery show us that he was on earth in rebellion against God's authority, and he was carrying out his own agenda.

Authority and Freedom

The Bible tells us that God, who is love, possesses all authority and power. He reigns over and is in control of all things, in all time and in all places. He also possesses all knowledge and wisdom. At the end of time, He will judge every human being, and His judgment will stand.

No one can take God's power or authority from Him. They are His to share with others as He sees fit according to His wisdom. Satan's initial conflict with God was over authority—who would possess it and who would be in control. Satan wasn't satisfied with what God had given him, so he grasped for more, wanting to be like God. In essence, he wanted to possess *all* God's authority and power so he could do whatever he wanted. Satan's title, "ruler of this world," indicates two things: (1) at some point before Lucifer fell, God gave him a measure of authority and power, and (2) his realm of authority included the earth. We know that Satan retained this authority over the world after his fall because Jesus referred to him as the "prince of this world." This title is used in the account of the devil tempting Jesus in the wilderness. At that time, Satan offered to give Jesus all the kingdoms of the world and their glory if Jesus would fall down and worship him. Jesus sent him packing with a few choice words of truth; but, what is noteworthy in that scene is that Jesus did not challenge his right to make the offer or his ability to deliver on it. Jesus' silence concerning this appears to be an acknowledgement that the devil was rightfully in possession of the kingdoms of this world and that they were his to offer.

It is not easy to talk about authority because we have a built-in lexicon with respect to this word that is different from God's. It is critical for us to recognize that the meanings we naturally give to the word "authority" and to other similar words such as "head," "rule," and "lord" do not match God's meaning. Because of our faulty and inaccurate understanding of what true authority really is, and of how it works, we misunderstand certain Bible passages and misapply them. If we wish to understand such passages correctly, we need to change our definition and understanding of authority so that our built-in lexicon matches God's.

In this writing, I will call our natural understanding of authority—that which matches the devil's practice and use of authority—"counterfeit authority." Until we ask the Lord to renew our minds to properly understand what He means by authority, we will not be able to understand the meaning God intends in Scriptures which use authority related words such as "head," "rule," "lord," "dominion," "kingdom," "submission," and "obedience." Instead, we will think wrongly about such Scriptures, and we will have wrong behavior as a result (Matt. 20:25, Mark 10:42, Luke 22:25).

The difference between true authority and counterfeit authority is determined by how it is used, or more precisely, by who is using it. When God uses His authority, because He is love, He exercises it in love. He loves the party on the receiving end of His authority, and He wisely uses His authority for their highest good. His use of authority is governed by His righteousness. He never does anything that is wrong. Whatever He does results in righteousness and peace.

When Satan uses authority (that which God gave him), he exercises it without love because he has no love. He does not love the party on the receiving end; and, what he does, he does for himself with his own benefit in view. He does not care for what is right, and he does what is wrong. Whatever He does produces unrighteousness and takes away peace. This is a condition produced by rebellion from God. Satan's counterfeit authority is fundamentally self-serving. It is a top-down hierarchical authority that dominates all who are below the topmost party in the hierarchy. Satan uses beings, both spiritual and human, in this kind of hierarchical system to carry out his evil purposes (Eph. 4:14). He is the party who is actually at the top of every hierarchy, but he chooses to stay hidden in the background as much as possible and work by trickery and deceit. His intent is to violate and take away people's freedom. Through his agents, he exercises either some form of overt, coercive, forceful control or some form of subtle, manipulative control. Counterfeit authority is always for the benefit of the party at the top in his war against God—the prince of this world. It will always have evidence of unrighteousness.

Among Christians, Satan has mastered the art of using word trickery to disguise counterfeit authority to the degree that it can be at work right under believers' noses in the name of God, bearing the label of the authority of God, and they cannot see it for what it really is. Satan, who wants to be God, has been able, time and again, to trick God's people into serving him and his agenda. He has been successful in causing believers to think that top-down, ruling, controlling, and freedom-robbing authority is God's authority and that believers need to submit to their leaders' directions without question. Examples abound in Christian history of Satan having worked in this way to get Christians to do his anti-God bidding. Well-known examples would be the Inquisition and the Crusades. Any Christian leadership which exercises authoritative control over God's people and does not respect their freedom and right to make their own decisions before God falls into this category. Such deceitful working is why the Bible tells us that Satan disguises himself as an angel of light and his ministers as ministers of righteousness (2 Cor. 11:13–15). Counterfeit authority is recognizable by its fruit, which may take time to manifest. It will ultimately bear the unrighteous characteristics of the one behind it—Satan. He:

- Operates from a basis of hatred, because he has no love

- Seeks to suppress, oppress, kill, and destroy whatever threatens or opposes him

- Has no regard for the needs or rights of others

- Takes no responsibility for the well-being of others

- Removes peace and brings turmoil and distress to all who are on the receiving end of his control

- Uses lies, trickery, subtlety, and deceit to get what he wants

- Is darkness, works in darkness, and spreads darkness

- Hates God and the Word of God and is in total rebellion against Him and His Word

- Lords it over everyone, including the demons and fallen angels under him in the unseen realm

- Has power over his subjects because of their sins

The strongest characteristic of counterfeit authority is that it imposes itself and doesn't respect a person's right to choose.

God's authority, on the other hand, is bottom-up, supportive authority. His everlasting arms are underneath, taking responsibility, powerfully protecting and accomplishing what is best for all those whom He loves (Deut. 33:27). True authority is rooted in humility and self-sacrifice (Phil. 2:5–11). It allows entreaty and questioning and asks for, not demands, willing cooperation. In Genesis 18:22–23, Abraham questioned God, entreated Him, and even changed His mind. God's way of exercising His authority is to instruct people and give them freedom to choose to obey Him. If they choose otherwise, He seeks to persuade them by giving them consequences. He waits patiently with great longsuffering after imposing consequences, giving them space to change their way of thinking and submit to Him willingly. God's authority reveals the character of God, who:

- Loves, because He is love

- Is not coercive or abusive

- Operates in the realm of freedom and respects the rights and freedom of others

- Is truthful and does not lie

- Is righteous and just

- Is love and light and reveals love and brings light with all His actions

- Always does what is best for others, even at great cost to Himself

- Disciplines by measured, purposeful consequences, and chastisement when necessary, to persuade people to do what is in their best interest

- Is willing to suffer wrong graciously for a very long time to give those He loves the opportunity to make right decisions, that is, to repent, turn, and yield to Him

- Brings life, light, joy, peace, and rest to those who choose to submit to Him

- Supplies whatever is needed to help those who choose to follow Him be able to do so

The strongest characteristic of God's authority is that it allows others to have freedom to choose within the boundaries He has set for them. He warns them not to violate those boundaries; and, if they do, He gives them consequences designed to help them change their minds and their behavior. In order for freedom to work, boundaries are necessary because there are multiple parties involved. God defines where one party's freedom stops and where another's starts. He gives the various parties the right to make their own choices—to have authority over their own choices—within the sphere which He has allotted to them.

In the Garden of Eden, God told Adam what he could not do and also told him the consequence that would come if he disobeyed. Adam and Eve had the freedom to choose to believe God or not. When they believed the lie of Satan instead and acted on it, they received the consequence that God had pronounced. God eventually sent His sinless Son to suffer death in mankind's place.

When Jesus came, He, too, had the freedom to make His own choice about doing His Father's will. He said, "I have the authority to lay my life down and to take it up again" (John 10:18). This means that He had authority to say "No" to dying on the cross. Whether He went to the cross or not was entirely His decision. He exercised His authority to choose to submit to His Father's will, which was to lay down His life for us. This exercise of authority by Christ reveals God's love for us and gives us the clearest and most powerful view of who God is and what true authority looks like. This is why people bow their knees to Jesus as Lord when they see the sacrifice that He made on the cross for them. Jesus Christ, God Himself, bleeding on the cross for our sins, is authority in action for our ultimate benefit. God Himself paid the price necessary to free us from the consequence of our sin and then gave us another choice: Believe the Son and what He has done to save you. That is the gospel. It is the result of God's exercise of true authority. He has paid the price to give mankind a second chance, but ... each person must choose to take it!

The concept of God's authority and man's freedom is not something that fallen man easily grasps or apprehends. It is easier to understand Satan's counterfeit authority, because that is the kind of authority human beings have experienced and seen exercised on the earth time and again as men rule over other men by coercion or manipulation.

A fundamental truth is that God respects and values all He creates. He also values having a true and loving relationship with His created beings—one like the relationship that exists with the Father, Son, and Holy Spirit. There is no possibility for Him to have such a relationship with His created beings if they are not free to choose to be, or not to be, in relationship with Him. The Father, Son, and Holy Spirit are in a perfect, harmonious, and freedom-based relationship. If God did not give his created beings the freedom to choose whether or not they want to participate in that relationship, He would be violating His own character. He knows that it is best for those whom He has created to choose Him, and He is confident that when they see Him as He really is, they will.

So, in this explanation about true and counterfeit authority, we can see what God's character is like and what Satan's character is like. Never forget the difference between God's way and Satan's way: God lets man choose; Satan's imposes. The difference between the two is the difference between breath and death. The wonder of wonders is that God has opened a door for us into eternal life. We can choose to enter through it and be saved. His exercise of authority on our behalf has opened the way for us to get back all that we lost—simply by choosing to believe what He has done for us.

The Prime Target in Satan's War: The First Woman, Eve

With this background and with these thoughts about authority, we return to the time that God created man. Satan realized that the only way to stop God's purpose for man having dominion over the earth was to cause man to do Satan's bidding instead. Thereby, man would disobey God and lose His relationship with God. Enslaved under the rule of Satan, man would also lose his power to subdue the earth.

Satan understood that God's authority was contained in His words, so his strategy against man was to craftily usurp God's words and slightly change them to accomplish his end. Through the serpent, Satan spoke a few such modified-God-sentences to Eve and deceived her. She was tricked into submitting to him and eating from the tree of the knowledge of good and evil. Adam followed her and disobeyed God by eating the fruit she offered him. They both became Satan's servants, subject to his evil authority (Rom. 6:16).

Satan thought he had won the day until he heard God's next words. God announced that He was putting hatred between the woman and the serpent, and between her seed and the serpent's seed. God also declared that the seed of the woman would crush the serpent's head, meaning Satan's head. Now, Satan had a new problem. He needed to find a way to prevent the woman from bringing forth such a seed. From that day, he hated the woman, and she hated him. From that day, she and her seed became the critical target in Satan's war against God.

Thousands of years later, in spite of all Satan did in the interim to thwart God's plan, at the time of Christ's death and resurrection, Satan saw God's promise concerning the seed of woman come to pass when a man named Jesus Christ rose from the dead. This man was God who had come in the flesh. He was a man who had no sin. He was the promised seed of woman. This man defeated the devil. Satan thought he had won with a masterful stroke when he had Jesus killed on the cross; but, to His surprise, Jesus walked right out of His grave. Satan had no power to hold him because He was sinless. Not only that, Satan saw that a harvest of many more godly men, more seed of woman, was beginning. Jesus had paid the debt for the sins of all mankind and taken away Satan's right to hold them in bondage. The door was open to freedom from the devil's control by faith in Christ's redemptive work.

From that terrifying day, Satan's new goal became to prevent people from hearing and believing the gospel and to hinder any who did believe from having a walk by faith in Him. His fear of such persons was great. Their existence was a tremendous threat to Him. He worked day and night to tempt them to return to a life of habitual sin, so that he could bring them back under his control.

Today, two millennia later, Satan is still fighting, even more fiercely, as he sees the day of the Lord approaching. He never stops his quest to hold believers in a state of bondage through deception, so that they will be ineffective in battle against him. He continues to use the same method of operation he has used against God's people from the beginning: misinterpreting and misusing God's words in order to deceive. In modern day vernacular, we might call his word trickery satanic spin.

The Power of One Word

Genesis 3:16 is part of the story of what happened to Adam and Eve in the Garden of Eden. A seemingly small, but very critical, change to the meaning of *one word* in this verse took place in a sixteenth century translation. This change made it possible to conceal the most likely scenario of what happened during and immediately after man's fall. It also made way for the enemy to offer a view of God's character which was false. Another part of Genesis 3:16, which was also poorly translated, afforded the way for interpreters and teachers to say that God had cursed woman. Finally, a third part of Genesis 3:16 came to be understood as an imperative or command when, grammatically, it was not. These three translation problems made it possible for the devil to use this verse to fight against and subdue women, and to do so in the name of God.

Problem 1 in Genesis 3:16: Turning or Lust?

The translation of this verse now stands in the King James Version of the Bible as follows:

> Unto the woman he saith, "I will greatly multiply thy sorrow and thy conception[3]; in sorrow thou shalt bring forth children; and thy desire shall be to thy husband and he shall rule over thee" (Gen. 3:16, KJV).

---

[3] According to Bushnell, this is a translation error: The word "conception" does not exist in the Hebrew. The word should be "sighing." A detailed explanation of this error is found in paragraphs 120–121 of *God's Word to Women*.

After studying this verse in Hebrew and reviewing the historical development of all the translations of this verse over eighteen centuries, Katharine Bushnell found that its translations and resultant interpretations were the basis for a stronghold of wrong beliefs about man ruling over woman. She discovered that the devil had craftily used natural male bias to torque the translation just enough to lay a foundational false belief about woman. After much careful study of the verse in Hebrew, she concluded that an accurate translation of this verse would be:

> Unto the woman He said, "A snare has increased thy sorrow and thy sighing. In sorrow thou shalt bring forth children. Thou art turning away to thy husband and he will rule over thee.[4]

---

[4] See Bushnell's *God's Word to Women,* paragraphs 117, 119, and 124 for a detailed explanation of her suggested translation.

She discovered that the Hebrew word, *"teshuqah,"* was translated "turning" in the earliest translations. It remained "turning" for sixteen centuries until Pagnino's Latin version changed it to "lust." It then read, "Your lust shall be to your husband and he shall rule over you." In the seventeenth century, the King James Version softened the translation by using the word "desire," which is a more genteel rendering with a similar meaning as Pagnino's word "lust". Now, in the twenty-first century, the word, "desire," is used in the vast majority of English Bibles.

Of note is the fact that the International Standard Version has in recent years resumed the use of the word "turning" and has translated Genesis 3:16 as follows:

> I'll greatly increase the pain of your labor during childbirth. It will be painful for you to bear children, since your trust is turning toward your husband, and he will dominate you. (Gen. 3:16, ISV)

Although this translation sounds awkward and falls short of clarity, it is an improvement because the meaning given to *teshuqah* is that of the Hebrew meaning (turning).

Just as a small finger held up between the eye and the sun can completely block the orb of the sun from view, the one word change from "turning" to "desire" has blocked a proper understanding of the account of the Fall in Genesis 3. The word "turning" in Genesis 3:16 reveals that it was Eve's choice to "turn" from God to Adam. This reference to her turning to him may mean that she was not driven out of the garden with Adam, but that she chose to follow him out. Regardless, in this verse, God was warning Eve that, because of her turning to Adam, Adam would rule over her. Rather than a command for the man to rule over woman, this was a warning to Eve of what was going to happen to her as a consequence of her choice. Whether she went out of the garden of her own volition or not, it is clear that God saw her turning away from Him to Adam and warned her of the danger of doing this. (For more detail on Genesis 3, see paragraphs 66–74 of Bushnell's book.)

In light of the earlier explanation about authority and freedom, it should be no surprise why Satan wanted to remove the word "turning" from Genesis 3:16. It showed Eve exercising her own authority, her God-given freedom, to make a choice. Satan saw to it that this word was replaced with a crude word, "lust," meaning inappropriate sexual desire. In this way, he brought about a change in the understanding of the first part of the verse that made it possible for the latter part, "he shall rule over you," to be misinterpreted as an imperative, a command, one that appeared to be given by God for man to rule over woman. The reason for this was, according to subsequent interpreters, so that man could keep his wife *and her lust* under his control.[5] It was a master stroke of the devil to win men fully into his woman-subduing camp by making it not only convenient for them, but a matter of obedience to God. It is strangely ironic that males—the gender that is known for out-of-control male lust—were behind a translation that said they had to dominate women because of their out-of-control female lust!

---

[5] See Bushnell's Lessons 13–22 in *God's Word to Women* for her full explanation of Genesis 3:16 translations and her insights on the account in Genesis 3.

The discovery of the correct meaning of this one word opens the way for revelation and understanding that has the potential to benefit millions of women and men and their marriages. It can wake up millions of Christian women and empower them to become women of *chayil* who, in the light of how God really sees them, will be able to do their part in paving the way for the second coming of Christ. Much more will be said about this potential, but first we need to look at two other problems with the modern understanding of Genesis 3:16.

Problem 2 in Genesis 3:16: Is Woman Cursed?

Bushnell also noted that nowhere in the Bible did God curse Eve; rather, God cursed only two things: the ground and the serpent. She also noted that nowhere does the Scripture say that God put Eve out of the garden. It does plainly say, however, that He drove Adam out of the garden and that He gave a consequence that was specifically tailored to fit with what Adam's job had been in the Garden of Eden—to cultivate and guard it. The truth is that, at the time of the Fall, God blessed woman and her seed in the pronouncement that He made to the devil. After hearing God's pronouncement to the serpent, Adam called his wife, "Eve," which means the mother of all living.

Neither did God curse Adam; however, He did place the responsibility for the Fall with him when He said, "Cursed is the ground thanks to you" (Gen. 3:17, NET). Upon examination of corresponding New Testament verses, it can be shown clearly that God's Word holds Adam, not Eve, responsible for the Fall (Rom. 5:12–19).

Problem 3 in Genesis 3:16: Did God Mandate that Man Rule Over Woman?

After a detailed explanation about the translation of the phrase, "shall rule over thee," Bushnell concludes:

> Thus we see that the context does not prove that this "shall be" of the sentence translated, "thy desire shall be to thy husband" is imperative. We can assert positively that this sentence is a simple future or present, warning woman of the consequences of her action. So it is rendered in all the ancient versions; never as an imperative. As a prophecy it has been abundantly fulfilled in the manner in which man rules over woman, especially in heathen lands. (Bushnell, para. 127)

So, rather than a mandate or a command, this phrase was a prediction of what would happen to woman if she made the choice to turn away from God and look to her husband to meet her needs. The belief that this phrase is God's decree for man to subdue woman is responsible for many centuries of the suppressive rule of men over women. The realization that the primary Old Testament support for woman's subjugation is an errant belief born of a faulty translation should greatly sober all of us.

Satan's Strategy Exposed

The broadly–accepted, modern-day translation of Genesis 3:16 exposes Satan's motive and strategy for any who would look closely at it and its long-term fruit. The corrupted translation reveals what Satan wanted to hide: truth about the character and ways of God and truth about man's freedom. The message conveyed by Genesis 3:16 as it now stands slanders God. It does not convey the truth about Him. God did not force or demand submission from man before or after his fall. A proper translation of this verse shows that God did not force Eve to submit to Him, but allowed her the freedom to make her own decision about who she would turn to and depend upon.

Satan wanted to hide the fact that, even after the Fall, Eve was still a free being who was able to choose whom she would follow. He wanted to hide God's way of dealing with man's fall and to defame God in the process. The truth is that when God saw Eve turning towards Adam and away from Him, His way was to warn her that there would be consequences she would not like ... and there were. She found herself living in the shadow of death, being ruled over by her husband. Neither did God force fallen Adam to submit to Him. Rather, God put Adam out of the garden with a serious consequence. He, too, found himself living in the shadow of death, being ruled over by the devil, tilling the cursed ground by the sweat of his brow so he could provide for himself.

These consequences show us that God is in control of the big picture, and the way He exercises His control is not by lording it over to get His way, but by allowing what is in our best interest to happen so we can learn to make the right choices. God suffers long on our behalf, always having our highest good in view. His way of gaining us is to allow us to reap what we sow.

In summary, God's light shining on the changed translation of Genesis 3:16 shows us the difference between God's way and Satan's way, between the way of one who has true authority and one who has counterfeit authority. God respects the freedom He gave man, and He persuades with words and consequences for man's benefit. Satan respects no one and doesn't persuade any one for their benefit; rather, he dominates them for his own selfish ends. The mistranslation of Genesis 3:16 supports and promotes Satan's method of ruling by domination and, at the same time, it reveals the character of Satan.

The commonly accepted translation of Genesis 3:16 sounds not only like God sanctioned man's domination of woman, but that He ordained it. In actuality, this was Satan playing a counterfeit authority card. It is time for this evil card to be removed from the Bible along with all the cards that followed its suit!

It is very significant that Genesis 3:16 is the only verse in the Old Testament that can be found to support the concept of man ruling over woman.[6] It is also significant that it took many centuries (from approximately 300 B.C. to 1528 A.D.) for the meaning of the Hebrew word, *"teshuqah,"* in Genesis 3:16 to be changed, through translations, so that it did not convey its correct Hebrew meaning, "turning."

---

[6] Another Bible passage that some might claim as Old Testament evidence that God has given a husband rule over his wife is Numbers 30:6–15. Bushnell provides a thorough explanation of why this passage cannot be considered as such evidence (Bushnell, para. 172–188). In brief, Numbers 30:6–15 is about cases in which vows were made by female family members who had no independent means. Bushnell says, "In those days as in these, the young daughter and the wife would not have much property under their own control, and hence the father and husband would stand in such relation to them as to be able, to a large extent, to control their vows." There were limitations put on the father's or husband's control over vows, however. Moses' handling of the problem that is addressed in this Numbers 30 passage is similar to how Paul and Peter handled the problem of Christians who were

slaves. All three—Moses, Paul, and Peter—were dealing with societal problems whose roots were in the Fall of man. Moses addressed a societal situation that had developed because of Satan's hatred for women. Paul and Peter addressed a societal situation that had developed because of mankind becoming the slave of the devil. Paul and Peter gave instruction concerning how Christians who were slaves should behave. The fact that Paul and Peter addressed the problem of slavery does not legitimize the practice of slavery, nor does it mean that God approves of slavery. Similarly, the fact that Moses gave instruction concerning women and their lack of property, and their husbands' rights over property, does not mean that God approves of husbands ruling over wives.

Katharine Bushnell designed a chart that shows the various meanings ascribed to the Hebrew word, *"teshuqah,"* from the time of the Greek Septuagint translation (250 B.C.–300 B.C.) to the Revised Version (1884 A.D.) (Bushnell, para. 128). It shows that the meaning of the Hebrew word, *"teshuqah,"* was rightly conveyed as "turning" by most translations until 1528, when Pagnino's Latin translation was published and conveyed the meaning "lust." After that, translations adopted Pagnino's meaning of "lust" until the Geneva, Authorized, and Revised Bible translations, which conveyed the meaning "desire." Bushnell gives a lengthy explanation of the translation history (Bushnell, paras. 128–145).

The bottom line is that translations gave Satan the opportunity to change the meaning of the Hebrew word, *"teshuqah,"* in such a way as to obscure God's gracious way of using authority. He succeeded in bringing about translations that supported the distorted idea of a dominating, authoritarian God who expected a man to rule over his wife.

A modern-day perversion of Genesis 3:16 presents an even more errant understanding: "You will desire to control your husband, but he will rule over you" (NLT). According to this modern Bible version, the woman, as a result of the Fall, has a strong desire to control her husband, but she won't be able to do so! This idea of woman wrongly desiring to control her husband was introduced by a Christian woman named Susan Foh in 1975 in an attempt to fight against godless feminism! According to Foh:

The woman has the same sort of desire for her husband that sin has for Cain, a desire to possess or control him. This desire disputes the headship of the husband.... The woman's desire is to control her husband (to usurp his divinely appointed headship, and he must master her, if he can...). Her desire is to contend with him for leadership in their relationship. This desire is a result of and a just punishment for sin, but it is not God's decretive will for the woman. Consequently, the man must actively seek to rule his wife. (Foh)

Foh's paper and interpretation further highlights the confusion surrounding this verse! Just this year, in 2016, the English Standard Version has come out with a revision which they call the ESV Permanent Text Edition. Only 52 words, out of more than 775,000, were changed in it. Some of the changed words are found in Genesis 3:16, making the errant understanding stronger:

I will surely multiply your pain in childbearing; in pain you shall bring forth children. Your desire shall be contrary to your husband, but he shall rule over you. (Gen. 3:16, ESV)

It is unfortunate that the decision was made that all the text of the ESV Permanent Edition Bible will remain unchanged in all future editions printed and published by Crossway (ESV Permanent).

A New Perspective on Adam and Eve

After examining the faulty translation of Genesis 3:16, it's time to revisit the story of Adam and Eve and see how an improved, more accurate translation of this verse can bring new understanding to the account. The new perspective that I am about to present may bring a sudden mind-awakening jolt to those who hold to the traditional interpretation of events found in Genesis 3 and 4. Such a jolt may be necessary to bring attention to the truth that is hiding under the carefully placed, stationary, cobweb-covered, traditional understanding. The new perspective turns the centuries-old spotlight away from the woman's role in the Fall and brings it to rest on the man's role, one which has remained hidden in the shadows. It also offers a pragmatic look at what happened to the first couple and their family after they began life outside of Eden. I believe that you will be surprised, as I was, at how the new perspective finds a much stronger footing in the text of the Bible than the traditional one does. Also, the new perspective is a more realistic one, in that the fallen patterns of behavior seen in the first family have been replicated over and over again in millions of fallen marriages and families on this earth since the Fall of man.

In the pristine Garden of Eden, we meet four characters in Genesis 3: God, Adam, Eve, and the serpent. Their interactions create a serious problem with long-term consequences:

1 Now the serpent was more subtle than any beast of the field which the LORD God had made. And he said unto the woman, Yea, hath God said, Ye shall not eat of every tree of the garden?

2 And the woman said unto the serpent, We may eat of the fruit of the trees of the garden:

3 But of the fruit of the tree which [is] in the midst of the garden, God hath said, Ye shall not eat of it, neither shall ye touch it, lest ye die.

4 And the serpent said unto the woman, Ye shall not surely die:

5 For God doth know that in the day ye eat thereof, then your eyes shall be opened, and ye shall be as gods, knowing good and evil.

6 And when the woman saw that the tree [was] good for food, and that it [was] pleasant to the eyes, and a tree to be desired to make one wise, she took of the fruit thereof, and did eat, and gave also unto her husband with her; and he did eat.

7 And the eyes of them both were opened, and they knew that they [were] naked; and they sewed fig leaves together, and made themselves aprons.

8 And they heard the voice of the LORD God walking in the garden in the cool of the day: and Adam and his wife hid themselves from the presence of the LORD God amongst the trees of the garden.

9 And the LORD God called unto Adam, and said unto him, Where [art] thou?

10 And he said, I heard thy voice in the garden, and I was afraid, because I [was] naked; and I hid myself.

11 And he said, Who told thee that thou [wast] naked? Hast thou eaten of the tree, whereof I commanded thee that thou shouldest not eat?

12 And the man said, The woman whom thou gavest [to be] with me, she gave me of the tree, and I did eat.

13 And the LORD God said unto the woman, What [is] this [that] thou hast done? And the woman said, The serpent beguiled me, and I did eat.

14 And the LORD God said unto the serpent, Because thou hast done this, thou [art] cursed above all cattle, and above every beast of the field; upon thy belly shalt thou go, and dust shalt thou eat all the days of thy life:

15 And I will put enmity between thee and the woman, and between thy seed and her seed; it shall bruise thy head, and thou shalt bruise his heel.

16 Unto the woman he said, I will greatly multiply thy sorrow and thy conception; in sorrow thou shalt bring forth children; and thy desire [shall be] to thy husband, and he shall rule over thee.

[16 Bushnell's translation:[7] Unto the woman He said, "A snare has increased thy sorrow and thy sighing. In sorrow thou shalt bring forth children. Thou art turning away to thy husband and he will rule over thee.]

17 And unto Adam he said, Because thou hast hearkened unto the voice of thy wife, and hast eaten of the tree, of which I commanded thee, saying, Thou shalt not eat of it: cursed [is] the ground for thy sake; in sorrow shalt thou eat [of] it all the days of thy life;

18 Thorns also and thistles shall it bring forth to thee; and thou shalt eat the herb of the field;

19 In the sweat of thy face shalt thou eat bread, till thou return unto the ground; for out of it wast thou taken: for dust thou [art], and unto dust shalt thou return.

20 And Adam called his wife's name Eve; because she was the mother of all living.

21 Unto Adam also and to his wife did the LORD God make coats of skins, and clothed them.

22 And the LORD God said, Behold, the man is become as one of us, to know good and evil: and now, lest he put forth his hand, and take also of the tree of life, and eat, and live for ever:

23 Therefore the LORD God sent him forth from the garden of Eden, to till the ground from whence he was taken.

24 So he drove out the man; and he placed at the east of the garden of Eden Cherubims, and a flaming sword which turned every way, to keep the way of the tree of life. (Gen 3:1–24, KJV)

---

[7] See Bushnell's *God's Word to Women*, paragraphs 117, 119, and 124, for a detailed explanation of this translation.

In this account, God does not tell us everything. He gives us just enough information about the characters and the plot to capture our attention and cause us to think, ask questions, and diligently seek answers. We cannot help but want to understand the Fall of man, because it has so greatly impacted all of us.

Eve: The First One Deceived, but Not Responsible for the Fall

As we look carefully at the account, we find something in verse 6 that immediately calls into question the traditional teaching about it:

> And when the woman saw that the tree was good for food, and that it was pleasant to the eyes, and a tree to be desired to make one wise, she took of the fruit thereof, and did eat, and gave also unto her husband with her; and he did eat. (Gen. 3:6, KJV)

This verse has been used to lay responsibility for the Fall solely at the feet of woman. However, the words, "gave also unto her husband with her," show that Adam, the man that God had charged to cultivate and guard the garden, the one who was older than Eve, was actually with her when she was tempted. He stood there silently and watched her take of the fruit and eat!

Even though the woman knew it was wrong to eat of the tree, and even though she was involved in the Fall, nowhere does the Bible hold her responsible for it. Possibly, this is because she was less mature, having been formed later than Adam, and possibly because there is no record that God had given her a direct command not to eat of the tree, as He had Adam. She had not yet been formed when Adam was given this command, so Eve may have only heard it later from Adam. Secondhand hearing may account for her having added the words, "neither shall ye touch it," when she repeated it to the serpent. Adam's accountability, however, is plainly spelled out in the Bible in the following verse which Paul wrote to Timothy:

> ... and Adam was not deceived, but his wife was thoroughly deceived, and so became involved in transgression. (1 Tim. 2:14, WNT)

In other words, Adam knew he was doing wrong (he was *not* deceived); and, therefore, he was in blatant disobedience to a direct command given by God to him. In Genesis 3:17, God says that Adam hearkened to his wife. This tells us that Adam had a choice, and he chose to take the fruit from her. Paul further clarified Adam's accountability: The Greek word that Paul used to describe Eve shows that when he read the Genesis account, he understood that the woman was "thoroughly deceived." He also understood that the man was not deceived. The man was disobedient. Therefore, the man, Adam, not the woman, was responsible for the Fall. Paul specifically pointed out this fact in his letter to the Romans:

> Therefore, just as through one man sin entered the world, and death through sin, and thus death spread to all men, because all sinned ... 14 Nevertheless death reigned from Adam to Moses, even over those who had not sinned according to the likeness of the transgression of Adam, who is a type of Him who was to come.... by the one man's offense many died ... by the one man's offense death reigned through the one ... (Rom 5:12, 14–15, 17, NKJV)

As Charles Trombley wrote in *Who Said Women Can't Teach?*:

> More than eight times, Paul said that one person caused the Fall, and twice he named that person as Adam. Adam was not deceived states Paul. That's why Christ is called the Last Adam and not the Last Eve, clearly implicating the first man as the cause of sin and death. (Trombley, 102)

Bushnell's commentary on Adam's and Eve's responses to God when confronted with their sins provides further understanding of why God's Word holds Adam responsible for the Fall:

> I think we are warranted in drawing a contrast between these two answers, for in them we find a clue to what follows. Both confess, *"I did eat,"* and both tell truthfully the *immediate* influence that led to the eating. So far they are equal. But Adam is led on to say more. There was a remote cause for his downfall, through Eve,—Satan. But Adam does not, like Eve, mention Satan; and yet he

does not remain silent as to a remote cause; he accuses God to His face of being Himself that remote cause,—in giving the woman to be with him. And the worst feature of the case consists in the fact that Satan was present, or near-by, at the interview, and could not have been overlooked, excepting wilfully, if a remote cause was to be mentioned at all. Satan must have rejoiced as much in Adam's attitude towards God in charging Him with folly, as in Adam's attitude towards himself, the tempter, in shielding him from blame. Is it not this scene, this conduct on the part of Adam, to which Job refers (31:33) when he complains, "If, like Adam, I covered my transgressions by hiding mine iniquity in my bosom?" Dr. Lange says (see par. 36), "Adam must watch and protect" the garden from an "existing power of evil." Is not this the reason why Adam does not mention Satan, who has been let inside? (para. 69, Bushnell)

Adam: The First Man To Lie and Blame

Adam was the first man on record in the Bible to lie to God, and he was also the first man to blame someone else. His lie was one of omission. When God directly asked Adam about what had happened, Adam failed to tell the whole truth. God asked him three questions: "Where are you?" "Who told you that you were naked?" and "Have you eaten of the tree of which I commanded you not to eat?" In answer to the first question, Adam said that when he heard God's voice, he was afraid because he was naked so he hid himself. He did not answer the second question, "Who told you that you were naked?" With this second question, God appears to have given Adam an opportunity to admit that there was another party involved—the serpent. Adam's non-answer not only hid the serpent's role in the event, it also hid evidence of Adam's failure to guard the garden. When Adam responded to God's third question, he did so by blaming his wife for giving him the fruit of the forbidden tree, leaving her holding the proverbial bag. Not only this, when Adam blamed Eve, he referred to her as the woman whom God had given to him! In so doing, he was indirectly pointing to God as the one at fault!

Adam: Stumbled Before Falling

There is a plausible explanation for Adam's non-response to God's second question. According to Bushnell, more than one theologian has suggested that Adam had already stumbled before the fatal eating of the forbidden fruit:

> Attention to some of these matters has been called by more than one theologian, only to be ignored by the generality of Bible expositors. For instance, William Law, a learned theologian and one of the most accomplished writers of his day, declares: "Adam had lost much of his first perfection before his Eve was taken out of him; which was done to prevent worse effects of his fall, and to prepare a means of his recovery when his fall should become total, as it afterwards was, upon eating of the earthly tree of the knowledge of good and evil. 'It is not good that man should be alone,' saith the Scripture. This shows that Adam had altered his first state, had brought some beginning of evil into it, and had made that not to be good, which God saw to be good, when He created him."

> The late Dr. Alexander Whyte, of Edinburgh, in his book, Bible Characters, set forth some of the views of William Law, and also of an earlier writer, Jacob Behman, the great German philosopher (whose writings Wesley, in his days, required all his preachers to study). Whyte quotes Behman as teaching,—

> > There must have been something of the nature of a stumble, if not an actual fall, in Adam while yet alone in Eden ... Eve was created [he should say, "elaborated"] to 'help' Adam to recover himself, and to establish himself in Paradise, and in the

favor, fellowship and service of his
Maker." (Bushnell, paras. 32–33)

It is also possible that the "not good" assessment by
God was due to the fact that Adam was being tempted to
eat of the forbidden tree. Temptation is not a sin, but it
could be rightly considered something that is not good.
James says of temptation:

> 14 But each one is tempted when he is drawn
> away by his own desires and enticed. 15 Then,
> when desire has conceived, it gives birth to sin;
> and sin, when it is full-grown, brings forth death.
> (James 1:14–15, NKJV)

Bushnell explains that the Hebrew word for "alone" in
the phrase, "it is not good that the man should be alone,"
means "in-his-separation." Strong says this word means
"to be separate, isolated." Briggs-Driver says it means
"cause to withdraw, separate, disunite, divide into parts,
go alone, act independently." Bushnell suggests that if
God's meaning was simply that it was not good for Adam
to be only one being (the common understanding), the
Hebrew word that is used in Joshua 2:20, which means
exactly that, would have fit (Bushnell, para. 31). Bushnell
asks, "and from whom was Adam 'in separation' but from
God?" If Adam was *withdrawing, separating, disuniting,
dividing, going alone, or acting independently* from God,
this certainly would have been "not good." This would be
the reason God took Eve out of Adam. She was made to
be a help[8] to him.

---

[8] Many believe that when the Bible refers to woman helping man, it means she
is an inferior being given to him to help him with domestic affairs such as
cooking, cleaning, washing clothes, etc. The Hebrew word for "help," however,
is the word that is used to refer to God as our help. Such help is not that of an
inferior. Furthermore, there were no such domestic duties in Eden. There was
no cooking because food hung on the trees ready to eat. There were no
clothes to wash because they didn't wear clothes. There was no filth to clean
because they were in the paradise of God.

Adam's failure to answer God's second question,
"Who told you ..." is evidence that things were not as
good as they should have been between God and Adam.
Bushnell points out a verse in Job which refers to Adam

covering his transgressions and hiding iniquity in his bosom (Job 31:33, KJV). What transgressions did Adam cover and what iniquity did he hide in his bosom? Could it not be that he covered and hid communications with the serpent which had affected his relationship with God?

Also, remember, Adam was with Eve and stood silently watching the serpent trick her. Why didn't Adam speak up and protect her? Was he silent because he had already been tempted by the serpent to consider this same action? Was he thinking that if Eve took the fruit from the tree, technically, it would be her, not him, who would be in disobedience? (This kind of pre-thinking would help explain why he so easily blamed Eve.) Of course, this is speculation, but it does fit well in the new perspective. (I might also point out that the commonly accepted interpretation of what happened in Genesis 3 is also speculative and can easily be shown to be inaccurate when the whole passage is carefully examined.) One thing is clear: An explanation for Adam's two glaring silences is in order: (1) Why was Adam silent when Eve was succumbing to temptation? (2) Why was he silent when God asked him a straightforward question about another party, another source of information, being present in the garden?

Adam's only source of information in the Garden of Eden was supposed to be God, with whom he was in daily fellowship. The devil, realizing the purpose that God had for man (to subdue the earth—his domain), had reason to gain access to man and work to derail God's purpose. So, it is not far-fetched to suggest the possibility that he had spoken with Adam previously, engaged him in seemingly innocent conversation (as he also later did with Eve), and offered his target some statements that were slightly different from God's so that he could ensnare him.

In this scenario, when Satan failed in his attempt to seduce Adam, he made an indirect move on Adam by going after Eve. He succeeded in deceiving her. Eve then finished the job for Satan when she offered the fruit to Adam. He had not hearkened to the serpent, but he did hearken to his wife. Later, under the light of God's scrutinizing questions, Adam wanted to hide his failure to guard the garden and also his culpability in what had happened. If he had pointed to the serpent as the cause, the fact that Adam had not guarded the garden well would have become apparent. He chose silence as the best option, perhaps to cover his own guilt.

Eve: The First Woman Enabler

Now we come to the scene outside the Garden of Eden. In what follows (indented and italicized), I present a *likely expanded* scenario of what happened to the first couple once they were outside the Garden of Eden. The strongest evidence that this scenario is a likely one is found in the fact that similar versions of it have been repeated consistently in marriages since the time of the Fall of man—including my own. My new perspective on what happened outside of Eden is written as if it is an actual account. I also have inserted some commentary about my new perspective.

> *In the garden, both Adam and Eve admitted that they had eaten the fruit of the tree. Then, God shed the blood of an animal and clothed them with its skin.*

There is no biblical record that Adam had a change of mind and repented for blaming both Eve and God. Nor is there a record that he repented for his lie by omission—committed when he failed to answer God's second question and expose the serpent's involvement. So, when God drove Adam out of the garden, he was still guilty of these things.

> *When God drove Adam out of the garden, He cursed the ground and told Adam that he would bring forth fruit from it by the sweat of his brow. Once outside of Eden, Eve witnessed Adam's upset and wanted to help him. She loved him, having been taken out of him, and having been with him daily in the garden. She knew that she had been given by God to Adam to be his companion and helper, so she wanted to do her best for him.*

> *Eve soon found, however, that she was living with and trying to "help" a man who not only had blamed both God and her for what had happened*

in the garden, but also one that was still continuing to do so. Adam was upset, even angry, about all that had happened and about God driving him out of the garden.

When Cain was born, Eve thought he was the seed God had promised, as shown by what she said when he was born ("I have gotten a manchild with [the help of] the Lord" [Gen. 4:1, NASB]). However, it eventually became evident that Cain was not the promised seed, but rather he was a seed of the serpent.

By looking at what eventually happened with Cain, it can be deduced that Adam took a prideful attitude concerning his ability to carry out God's pronouncement concerning tilling the ground. Cain, whom the Bible tells us was a tiller of the ground, no doubt learned how to till the ground from Adam. Pride in the work that his father had taught him to do would explain the anger Cain felt when God did not respect his offering. Cain's attitude and anger is strong evidence that his father had a proud "can-do" attitude that he had passed on to his son.

Eve loved Adam and was doing her best to help him, but she was expecting him to reciprocate and meet her needs! However, there was nothing but disappointment in that department because he had not repented for blaming her (and God) in the garden.

As is true in fallen human experience, unrepentant man, like Adam, is good at blaming others and cursing God as he struggles to bring forth food and make a living from a cursed ground. Women do their best to help such husbands, like Eve no doubt did.

Eve tried to help Adam by finding ways to pacify him and make things better. At the same time, she was growing more and more troubled as she observed that Adam's behavior and prideful attitude was being passed on to Cain by example. Cain was also prone to treat her poorly like his father did.

Such distressing experiences caused her to begin to want to talk to God and seek His help.

When she called out to Him, God showed her the way to have fellowship with Him. He reminded her of the lesson He gave them both shortly after their fall in the Garden of Eden when he offered a blood sacrifice for their sin by killing an animal and clothing them with its skin. She understood. She began to have frequent visits with God. She told Him about all her troubles with Adam and Cain. God reminded her of His warning of what would happen if she turned to Adam to meet her needs. This began to make sense to her, and she determined she would learn to look to God and trust Him. When she talked to God about Adam's blaming of her in the garden, God told her to talk to Adam about it.

This would be true to the principle found in Leviticus 19:17 and in Matthew 18:15, which certainly existed in God's thought *(logos)* before it appeared in the law of Moses and before it was spoken by Jesus.

Eve tried to talk to Adam about what had happened in the garden, but he would not engage in conversation. She had begun to hope that if Adam would also talk to God through the means of a blood sacrifice, he would be changed for the better. However, whenever she tried to approach him with his need to get right with God, he would not talk about it. If she pressed him, he became angry and made her afraid. Adam clearly did not want to hear what she had to say about God or their expulsion from the garden. Eve soon began to lose hope and feel that Adam was beyond help, stuck where he was; and, therefore, she was also stuck. All she could do was continue to try to make the best of things.

When Abel was born, because of what she saw happening to Cain, she decided to take her second son under her wing and teach him how to have fellowship with God through a blood sacrifice. Abel, therefore, understood the need for having animals to sacrifice, and he became a keeper of sheep.

Man did not yet eat meat because meat-eating did not begin until after Noah and the flood (Gen. 9:3), so the only other reason to keep sheep would have been for clothing. Because of his proper approach to God, by shedding of blood, Abel was the first godly male seed. The New Testament teaching about marriage shows us that it only takes one godly person in a marriage relationship to insure that the children are sanctified (1 Cor. 7:14), so Abel was a sanctified child because his mother had turned back to God.

> *Adam had begun to notice a difference in Eve after she began to talk to God again. He wasn't sure he liked it. As time passed, he didn't tell Eve, but he began to have some thought about approaching God for himself. One day, he had the idea to send Cain to take an offering to God from the fruit of the ground. On that same day, Abel also made an offering to God—an animal offering. This did not go as well as Adam and Cain expected. God did not accept Cain's offering, but He did accept Abel's. When Cain saw this, he became angry. God asked him, "Why are you angry? Why is your countenance fallen? If thou doest well, shalt thou not be accepted? and if thou doest not well, sin lieth at the door. And unto thee shall be his desire, and thou shalt rule over him"* (Gen. 4:7).

There are many diverse translations for Genesis 4:7. Commentators explain that it is very difficult to determine the meaning of the last part of this passage. Here are some of the translations:

> if thou doest not well, sin coucheth at the door: and unto thee shall be its desire, but do thou rule over it (ASV)

> And if you do not do well, sin is crouching at the door; and its desire is for you, but you must master it (NASB)

> and if thou dost not well, at the opening a sin-offering is crouching, and unto thee its desire, and thou rulest over it (YLT)

But if you do not what is right, sin is crouching at the door. It desires to dominate you, but you must subdue it (NET)

and if you do wrong, sin is waiting at the door, desiring to have you, but do not let it be your master (BBE)

In Hebrew, the word in Genesis 4:7 that is translated "sin" can also be translated "sin offering."[9] In this verse, the word that is translated "desire" is the same Hebrew word *(teshuqah)* that occurs in Genesis 3:16, which we have seen should be translated "turning" instead of "desire." So, Genesis 4:7 could have been translated:

Why are you angry? Why is your countenance fallen? If thou doest well, shalt thou not be accepted? and if thou doest not well, there is a sin offering at the gate; it will turn to you so you can subdue it.

---

[9] Hebrew 2403 *(chattah)* an offense (sometimes habitual sinfulness) and its penalty, occasion, sacrifice, or expiation; also an offender:—punishment (of sin), purifying (-fication for sin), sin (-ner, offering).

This translation fits very well in context. It would mean that God told Cain what he should do in order for God to be pleased with his offering. Not only that, God told him that He had provided a sin offering (an animal) for Cain. There was one at the gate, one that would turn to Cain, so he could more easily capture and kill it. However, Cain needed to do his part. His part was to obey, go to the gate, and have dominion over the sin offering by killing it.

Cain, like his father, did not answer God's questions nor did he take the way of escape God offered him. Instead of killing the sin offering, Cain left the presence of God and, in jealous anger, killed his brother Abel.

As Jesus later said to the Pharisees, "Ye are of your father the devil, and the lusts of your father ye will do. He was a murderer from the beginning ...." (John 8:44, KJV). Cain was the first of many men in history who fit this description. Such were the religious men to whom Jesus spoke these words. Like Cain, who murdered Abel, they eventually murdered Jesus.

Fallen men today proudly believe themselves to be independently capable of accomplishing whatever is set before them. They remain silent when they should speak. They blame others instead of themselves. They resist God and carry out base reactions instead of accepting the sacrifice God has provided for them in Christ. They are walking in the footsteps of the first fallen man and his first son. Such men are the seed of the serpent referred to in Genesis 3:15.

Eve: The First Woman of Chayil

On the fateful day that Cain killed Abel, the first family was suddenly thrown into a terrible crisis. Eve, in her grief and agony over losing both of her sons in one day[10]—one to death and one sentenced by God to wandering—finally reached the end of her enabling rope. Eve was finished with her hurt-filled relationship with Adam. She knew that she would not spend another day expecting him to meet her emotional and physical needs. No more would she hope that he would do the right thing for her and for himself. No more would she try to help him get right with God. She would no longer accept his blaming of her or his poor speaking about God. She made a thorough repentance to God for having turned away from Him to Adam. This time, she made her turn back to God with her whole heart, having decided to look to Him alone to meet all her needs. Thus, she broke the hold Adam had over her heart. She handed him over to God. She realized that only God could help him, but she hardly cared anymore whether He did or not.

---

[10] The first woman of *chayil* experienced a full dose of the sorrow that Genesis 3:16 stated that she and her progenitors would have in bearing and rearing sons in the world. The Hebrew word for "children" (H1121, *"ben"*) in Genesis 3:16 is typically translated, "son," referring to male children. So Bushnell's rendering of the verse could have been, "In sorrow and sighing shall you bring

forth sons." This certainly was a true statement for Eve, because one of her sons killed the other.

As any wife and mother understands, horrible circumstances like those Eve faced cause a woman's heart to turn cold towards her husband and cause her to withdraw.

> *When Eve withdrew, she left Adam to face himself and find his way out of his problem all by himself. With the passage of time, however, and with God's help, she found the wherewithal to communicate frankly and thoroughly with Adam. After all, he was trying to talk to her now and said he wanted to hear what she had to say. She spelled out the whole truth to him about how she had been hurt by what he had done in the garden. He had protected himself and sacrificed her. She asked why he stood by and watched while she was listening to the serpent and did nothing to warn her. Why did he hide his own failure in the matter? Why had he been unwilling to tell God about the serpent's involvement? How had he dared to imply that God was the one at fault? Finally, she let him know that she held him responsible for Cain having become a proud and angry man—a murderer—a man capable of killing his own brother! She was no longer willing to continue with a man who would not get himself right with God and with her. She was done! Adam needed to make his own decision to turn to God.*

In this, she finally began to truly "help" her husband. Her strength in ending her enabling behavior, standing up to Adam, speaking the truth to him, and setting a proper boundary between him and her for his benefit, showed that she was a woman of *chayil*. The first indication that she was such a woman took place in the Garden of Eden, when she fearlessly named the serpent and exposed his involvement in their sin. Now, she had become the first woman to change her own behavior in such a way that her husband was left facing his responsibility for the crisis that he had caused. She left him in a position that he might recognize his need for God.

Adam: The First Man To Repent, Be Transformed, and Father a Lineage of Godly Males

Adam, as a result of Cain's murder of Abel, was now brought face to face with the role he had played in bringing about that murder. In one day, he had lost two sons; and, then, he had lost his relationship with his wife. He gradually began to see and admit to himself that the way he had brought up Cain lay at the root of Abel's murder. In her parting communication, Eve had "helped" make this fact crystal clear to him, and like it or not, he had to admit that she was right.

Thus, with Eve's help, Adam finally reached the place that he was able to admit that what he had done in the garden was wrong. He also realized that he had set a wrong example for Cain. When he repented to God and to Eve, his fellowship with God and his wife was restored, and his "seed of the serpent" relationship with the devil was broken.

The New Perspective Is a Fit

The new perspective of the first family fits well in the whole revelation of the Bible concerning God, man, woman, and the serpent.

A Fit with Centuries of Human Experience

There is abundant evidence that the new perspective fits with the general patterns of fallen male and female behavior seen for centuries in marriages and families: Fearful women enable, and proud men lie and murder. Such are the seed of the serpent who produce more seed of the serpent. We also see patterns of behavior in repentant males and females, those who turn back to God and look to Him. They become godly seed who produce more godly seed.

Some might say that my portrayal of Eve's response to Abel's death is nothing more than speculation. However, it is also nothing more than speculation to say she just coasted through this situation without ever blinking an eye. It is also speculation that she immediately had sex with Adam again and bore him another son. Yes, the Bible account appears to read that way, but as students of the Bible know well, God does not always spell out every detail in biblical accounts. He sometimes leaves us to draw rational conclusions based on our human experiences. My conclusion is that Eve was inconsolable over the death of Abel and over God's sentence on Cain. She would never have let Adam near her again without his full and complete repentance for his part in what had happened. This is not only rational, it is supportable by centuries of human experiences between husbands and wives. Although nothing much seems to interfere with a man's ability to have sexual relations, it is not so with women. When things are not right between a woman and her husband, any possibility of willing sexual intimacy disappears like a startled deer into the woods of you-will-not-touch-me-or-even-look-at-me-again.

Futhermore, there is evidence in the Bible that a repentance scenario like the one in the new perspective, or very similar to it, did take place with Adam. The evidence is found in the next record in the Bible about Adam and Eve after the murder of Abel. The Bible says that Adam knew his wife, Eve, and Seth was born. Seth, as many Bible expositors acknowledge, was the first in the line of godly male seed of woman.

> And Adam knew his wife again; and she bare a son, and called his name Seth: For God, [said she,] hath appointed me another seed instead of Abel, whom Cain slew. (Gen. 4:25, KJV)

As previously explained, without Adam's full and convincing repentance to Eve, Seth would not have been conceived (unless, of course, by rape—in which case the Bible text probably would not have used the word, "knew" (H3045), but a word such as "force," as seen in Esther 7:8 and Deuteronomy 22:25). Eve would not have been willing to let Adam near her unless she was convinced that Adam had taken responsibility for everything that had brought them to the terrible day of Abel's murder, and she had heard convincing words of repentance from his mouth. The fact that Seth was conceived is strong evidence of Adam's genuine repentance. Another verse provides further evidence that Adam repented and also that he had a transformational change in his character.

> And to Seth, to him also there was born a son; and he called his name Enos: then began men to call upon the name of the LORD. (Gen 4:26, KJV)

Sons typically model the behavior of their fathers. Adam's first son, Cain, modeled the behavior of his unrepentant father. Adam's third son, Seth, would have likewise modeled the behavior of his father. It is likely that Seth watched his father, Adam, who was now a repentant man, humble himself again and again as he learned not to proudly trust in himself and his abilities, but in God. Witnessing Adam's good example, Seth would have learned that he should not be prideful and independent, but humble and dependent on God.

Then Seth had a son, Enos. Seth modeled this same behavior for Enos. Genesis 4:26 says that in the generation of Enos men began the practice of calling on the name of the Lord. The fact that the progeny of Adam's son, Seth, called on the name of the Lord is further evidence of Adam's repentance.

A Fit with the Gospel Message

The new perspective on the first family also fits well with the gospel message of the New Testament. It contains a miniature picture of Christ's redeeming and transforming work among mankind.

Cain killing his brother Abel is a picture of the Jews (brethren of Jesus in God's family) crucifying Jesus. In both cases, Satan, whom the Bible calls a murderer from the beginning, was the instigator. In the Genesis 3 murder, Satan intended to thwart God's plan; but instead, he helped it along. Cain's act of murder opened the way for Adam's repentance, and men began to call on the name of the Lord. In New Testament times, Satan intended to thwart God's plan when he had Jesus crucified; instead, he again opened the door for men to repent and begin to call upon the name of the Lord. Also, Cain's act of murder opened the way for Adam's transformation, just as Christ's death and resurrection has opened the way for believers in Christ to be transformed.

After Eve decided to no longer be a bondwoman who was enslaved to her husband (who himself was in slavery to the devil), and after she took her place as a free woman who was completely dependent on God, Adam also turned back to God. Then, these two repentant and free beings produced Seth, who became a godly man like his father. Seth, then, also brought up a godly son.

Adam and Eve's marriage relationship was healed and restored when both returned to God. When husbands and wives get their individual relationships right with God first, and then get their relationships right with each other, they can produce a godly lineage.

A Fit with the Redemptive Message of the Old Covenant

It is noteworthy that the first family story matches up with the old covenant requirement that the male have his flesh cut off.

> 9 Then God said to Abraham, "As for you, you must keep the covenantal requirement I am imposing on you and your descendants after you throughout their generations. 10 This is my requirement that you and your descendants after you must keep: Every male among you must be circumcised. 11 You must circumcise the flesh of your foreskins. This will be a reminder of the covenant between me and you. 12 Throughout your generations every male among you who is eight days old must be circumcised, whether born in your house or bought with money from any foreigner who is not one of your descendants. 13 They must indeed be circumcised, whether born in your house or bought with money. The sign of my covenant will be visible in your flesh as a

permanent reminder. 14 Any uncircumcised male who has not been circumcised in the flesh of his foreskin will be cut off from his people—he has failed to carry out my requirement." (Gen. 17:9–14, NET)

In the garden, the man's fall was different from the woman's in that she fell as a result of being deceived (1 Tim. 2:14), whereas the man fell because of his decision to knowingly disobey God (Rom 5:12, 14–15, 17–19). Afterwards, Eve answered God's question with a full disclosure of what she had done. She also exposed the serpent's involvement. Adam did not make a full disclosure, and he took no responsibility for his role. Instead, he blamed both his wife and God. He did not even mention the serpent's involvement. When God drove him from the garden, he had not repented for these things. Once outside, living in his fallen flesh, Adam fathered the first murderer. Adam's fallen behavior had to be "cut off" by repentance before he could father godly seed. God later commanded that Abraham be circumcised. His circumcision, and that of all his male descendants, was a reminder of the covenant between God and man. Circumcision was necessary for Abraham's lineage to be godly and meet God's requirement for holiness. In Romans 2:29, Paul tells us that true circumcision is of the heart. This can be understood to mean that every believer must have a heart that is circumcised (the "flesh" cut off) in order to bring forth godly fruit.

A Fit with the Redemptive Message of the New Covenant

Adam and Eve, two fallen beings who were in bondage to Satan, produced the first seed of the serpent and, as a result, a lineage of fallen men like Cain has continued on the earth to this day. However, the Genesis 4 story ended with two repentant and free beings who had turned back to God, producing the first godly seed of woman through whom ultimately Jesus Christ came.

A Fit with the Free Woman Message of Galatians

Paul's words to the Galatians fit with the new perspective on Genesis 4 where two free beings produced a godly seed. In Galatians, Paul explains that those under the new covenant were free. He refers to them as the "Jerusalem which is above which is free and is the mother of us all." They are like Isaac who was born of a free woman. He also explains that those under the old covenant were in bondage. He refers to them as the "Jerusalem that now is, and is in bondage with her children." They are like Ishmael who was born of a woman in bondage.

Paul makes it plain that under the new covenant, both men and women have been set free from the bondage of the devil by Christ's once-for-all sin offering. As they stand in that freedom, they can bear fruit that is holy and acceptable to God.

A Fit with the Marriage Picture in Ephesians

In Ephesians 5, Paul describes how Christ gave himself for the church by laying down his life for her. He wrote that this is what a new creation husband should do. If a husband is walking with Christ and living according to the Spirit, his treatment of his wife will be in stark contrast to that of Adam at the time of the Fall. In Genesis, Adam sinned by sacrificing his wife and protecting himself from being exposed. In so doing, he did not love and cherish her, but hated and hurt her. Ephesians points to what Christ, the last Adam, did for the church, and says that this is a picture of what a new creation Christian husband should do for his wife. A new creation husband is one who does what Adam failed to do. He lays down himself for the benefit of his wife. Speaking of marriage in this way, Paul says this is a great mystery, but he is talking about Christ and the church.

Paul also said that the woman should see that she respects her husband (Eph. 5:33). To have respect for people is to admire them deeply as a result of their abilities, qualities, or achievements. This is a feeling one person has about another person. Feelings of respect cannot be demanded, because it is not possible to feel respect for someone whose behavior is bad, evil, or wrong. It is another thing to *treat* someone respectfully. Even the worst person deserves to be *treated* respectfully simply because he or she is a human being created by God.

Paul said that a wife is to see that she respect her husband. I believe that he meant a wife should see that she feel true respect for her husband (not only treat him respectfully). This can be understood to mean that she has some responsibility in the matter of being able to respect him. If she has a husband whose way of life is undeserving of respect, she is not free just to walk away from him. She should live with him in a way that will help him become worthy of respect. She must not support or enable his bad behavior. She should live as Peter advised and keep her own behavior in line with the truth of the Word of God (1 Pet. 3:1). In so doing, she would maintain an environment around him that God could use to help turn him to God. For example, if her husband tells her to do something that is immoral, or would cause her to disobey God—such as go with him to an idol temple and offer sacrifices to idols—to be true to the Word of God, she would not submit. This would become a living message of truth to him.

Today, many churches are made up of families who still live like the fallen first family. It is time for husbands and wives to begin to model Christ's behavior, as Paul described in Ephesians 5, in their marriage and with their children. When the church is filled with families where new creation husbands and wives relate to each other as Christ relates to His church, God will pour out his blessing, and the Spirit will have a free way on the earth to save and heal many people and relationships. Society will be improved because the Lord's presence among men and women always changes them and their society for the better.

A Fit with the Way to Address Offenses in Matthew

The new perspective of the Genesis account also stands well in light of what Jesus said in the New

Testament concerning how to deal with offenses with others in the family of God.

> 15 "If your brother sins, go and show him his fault in private; if he listens to you, you have won your brother. 16 But if he does not listen to you, take one or two more with you, so that BY THE MOUTH OF TWO OR THREE WITNESSES EVERY FACT MAY BE CONFIRMED. 17 If he refuses to listen to them, tell it to the church; and if he refuses to listen even to the church, let him be to you as a Gentile and a tax collector. (Matt. 18:15–17, NASB)

There is no question that Adam's blaming of Eve in the Garden of Eden would have offended Eve. When his blaming behavior continued outside the garden, and when Eve realized her own helplessness to continue living in that kind of environment with him, she would have asked for God's help. The Word stands forever true, so although it is not recorded in Genesis, the truth that Jesus gave in Matthew 18 about how to handle offenses among brethren would apply just the same then as now. Part of the help God would have given her would have been to show her that she needed to tell Adam that he was wrong to blame her in the garden. Presenting him with the fact that his sin had hurt her would be to *help* him in the right way. She couldn't change him herself, but God could use her words to work on Adam's desensitized conscience and possibly persuade him to repent.

A Fit with Practical Marriage and Family Life

As has been discussed, after the first couple ate of the forbidden fruit, Adam blamed the woman and indirectly blamed God. It was the devil, the accuser of the brethren, who sowed this blatant accusation against Eve, and the more subtle accusation against God, into Adam's mind. Adam accepted these fiery darts and voiced them to God. In this, Adam sinned further by believing the devil and blaming his wife and God.

Looking at the long history on this earth, we see that after man was driven out of the Garden of Eden, fallen men, as the seed of the serpent, have continued to listen to the devil and blame Eve (and God) when it suits them. By the time of Christ's coming, the Jewish leaders had magnified their blaming of Eve in the teachings of their oral tradition. They had declared all women to be cursed in ten different ways by God. They had justified their evil behavior toward women by saying that they were obeying God and doing His will with respect to women's punishment because of Eve's sin in the garden. We can also see in earth's long history, women who have followed in Eve's steps and enabled the suppressive behavior of fallen men by submitting to them out of fear for their own safety and security. Male dominating and female enabling patterns in marriage have been repeated millions of times. So, the new perspective of the Genesis story is a fit with practical marriage life.

The new perspective on Adam and Eve makes much more sense than the one that is traditionally given about the Genesis account. It also offers practical lessons for how a fallen marriage can become a godly one. Eve had to choose to move from a place of bondage under the rule of her fallen husband to a place of freedom under God's rule. She had to end her self-protective enabling and get out of God's way before He could open Adam's eyes to his true condition and bring him to repentance. Adam's repentance had to take place before the birth of Seth could take place. His repentance signaled the beginning of a line of godly males.

There is a clear lesson for women in this first Bible family scenario. Women cannot really help anyone until their own total and complete dependence is on God for everything. A woman, regardless of her particular circumstances, has to reach the point in life that she accepts the freedom God has offered her and repents of her enabling behaviors. She has to turn back to God with her whole heart and develop an intimate, daily relationship with Him. When she learns to look to Him alone for every need—physical, psychological, emotional, and spiritual—then she can become the strong, confident, capable woman of *chayil* that God intends her to be. Rightly related to God, she can help others, including men, turn to God. She can find her strong, yet appropriate voice, in situations that demand it. She can stand in her place as a believer and use the authority in the name of Jesus to bind the enemy and loose real, visible evidence of the kingdom of heaven on earth, starting first of all in her own family.

There is also a clear lesson for men. They can begin to be proper husbands, sons, and fathers of godly seed when they:

- See the pride at the root of their behavior

- Recognize their state of bondage to the devil

- Repent for their sins, in particular for the sins of lying by omission, of blaming their wives instead of loving and sacrificing themselves for them, and of slandering God

- Turn to God with all their heart and learn to humbly trust and depend on Him for everything

A Fit with the Condition of Society Today

As previously stated, the supposed Genesis 3:16 mandate by God for man to rule over woman has played a role in the modern-day feminist movement. If the truth of the freedom given to women by God had not been obscured, the destructive effects of ungodly feminism might not be rampant in society today.

Women who stand up and learn to be women of *chayil,* who have every need met by God, will not be like feminists who fight to get what is due them and blame men for discriminating against them. Instead, they will be strong, capable warriors against the devil. They will not be silent in the face of sin. Their voices of truth and matching actions will open the way for men to be convicted about how much they have hurt others, especially the women in their lives. As these men repent, they will become men who produce godly families. They will become a light to other men, showing them the way back to God.

A Fit with a High-level View of the Conflict between the Two Seeds Set in Motion in Genesis 3:15

By the end of Genesis 4, there are two seeds and two lineages of human beings on the earth: a godly one, Seth, and his descendants—the line of the promised seed of woman—and a serpentine one, Cain, and his descendants—the line of the seed of the serpent. It should be noted that there are males and females in both lineages. The godly line of Seth, under assault by the serpent, was gradually corrupted until they also became the seed of the serpent. God then judged the whole earth and saved one godly man, Noah, and his family. Noah's lineage also became corrupt over time, becoming the seed of the serpent. God then called a man named Abraham and through him began another godly line. By the end of the Old Testament period, Abraham's seed, the children of Israel, also had become corrupt. Finally, God sent His son, Jesus Christ—the promised seed of woman. He dealt a fatal blow to the head of the serpent and produced a godly line of believers from every tongue, tribe, and nation on the earth. This godly line, by God's grace, survives the assault by the serpent to the praise and honor and glory of God.

We have come to the end of our examination of the only lemon passage in the Old Testament, Genesis 3:16. We have covered the aftermath of the Fall and have met the first woman of *chayil*. Next, we will take a look at other women of *chayil* in the Old Testament.

Chapter 4
The Brave and the Bold: Many Women of Chayil

My heart rejoices in the Lord; My horn is exalted in the Lord. I smile at my enemies, because I rejoice in Your salvation. The adversaries of the Lord shall be broken in pieces; from heaven He will thunder against them. The Lord will judge the ends of the earth. (1 Sam. 2:1, 10, NKJV)

THE WOMEN WHO LIVED during the Old Testament period are described in many grape passages. They are "The Brave and the Bold" because, even though they were in the state of being ruled over by men because of the Fall, they were undaunted by their difficult situations. When it became necessary, they bravely and boldly spoke what was true according to God, or they demonstrated truth by their courageous actions.

Even though the Bible does not use the word *chayil* concerning all of them, the word *chayil* describes their qualities and characteristics. Because of this, I am referring to them as women of *chayil*. The first such woman, Eve, eventually saw her problem as an enabler and found the way out of it, becoming an example for all who would follow. She was the first of many other women in Old Testament times who did similarly: Sarah (spoke God's word to her husband and God told him to obey her), Zipporah (obeyed God's mandate when Moses had not done so and saved his life), Abigail (did what was right and did not submit to her husband), Naomi (returned to God's people after going with her husband to the Moabites), Ruth (told Boaz to do for Naomi what God's word commanded), Esther (risked her life to speak to the king and exposed the devil's work in Haman), Deborah (led Israel into battle when men would not), Jael (killed an enemy king with a tent peg), a mother in Israel (her wisdom saved her city), Bathsheba (taught Solomon about a woman of *chayil*), Hannah (helped purify the priesthood), and other women who were prophets (like

Huldah, who gave God's word to the king). These Old Testament women were women of force, strength, and ability; they were women of *chayil*. Next we will take a closer look at these women, and also make mention of a woman in the Bible who was strong, but bad.

Sarah

God used a free woman, Sarah, in Genesis 21:10–13 to tell the patriarch Abraham, her husband, that the son of a bondwoman could not be heir with the son of a free woman. God had changed this free woman's name to Sarah—a name that meant "chieftain"—indicating that she was not a weak or subjugated person. Abraham had been promised by God that he would have an heir through her; yet, many years passed, and she remained barren. Then, Sarah acted out of unbelief and suggested that Abraham get an heir by using her bondwoman, Hagar. Hagar had no voice in the matter because she was a slave. Ishmael was then born of Abraham and Hagar. His parents were a free man and a slave woman. When Ishmael was about thirteen years old, God fulfilled His promise to Abraham. Sarah conceived, and Isaac, the promised seed, was born. Isaac's parents, Abraham and Sarah, were a free man *and a free woman*. Isaac was the result of God's promise; Ishmael was not. Isaac was acceptable to God; Ishmael was not (Gen. 21:12, Rom. 9:6–8).

When Isaac was a young boy, Ishmael began to mock him. Sarah then went to Abraham and told him that Ishmael had to go. We can infer from this that she was sorry for the unbelieving part she had played in producing Ishmael, and that she was doing something to correct the situation for which she was responsible. God used her to help Abraham take steps to undo the damage they had done. God supported Sarah's statement to Abraham, "Cast out the bondwoman and her son: for the son of the bondwoman shall not be heir with the son of the free woman" (Gal. 4:30, Gen. 21:10, KJV). Abraham didn't want to do what Sarah said, but God told him to obey his wife, and he did.

It was Abraham's son by Sarah, a free woman, who was blessed. Ishmael, Abraham's son by Hagar, a bondwoman, was not accepted by God. If all that was needed for the earth to be blessed was to have Abraham's seed, then Ishmael fit that bill, and God could have blessed the earth through him. But the promise God made in the garden held. It was the seed of woman (seed born of the free woman as explained by Paul in Galatians) who was to be the one who would crush the head of the enemy. Isaac, the promised seed, came through Sarah, a free woman.

God honored Sarah in three ways: (1) He told Abraham to obey her words, (2) He blessed Isaac, her son, and (3) He had the apostle Paul quote Sarah's words in the New Testament book of Galatians and refer to them as "scripture" (Gal. 4:30–31).

Zipporah and Abigail

God recorded a life-changing event in both Zipporah's (Exo. 4:24–26) and Abigail's (1 Sam. 25:2–42) lives. These two women did the right thing when their husbands were in disobedience. In both accounts:

- The husbands had offended God and were in a situation requiring death.

- Both did something to correct the situation.

- The women ended up with godly husbands who were greatly used by God.

Zipporah

Zipporah had probably been involved in Moses' decision not to circumcise his son. Maybe she had suggested that he not circumcise the child, or maybe she just did not help him do what he knew he should have done. Either way, God ultimately came to Zipporah and let her know why He was seeking to kill Moses. Maybe He came to her because she was involved or maybe He could not get Moses to understand and respond, even when He was seeking to kill him. God apparently showed Zipporah Moses' disobedience, and she had to do something to save her husband. What she did showed Moses his disobedience. She circumcised their son with a sharp stone. This was much more difficult at the time because the child was older. She had to do what Moses should already have done. Circumcision is to cut off the flesh. I believe that the child represented the flesh of both Moses and Zipporah, since the son had come from both of them. When she cut off the foreskin, the result was that the fleshly disobedience of both of them was cut off. She had to do something that hurt her very much and was like a death to her. She was angry with Moses for having put her in the position that she had to do this, and she called him a bloody husband.

As women, we may find ourselves facing something similar to what Zipporah faced. We may realize that our husbands are walking in disobedience and living in their corrupt flesh while trying to obey and serve God. We may have to take an unpleasant action that is necessary to save our husbands from God's judgment.

Abigail

Abigail risked everything to turn a situation around. She paid attention when a young man referred to her husband, Nabal, as a son of Belial and told her that David was coming to kill him and many others in her family. Abigail saw how wrong her husband's behavior had been in the situation. She did not just stand by. She decided to do something behind her husband's back. She put herself in a position in which she might lose her life (at David's hands or her angry husband's hands or maybe even at God's hands). The lives of the others involved meant more to her than her own life; so, against her husband Nabal's wishes, she went to David to try and clear up the offense. She interceded for Nabal, admitting to David that Nabal was a fool. She took the blame for the situation, asking David's forgiveness. She gave him provision for his men, maybe even more than he had requested. She carried out what was just and righteous in the eyes of God based on her discernment of the situation. Her action was what Nabal really needed, not what he wanted. She did not tell Nabal what she was doing. Nabal was a proud man, and her action put him to shame. She was also shamed by having such a husband. Later, she told him what she had done, exposing him and his sin. His heart died and he became as stone. Ten days later, he died. She was without a husband. Then David sent for her and married her.

In these verses, Nabal symbolizes the old man and David the new man, the man in resurrection. Abigail symbolizes a woman of *chayil* who begins with a husband who is an old fool and, because of her strength to do the right thing in a bad situation, she ends up with a wonderful husband in resurrection. I believe Abigail's real motivation was for others, not for herself. She might have borne Nabal's abuse her whole life, but others were being affected. David and all his men were offended and were suffering hunger. Her household was in danger because of Nabal's behavior. She acted on their behalf. She didn't say, "I have to go along with Nabal; he is my husband. I have to act according to how he sees this situation."

Naomi and Ruth

God devoted a whole book of the Bible to a detailed account of two women, Naomi and Ruth. Naomi followed her husband and lived among the Moabites. Both of her sons married Moabite women. When Naomi's husband and both of her sons died, she turned back to God and returned to Israel. Ruth, her Moabitess daughter-in-law, made the decision to go with her mother-in-law to Israel and follow Naomi's God. Once there, Ruth gleaned in the fields to support Naomi. When she learned that a prominent Jewish man named Boaz was a relative of Naomi's and that he should have done something to take care of Naomi, Ruth took some bold steps in that direction. She made a marriage proposal to Boaz! In this way, she became a great, great, great ... grandmother of Christ. In Ruth 3:11, God calls Ruth a woman of *chayil*.

Esther

God devoted another book of the Bible to a woman (Esther). Esther risked her life to battle with God's enemy and save God's people. God chose Esther in advance of an attack by the enemy and set her in a place where she could save His people. Her self-sacrificing actions resulted in God's people being able to defeat those that hated them (Esther 4:14, 9:1).

Deborah and Jael

Deborah was a prophetess and a judge who led Israel into battle when a man refused to do so (Judg. 4:4). During the heat of battle, the enemy's king fled and sought refuge in Jael's tent. After he was asleep, Jael took a tent peg and drove it into his head and killed him. God used these two wise, courageous, and strong women to save Israel from peril (Judg. 4:21).

A Mother in Israel

A wise woman, a mother in Israel, saved her city through her wisdom. She advised the people of her city to cut off the head of Sheba the son of Bichri and throw it over the wall to Joab. His army was besieging her city because Sheba, a man who had lifted up his hand against King David, was hiding there. Her wisdom and bold action ended the conflict. Joab stopped his attack and returned to Jerusalem (2 Sam. 20:13–22).

Bathsheba

God used a woman, Bathsheba, to teach one of the wisest men that ever lived. In addition to being David's wife, Bathsheba was Solomon's mother. She taught him what he wrote in Proverbs 31. Proverbs 31:1 says that the oracle contains "the words that his mother taught him." I still remember how shocked I was when it dawned on me that the source of Proverbs 31 was Bathsheba, a woman who had committed adultery with David, and that she was the one who taught Solomon what he wrote about a woman of *chayil* (a woman whose price was far above rubies). Bathsheba understood the value of such a woman. In a sense, Bathsheba had been a victim of the King's lust. He saw her and had her brought to him. She did not seek him out, though some say she knew he could see her bathing on the roof and that she sought to attract him. However, the fact is that he had her brought to him, and he had his way with her. He was the King of Israel, a great and powerful man, and she came under his aura.

It is very interesting that she taught her second son that a woman of *chayil* was priceless. Maybe, after suffering the consequences of her sin—the loss of her husband Uriah and also the death of her first child with David—she realized that she had been a weak woman. She had not been strong enough to stand up to David and say, "No." She could have done this, because the Word of God forbade adultery. David might have been helped by this to stop his sin. So, after God gave Bathsheba another son, she taught this son the value of a woman of *chayil* and may even have encouraged him to find such a wife. Her teaching has been preserved in the Bible and has been read by untold numbers of people over the centuries.

Hannah

At a time when the priesthood had become corrupt, God used a faithful, praying woman named Hannah to change the situation. Eli, the priest, was faithful in his priestly service except that he would not discipline his wicked sons who were defiling the priesthood by their wicked ways.

Hannah, who was barren, begged the Lord over a long period of time for a child, promising that she would give the child to God. God answered her prayers and gave her a godly seed. Hannah kept her vow, and her son, Samuel, became the priest that took Eli's place when God took Eli's life and the lives of his wicked sons.

After her prayer was answered, Hannah was filled with praise for the Lord and rejoiced over her enemies. She also prophetically proclaimed:

6 "The Lord kills and makes alive;
He brings down to Sheol and raises up.
7 "The Lord makes poor and rich;

He brings low, He also exalts.
8 "He raises the poor from the dust,
He lifts the needy from the ash heap
To make them sit with nobles,
And inherit a seat of honor;
For the pillars of the earth are the Lord's,
And He set the world on them.
9 "He keeps the feet of His godly ones,
But the wicked ones are silenced in darkness;
For not by might shall a man prevail.
10 "Those who contend with the Lord will be shattered;
Against them He will thunder in the heavens,
The Lord will judge the ends of the earth;
And He will give strength to His king,
And will exalt the horn of His anointed." (1 Sam. 2:6–10, NASB)

Other Women

God used other women in the Old Testament who were strong, active, and capable:

- Miriam was a prophetess (Exo. 15:20).

- Huldah was a prophetess (2 Kings 22:14, 2 Chron. 34:22).

- Noadiah was a prophetess (Neh. 6:14).

- A woman of *chayil* was priced above rubies (Pro. 31).

- A woman of *chayil* was a crown to her husband (Pro. 12:4).

- Isaiah's wife was a prophetess (Isa. 8:3).

- Women were called out of their ease to put on sackcloth (usually a sign of repentance which implies praying or pleading) until the Spirit was poured out from on high (Isa. 32:9–15).

- Daughters of the people prophesied (Ezek. 13:17).

God also spoke in the Old Testament about women yet to come:

- A great host of women will publish the tidings of the word the Lord gave (Psa. 68:11, RV).

- Daughters and handmaidens will prophesy, and the Spirit will be poured out on them (Joel 2:28-29).

A Bad, Strong Woman

To close the Old Testament section, it is fitting to look at Jezebel, a woman who misused her strength as a woman. She was the wife of King Ahab, who was a king of the northern kingdom during the time of Elijah. She was a powerful, self-absorbed woman who carried her enabling of her wicked husband to the farthest extreme (1 Kings 21:9). She misused the power and position she had as Ahab's wife in order to keep him happy. She was controlled not by the Holy Spirit of God but by filthy, seducing spirits.

One account concerning Jezebel highlights her enabling ways. For the full account, see 1st Kings 21. In brief, Ahab coveted his neighbor's vineyard, but Naboth could not and would not sell it to Ahab because it was Naboth's ancestral inheritance. Jezebel found Ahab pouting and depressed because he could not get the vineyard. She then used her husband's name to deceive the elders and nobles in the city to do her bidding. They then framed Naboth using two false witnesses and had him stoned to death. Jezebel happily told Ahab the good news of Naboth's death. The news pleased him, and he went and secured the vineyard he had coveted.

If she had been a godly woman of *chayil,* she would have helped him by reminding him of the tenth commandment—you shall not covet. In so doing, she would have put God and His commandments before any desire to please her husband. Instead, Jezebel stands in the Bible as an example of the full development of fallen woman in her anti-God role. Ahab also shows the full development of a fallen man in his anti-God role.

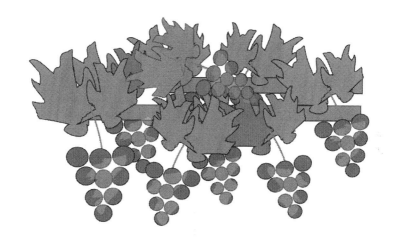

PART THREE:
THE NEW TESTAMENT ERA

Chapter 5
The Bent: Godly Women at the Time of Christ

IN THIS SECTION, first we will cover a little about the long period between the Old and New Testaments. Then, we will cover the many grapes found in the New Testament. After this, we will cover some history of Christian women's status in the church, and, lastly, we will cover the New Testament's seven lemons. The primary reason for presenting the material in this order is to make it possible to compare and contrast some things. Christ and Paul treated women differently from the mandates found in the seven lemon translations. The historical church, however, has mostly followed the mandates of the lemon translations.

I refer to the women who lived at the time of the coming of Christ as "The Bent" because of the condition they were in at the time He came. Their condition was a result of the changes that took place in Judaism during the days of mingling.

Some Necessary Background: The Days of Mingling

Remember that Genesis 3:16 conveyed the meaning of *teshuqah* as "turning" up until the 16th century. Also, in their native language, Old Testament Jews would have understood that the verb in the phrase, "shall rule over you" (as translated in the King James Version), was not a command verb but a verb showing a result. This means that they would have understood this verse differently than we do today. They would not have understood it as a mandate for men to rule over women, but as a description of woman's state of being as a result of her turning from God to her husband.

Old Testament women did not live under teachings that mandated their silence and submission to men. Instead, knowing well the story of Adam and Eve, Cain and Abel, and Seth, it was possible for them to consider Eve as the mother of all living and realize the important role she had played in bringing forth a line of godly men.

It is no wonder that Satan eventually brought about a translation change that not only obscured, but totally changed the true meaning of Genesis 3:16. He did not want New Testament women to discover its empowering secret. His subtle translation change took place sixteen centuries after Christ, near the end of the Dark Ages and near the time of the invention of movable type for the printing press, when the Bible was being translated into the languages of the common man. However, the groundwork for that sixteenth century change was laid centuries before in the long gap of time between the Old and New Testaments. During that four hundred year period, referred to as the "days of mingling," Satan was able to bring about profound changes in Jewish beliefs and teachings about women, greatly furthering his woman-subduing agenda.

When this long gap of time began, Satan had already seemingly gained the upper hand over God's people. Time and again, during the Old Testament period, he had been able to lead them into idolatry and defeat them. By the end of the Old Testament period, the relationship between the children of Israel and God had become so broken that God withdrew His manifest presence from them and went silent. Satan took full advantage of God's silence during the next four centuries. He realized that, even though God was silent, it was only a matter of time before He would begin to work again to produce the promised seed. Satan, therefore, turned his full attention to subduing woman and thwarting her ability to cooperate with God and bring forth the seed that was supposed to bruise his head.

In this four hundred year window of time, Satan used Jewish rabbi's lore (acquired knowledge or wisdom on subjects that were handed down by word of mouth usually in the form of stories or historical anecdotes [Encarta]) to introduce woman-subjugating changes to Jewish beliefs. The Jews were desirous of acceptance by the Greeks, among whom they were living, so Satan used Greek mythology and its practices to influence the rabbis.

For example, the rabbis overlaid the Greek myth of Pandora's box on the story of Eve and the "apple" (Bushnell, paras. 85, 118). Because the woman, Pandora, was considered to be the source of all human ills, Eve began to be portrayed likewise. (This thought about Eve has been perpetuated and survives today.) In this way, the Jews gradually developed an Oral Law, with many teachings that differed from the Word of God in the Old Testament, and they taught them to God's people as truth. The Oral Law was in use when Jesus came, and this is the law that He spoke strongly against, often referring to it as their traditions. Satan's persistent and purposeful behind-the-scenes work is evident in the fact that the Oral Law succeeded in subjugating Jewish women (Bushnell, paras. 8, 42–43). The Oral Law was later written down and became what is known today as the Talmud (Bushnell, para. 146 note).

Bushnell quotes Kalisch, who comments on the effect that the days of mingling had on the first translation of the Old Testament into Greek (the Septuagint), which took place from 300–200 B.C.:

> We should constantly bear in mind; in studying these Lessons, the point we have made: It was during the "days of mingling," especially, that the teaching got hold of the mind of the Jew, that his wife, merely because of her sex, was his inferior. It was during these days that the first translation of the Bible—the Septuagint Greek version—was made. This version, in some places, incorporated in its renderings the idea of woman's inferiority; and all other versions since have followed suit, more or less. "Men only need," says Dr. Beard, "to bring to the Bible sufficiently strong prepossessions, sufficiently fixed opinions, to have them reflected back in all the glamour of infallible authority" (Bushnell, para. 154)

A Taste of the Talmud

As stated earlier, I refer to the women who lived at the time of the coming of Christ as "The Bent" because of what had happened to them as a result of the changes that took place in Judaism during the days of mingling. Women of that day had a very low social status:

- In the Jerusalem temple, women were limited to one outer portion, the women's court, which was five steps below the court for men.

- A rabbi regarded it beneath his dignity to speak to a woman in public.

- Women were kept for childbearing and rearing and were always under the strict control of a man. (Hyatt, *In the Spirit,* 14)

Some statements from the Talmud show the reason for their *bent* condition:

- Let the words of the Law be burned rather than committed to women.... If a man teaches his daughter the Law, it is as though he taught her lewdness (*Sotah* 3:4).

- The woman, says the Law, is in all things inferior to man. Let her accordingly be submissive (*Apion* 2:210).

- Let a curse come upon the man who must needs have his wife or children say grace for him.

- Praised be to God that he has not created me a gentile; praised be God that he created me not a woman; praised be God that he has not created me an ignorant man ... (*Menahot* 43b)

- It is well for those whose children are male, but ill for those whose children are female ... At the birth of a boy all are joyful, but at the birth of a girl all are sad ... When a boy comes into the world, peace comes into the world; when a girl comes, nothing comes ... Even the most virtuous of women is a witch. (*Niddah* 31b) (Hyatt, *In the Spirit,* 13–14)

Bushnell explains more about the Talmud and its influence on translations:

Furthermore, if we may judge from the spirit of the teachings of the Talmud on the "woman question" (for the Talmud was then in the ascendancy, and the sayings of the rabbis considered more authoritative than Scripture itself), these amenders of the original text, as a class, held women in utter contempt. Dr. Paul Isaac Hershon (to quote one of the many witnesses to this statement) says: "The rabbis, over and over again, teach the utter inferiority of woman: they put a definite seal as it were on the degraded life of the female sex which for ages has been lived by women in the East as in the West." A certain Rabbi Yochanan, we are told, quotes the Mishnic (the Mishna is the most ancient and important part of the Talmud) rabbis as teaching that a man may do as he pleases with his wife: "It is like a piece of meat brought from the shambles, which one may eat, salt, roast, partially or wholly cooked." A woman once complained before Rav (a great rabbi) of bad treatment from her husband. He replied: "What is the difference between thee and a fish, which one may eat either broiled or cooked?" But Jews alone did not hold women in contempt at that time in human history. It was an unfortunate time, as regards women, for fixing the sense of the Holy Scriptures. (Bushnell, para. 8)

In one of her lessons entitled, "Shall Women Keep Silence?" Bushnell wrote:

That the Talmud, unlike the Old Testament, did remand women to silence admits of no doubt. "Out of respect to the congregation, a woman should not herself read in the law." "It is a shame for a woman to let her voice be heard among men." "The voice of a woman is filthy nakedness." These are some, out of many, of its sayings. As to asking questions: A wealthy Jewess ventured to ask once, of the great R. Eleazer, "Why, when the sin of the golden calf was but one only, should it be punished with a three-fold death?" We imagine the question was beyond his stock of knowledge, for he replied: "A woman ought not to be wise above her distaff." One Hyrcanus protested, aside, to R. Eleazer, because the lady who was thus reproved might withhold her tithes, in retaliation, and they amounted to considerable. R. Eleazer replied: *"Let the words of the law be burned rather than committed to woman."* This was accepted as a sort of judicial utterance, for future generations, among the Jews. (Bushnell, para. 202)

According to the Talmud, ten curses were uttered against Eve:

1. 'Greatly multiply' refers to catamenia [menstruation], etc.;

2. 'thy sorrow' in rearing children;

3. 'thy conception';

4. 'in sorrow shalt thou bring forth children';

5. 'thy desire shall be unto thy husband'; [followed by language too coarse for reproduction, leaving no doubt of the rabbinical interpretation of "desire"];

6. 'He shall rule over thee' [more, and fouler language];

7. she is wrapped up like a mourner, i. e.

8. dares not appear in public with her head uncovered;

9. is restricted to one husband, while he may have many wives;

10. and is confined to the house as to a prison. (Bushnell, para. 106)

Bushnell notes that Eve was never cursed and that Christ became a curse for us. She explains that nonetheless, Christian theologians still adopted certain of the ten curses from the Talmud to levy against woman, and she refers to Dean Alford's words as representative of this:

Notice that Dean Alford names at least *three curses* from which, he says, woman is to suffer. But why did he not set forth all ten of them,— especially that one that declares that man was also to be awarded the privilege of practicing polygamy because of Eve's sin? Christian theology *dares not set* forth the whole of the Talmudic teaching as to the "curses" of woman, in these enlightened days. It only ventures as far as the subordination of woman to the sensuality of man. To set forth the whole ten curses would effectually secure the condemnation of the whole, including the parts theology would keep. (Bushnell, para. 105)

New Testament Grapes during Jesus Time

When Jesus came, he set free the Jewish women who had been bowed down by the oppressive teachings of their rabbis. We can see clearly God's estimation of woman by Christ's treatment of them.

First of all, Jesus was born of a woman and God announced His birth through two women. Throughout all of His life, Jesus' treatment of women exposed the darkness of the Jewish teachings and showed people the truth about how God saw and felt about women. His living demonstrated to his male disciples how they should treat women. Through the involvement of women at every stage of His life, including his death and resurrection, God gave clear testament to His high regard for women.

Elizabeth and Mary Spoke of Jesus as Lord before His Birth

See the account of Elizabeth and Mary and their high praise, pre-birth announcement of Jesus in Luke 1:41–55. It is noteworthy that the Lord's four hundred year period of silence was broken by God's interaction with two women. The first was Elizabeth. Through her, God announced the coming of the Messiah's forerunner (Wiles, 26). Next, was Mary, a lowly Jewish woman who was a virgin. She bore the promised seed of woman, the Messiah, and was willing to bear the shame associated with being pregnant outside of wedlock. She responded to God's visitation with these words, "Be it unto me according to Your word."

Anna Announced Jesus as the Promised One after His Birth

A prophetess named Anna prophesied and spoke of Jesus to all who looked for redemption in Jerusalem (Luke 2:36–38).

Numerous Women Traveled with Jesus and Ministered to Him

Jesus ministered to women, traveled with them, and was ministered to by them:

> 2 And certain women, which had been healed of evil spirits and infirmities, Mary called Magdalene, out of whom went seven devils, 3 and Joanna the wife of Chuza Herod's steward, and Susanna, and many others, which ministered unto him of their substance. (Luke 8:2–3, KJV)

> 40 There were also women looking on afar off: among whom was Mary Magdalene, and Mary the mother of James the less and of Joses, and Salome; 41 (who also, when he was in Galilee, followed him, and ministered unto him;) and many other women which came up with him unto Jerusalem. (Mark 15:40–41, KJV)

Mary Commended for Sitting at the Feet of Jesus To Learn

In the face of rabbis who had shut women out from learning the Torah, Jesus announced that Mary's choice to sit at his feet and learn His words was the best choice and that no one would take that good part away from her (Luke 10:38–42).

> He praised Mary for being a learning disciple, a student, (sitting at his feet); He withheld praise from Martha for doing "women's work." (Hyatt, *10 Things,* 37)

> ... Jesus was prohibited [by the Jewish Oral Law of His day] from teaching women theology. But He did. (Hyatt, *10 Things,* 22–23)

Women Used in the Parables of Jesus To Represent God

God was likened to a woman sweeping her house to find a lost coin (Luke 15:8–10), and God was likened to a mother hen (Matt. 23:37).

A Woman Engaged by Jesus in Conversation

In defiance of the Oral Law of the Jews, showing that He did not view women at all as they did, Jesus spoke in a public place to a Samaritan woman at a well (John 4:6–29). She was the first person to whom He revealed that He was the Messiah. Jesus broke three Jewish rules by speaking with her as He did: As a Jew, He spoke to a Samaritan; as a man, He spoke to a woman in a public place; and He taught a woman theology. John 4:27 says that His disciples marveled that He spoke to a woman. (Hyatt, *10 Things,* 22–23)

A Woman Brought Forward by Jesus in the Synagogue

In opposition to their traditions, Jesus brought a woman forward in the synagogue before a group of rejecting, religious men. She had been bound by Satan and had been bent over with a spirit of infirmity for over eighteen years. He healed her and let her testify of God's glory in front of them (Luke 13:10–16).

Mary Magdalene Received and Memorialized by Jesus

Jesus let a woman with a very sinful past kiss His feet and anoint Him with oil in front of others who were critical of Him for this:

> 6 And when Jesus was in Bethany at the house of Simon the leper, 7 a woman came to Him having an alabaster flask of very costly fragrant oil, and she poured it on His head as He sat at the table. 8 But when His disciples saw it, they were indignant, saying, "Why this waste? 9 For this fragrant oil might have been sold for much and given to the poor." 10 But when Jesus was aware of it, He said to them, "Why do you trouble the woman? For she has done a good work for

Me. 11 For you have the poor with you always, but Me you do not have always. 12 For in pouring this fragrant oil on My body, she did it for My burial. 13 Assuredly, I say to you, wherever this gospel is preached in the whole world, what this woman has done will also be told as a memorial to her. (Matt. 26:6–13, NKJV)

Mary Shown Tender Love by Jesus during His Death

In his greatest time of suffering, nailed to the cross, Jesus saw His mother standing there, watching in agony as He was dying. Even though He knew that she would be comforted and made joyful by His resurrection in a few short days, He still took thought for her feelings in those few black and sorrowful days of terrible loss. He told her to look to John as her son and told John to take care of her as his mother. Her pain was only going to be for a few days, but He didn't want her to be without comfort even for those days (John 19:26–27). (Should we ever doubt His care for us in all our afflictions?)

A Gentile Woman Cared For by Jesus

A Syro-Phoenician woman came to Jesus and worshipped him, begging him to cast the demon out of her daughter. Jesus told her He was only sent to the lost sheep of the house of Israel. She reasoned with him by likening herself to a dog under the table of his master waiting for crumbs. He commended her saying, "O woman, great is your faith: let it be unto you as you desire," and her daughter was healed from that hour (Matt. 15:22–28, Mark 7:26).

Women Were First To Testify to the Death and Resurrection of Jesus

God had women present at the death of Jesus and after His resurrection, and He had them testify of what they saw; otherwise, there would be no record of some events, including those surrounding the resurrection itself. This is interesting because,

In Roman and Jewish law, the testimony of a woman was not permitted as evidence. Jesus, by this action, was cutting through remnants of prejudice that was yet remaining in His male disciples towards his female disciples. He was showing women that a new day had dawned. (Hyatt, *10 Things,* 31)

The following excerpts from the Bible reveal the details that we would be missing if it were not for the accounts of women, including one in which the women were to give instructions to the brethren.

45 And when he knew [it] of the centurion, he gave the body to Joseph. 46 And he bought fine linen, and took him down, and wrapped him in the linen, and laid him in a sepulchre which was hewn out of a rock, and rolled a stone unto the door of the sepulchre. 47 And Mary Magdalene and Mary [the mother] of Joses beheld where he was laid. (Mark 15:45–47, KJV)

1 In the end of the sabbath, as it began to dawn toward the first [day] of the week, came Mary Magdalene and the other Mary to see the sepulchre. 2 And, behold, there was a great earthquake: for the angel of the Lord descended from heaven, and came and rolled back the stone from the door, and sat upon it. 3 His countenance was like lightning, and his raiment white as snow: 4 And for fear of him the keepers did shake, and became as dead [men]. 5 And the angel answered and said unto the women, Fear not ye: for I know that ye seek Jesus, which was crucified. 6 He is not here: for he is risen, as he said. Come, see the place where the Lord lay. 7 And go quickly, and tell his disciples that he is risen from the dead; and, behold, he goeth before you into Galilee; there shall ye see him: lo, I have told you. 8 And they departed quickly from the sepulchre with fear and great joy; and did run to bring his disciples word. 9 And as they went to tell his disciples, behold, Jesus met them, saying,

All hail. And they came and held him by the feet, and worshipped him. 10 Then said Jesus unto them, Be not afraid: go tell my brethren that they go into Galilee, and there shall they see me. (Matt. 28:1–10, KJV)

55 And the women also, which came with him from Galilee, followed after, and beheld the sepulchre, and how his body was laid. 56 And they returned, and prepared spices and ointments; and rested the sabbath day according to the commandment. 1 Now upon the first [day] of the week, very early in the morning, they came unto the sepulchre, bringing the spices which they had prepared, and certain [others] with them. 2 And they found the stone rolled away from the sepulchre. 3 And they entered in, and found not the body of the Lord Jesus. 4 And it came to pass, as they were much perplexed thereabout, behold, two men stood by them in shining garments: 5 And as they were afraid, and bowed down [their] faces to the earth, they said unto them, Why seek ye the living among the dead? 6 He is not here, but is risen: remember how he spake unto you when he was yet in Galilee, 7 Saying, The Son of man must be delivered into the hands of sinful men, and be crucified, and the third day rise again. 8 And they remembered his words, 9 and returned from the sepulchre, and told all these things unto the eleven, and to all the rest. 10 It was Mary Magdalene, and Joanna, and Mary [the mother] of James, and other women [that were] with them, which told these things unto the apostles. 11 And their words seemed to them as idle tales, and they believed them not. (Luke 23:55–24:11, KJV)

8 Then went in also that other disciple, which came first to the sepulchre, and he saw, and believed. 9 For as yet they knew not the scripture, that he must rise again from the dead.

10 Then the disciples went away again unto their own home. 11 But Mary stood without at the sepulchre weeping: and as she wept, she stooped down, [and looked] into the sepulchre, 12 And seeth two angels in white sitting, the one at the head, and the other at the feet, where the body of Jesus had lain. 13 And they say unto her, Woman, why weepest thou? She saith unto them, Because they have taken away my Lord, and I know not where they have laid him. 14 And when she had thus said, she turned herself back, and saw Jesus standing, and knew not that it was Jesus. 15 Jesus saith unto her, Woman, why weepest thou? whom seekest thou? She, supposing him to be the gardener, saith unto him, Sir, if thou have borne him hence, tell me where thou hast laid him, and I will take him away. 16 Jesus saith unto her, Mary. She turned herself, and saith unto him, Rabboni; which is to say, Master. 17 Jesus saith unto her, Touch me not; for I am not yet ascended to my Father: but go to my brethren, and say unto them, I ascend unto my Father, and your Father; and to my God, and your God. 18 Mary Magdalene came and told the disciples that she had seen the Lord, and [that] he had spoken these things unto her. (John 20:8–18, KJV).

Women Received the Holy Spirit on the Day of Pentecost Just as the Men Did

That which was promised by the Father, the outpouring of the Holy Spirit, took place for the Jews on the day of Pentecost. That outpouring began the New Testament period in which many men and women would prophesy and preach the message of Christ's resurrection from the dead, just as Peter did that first day when he stood and declared:

16 But this is that which was spoken by the prophet Joel, 17 And it shall come to pass in the last days, saith God, I will pour out of my Spirit upon all flesh: and your sons and your daughters

shall prophesy, and your young men shall see visions, and your old men shall dream dreams: 18 And on my servants and on my handmaidens I will pour out in those days of my Spirit; and they shall prophesy: (Acts 2:16–18, KJV)

Peter announced that they were witnessing the Holy Spirit being poured out on men and women as a result of Christ's resurrection from the dead after having been crucified by wicked men. Peter's message brought conviction on those who heard it to such an extent that the hearers asked Peter and the rest of the apostles what they should do:

37 Now when they heard [this], they were pricked in their heart, and said unto Peter and to the rest of the apostles, Men [and] brethren, what shall we do? 38 Then Peter said unto them, Repent, and be baptized every one of you in the name of Jesus Christ for the remission of sins, and ye shall receive the gift of the Holy Ghost. 39 For the promise is unto you, and to your children, and to all that are afar off, [even] as many as the Lord our God shall call. 40 And with many other words did he testify and exhort, saying, Save yourselves from this untoward generation. (Acts 2:37–40, KJV)

It is noteworthy that the Father gave the Holy Spirit when Peter and the apostles were no longer part of the woman-suppressing religion of the Jews. The male disciples had seen the truth of God's view of woman demonstrated in Jesus' treatment of women and they had changed accordingly—repented, if you will. They understood that Jesus' coming had changed things. They remembered that He had sent a woman, Mary, to tell them the good news of His resurrection. So when they waited in Jerusalem for the promise of the Father, they did so *with the women* (Acts 1:14).

Do you think that, if Peter and the other apostles had told the women not to wait with them in Jerusalem, but to go home, the women would have silently departed? There is no way Peter and the others could have sent the women away. These women loved Jesus intensely; they were pursuers. They were the ones who went to the sealed tomb after Jesus died. Maybe they were watching to see if He was going to rise from the dead, as He had said. They were the first to know that He had risen, and at least one of them was the first to see and talk to Him afterward. They believed that He would send them the promise of His Father if they tarried in the city of Jerusalem as He told them (Luke 24:49). They would have acted on what they knew to be true. Having been with Jesus and having loved Him even in death, they would never have accepted their Jewish brothers telling them that they were not allowed to receive the promise of the Father because they were women!

What Peter and the other apostles did by including the women was completely against the tradition of the Jews, who would not permit a woman to learn God's Word or teach it, much less agree with them receiving the Spirit of God and prophesying! On the day of Pentecost, the apostles witnessed the promise of the Holy Spirit poured out on both men and women alike, and they also heard both men and women prophesy. This is why Peter explained this phenomenon to be the fulfillment of Joel's prophecy hundreds of years before concerning the sons and daughters of God.

Some New Testament Grapes during the Early Church Period

New Testament women were set free by Jesus. Chapter 3 of Hyatt's book, *In the Spirit We're Equal,* covers the freedom of women in the early church. Both men and women were present in the upper room on the Day of Pentecost (Acts 1:13–26).

> The Holy Spirit confirmed the egalitarian pattern demonstrated by Jesus, when, on the Day of Pentecost, women were equal recipients of the Pentecostal outpouring (Acts 2:1–5, 17–18) (Hyatt, *In the Spirit*, 21)

> In Romans 16:1–15, Paul specifically greets ten women by name, including Phoebe, Prisca, May,

Junia, Tryphaena, Tryphosa, Persis, the mother of Rufus, Julia, and the sister of Nereus. (Hyatt, *In the Spirit*, 22)

Paul mentions women as being co-laborers or coworkers (Greek, *sunergoi*) with him in ministry (1 Cor. 16:16, 19; Rom. 16:1–16; Phil. 4:2–3). (Hyatt, *In the Spirit*, 28)

Two Women Targeted by the Spirit

Paul and Silas traveled through Phrygia and Galatia, and they considered going to preach the word in Asia; but the Spirit forbade them to go there. They went on to Mysia. From there, they wanted to go into Bithynia, but the Spirit did not allow them to go there either. Then, when they arrived in Troas, God called Paul through a vision to go over into Macedonia. So, Paul and Silas went to Philippi in Macedonia. There the Spirit led them to speak to a group of women:

> 13 And on the sabbath we went out of the city by a river side, where prayer was wont to be made; and we sat down, and spake unto the women which resorted [thither]. 14 And a certain woman named Lydia, a seller of purple, of the city of Thyatira, which worshipped God, heard [us]: whose heart the Lord opened, that she attended unto the things which were spoken of Paul. 15 And when she was baptized, and her household, she besought [us], saying, If ye have judged me to be faithful to the Lord, come into my house, and abide [there]. And she constrained us. (Acts 16:13–15, KJV)

So, the first convert in Macedonia was a woman. She opened her home to Paul and Silas. Immediately after this, a damsel who was possessed with a spirit of divination began to follow Paul and Silas about proclaiming who they were. Paul commanded the spirit to come out of her, and she was delivered. This upset her masters because they were using her demonic ability to make money.

It is noteworthy that the Scripture tells us that the Spirit prevented Paul and Silas from going to two different places and then led them by a vision to another place—specifically to a group of women. God seems to be making a statement about his view of women's place in the Spirit's move on earth—women were going to be used by Him the same as men. There was no male or female in Christ. Not only did the Spirit begin the church in Philippi through a woman and her household, He also delivered a woman there from bondage to an evil spirit and her human masters.

Priscilla Labored with Paul

When Paul mentioned Priscilla in writing, he put her name before the name of her husband, Aquila, which was, according to some biblical commentary, an indication of her value in the church.

Phoebe Commended by Paul

Ray Munson wrote in the "Foreword" to *God's Word to Women:*

> Paul calls Phoebe deacon of the church at Cenchrea and orders the church at Rome *"to assist her* [men and all] in whatsoever business she hath need of you" (Rom. 16:2). (Bushnell, iv)

Philip's Daughters Prophesied

Paul stayed in the house of Philip who had four virgin daughters who all prophesied (Acts 21:9), and there is no record that he said anything against this. If women were supposed to keep silent in the churches, then shouldn't Luke, the author of Acts, have made this observation? Shouldn't Paul have pointed out in one of his letters that Philip's daughters were doing something wrong?

Two Women Responsible for Timothy's Faith

Paul gave credit to Timothy's grandmother, Lois, and his mother, Eunice, for the sincere faith that Timothy had. They were responsible for his knowing the Holy Scriptures from childhood (2 Tim. 1:5, 3:15).

Chapter 6
The Beaten: Christian Women after the Ascension of Christ

Your word is a lamp to my feet and a light to my path.
(Psa. 119:105, NKJV)

And the word of the LORD was rare in those days; [there was] no
widespread revelation.
(1 Sam. 3:1, NKJV)

I AM REFERRING TO THE CHRISTIAN WOMEN that were born and lived in the centuries after Christ's ascension as "The Beaten," because history shows that shortly after the beginnings of the early church, in which women were being set free by the gospel, Satan began a strategy to suppress women believers. He was gradually able to create a very dark environment on the earth in which he continued and even increased his suppression of women. He gradually was able to conceal the truth of the word of God from people and its transforming light by removing it from their apprehension and by misinterpreting and misapplying it through the pulpits of the male clergy of the day—many of whom he had usurped. We refer to that long period of history on the earth as the Dark Ages. The following gives evidence of the detrimental effect this progressive darkness had on women.

The Paradox

One cannot help but notice the historically observable paradox that, after Christ brought deliverance for everyone from the bondage of sin and death, Christian women were treated as if this deliverance had not occurred for them. Actually, they were treated worse than Old Testament women.

Bushnell informs us that:

Occasionally a Bible expositor comments on the seemingly narrower sphere allotted to women under the Gospel than was accorded them under the law. Kalisch says: "The New Testament is ... even more rigorous than the Old; for whilst it commands the woman *'to learn in silence with all subjection, but not to teach, nor to usurp authority over the man, but to be in silence,'* she was in the Old Testament admitted to the highest office of teaching, that of prophets, as Miriam, Deborah and Huldah." (Bushnell, para. 153)

In the early first century church, women experienced a measure of freedom, as seen in Jesus' treatment of them and in Paul's. However, in a relatively short time, the Oral Law's perverted teachings about women surfaced through the Judaizers—Jews who had accepted Christ but who still adhered to some of the teachings of the Oral law. The Judaizers sought to influence the new believers to continue to operate under the Oral law's teachings. They also influenced the founding church fathers. These second and third century clerics, having lost the knowledge of the Hebrew language (which had become by their time almost a dead language), sought to learn about the Hebrew language directly from those who knew it— the Jewish rabbis—men who were proponents of the Talmud's (written version of the Oral Law) teachings (Bushnell, paras. 16, 19). Thus, these Christian clerics came under the influence of Jewish Talmudic views. So, although in the early church women were liberated, Judaizers and some of the early church fathers, who adopted and promoted some of the Talmudic teachings about women, were used by the devil to bring women back into bondage and ultimately into a state much worse than the state of women during Old Testament times.

I recommend the book, *In the Spirit We're Equal*, by Susan C. Hyatt, for a detailed historical overview of women in New Testament Christian history. She covers that history by looking at it in four basic periods of time: The early church (first century), the early centuries of the church (second, third, and fourth centuries), the Dark Ages (fifth through fifteenth centuries), and the Reformation (sixteenth century forward). In the following, I present an overview of some enlightening highlights from her writing and research, beginning with the second century. As a matter of history, I will include the names of some of the men in early centuries who were used by Satan as instruments to oppress women.

To avoid misunderstanding, if possible, it needs to be stated up front that anyone, male or female, non-Christian or Christian, who participates in the suppression, oppression, or abuse of women is a person who is expressing the fallen, Adamic nature. All such persons are the seed of the serpent that are used by the devil to "bruise the heel" of the seed of woman. To help keep this fact in view, when possible and suitable, I will use the term "seed of the serpent" instead of the word "men."

Some Clarification about the Word "Equal"

Some of the quotes found in this chapter make use of the word "equal" with respect to the relationship between male and female believers. Therefore, before continuing, I feel it is important to give some necessary clarification about my position with respect to two main schools of thought about the roles of men and women that exist in Christian circles today. The two schools of thought are complementarian and egalitarian. There are also schools of thought that are slightly modified variations of these two schools.

In general, complementarians believe that women and men have particular God-ordained roles that are unique and distinct, and that functions and roles which involve authority belong with the male. They believe that respective male and female roles are designed by God to complement each other and, therefore, males and females can work harmoniously together to serve God within the parameters set by God.

Egalitarians mostly reject the complementarian position. They consider Christian males and females to be equal with respect to their possible functions and roles as believers. They believe that authority is not gender specific. They believe that males and females can work harmoniously together to serve God within an egalitarian framework.

I do not accept the complementarian position, and, if forced to choose, would come down more on the side of egalitarians. However, I do not feel comfortable with the heavy use of the word "equal" in the egalitarian movement or with some of their ways of discussing and explaining their position, at least with respect to material I have read thus far. Like the egalitarians, I strongly believe that in Christ there is neither male nor female and that God views male and female believers as equal in value and rights by virtue of being human beings. I also believe that the functions and roles of males and females are completely determined by the gifts and leading of the Holy Spirit, which are given to each person by God. I also believe that the Spirit does not distribute these gifts equally or with gender considerations. It is this—the fact that the Spirit does not equally distribute gifts and leading—that causes me to object to the heavy use of the terms "equal" and "egalitarian." In other words, with respect to their Spirit assigned functions and roles, believers *are not treated as equal* by God. Some persons are given greater gifts, some lesser gifts. God's valuation of the core worth of persons is the same whether male or female, but His distribution of gifts is not equal.

It is this kind of confusion that causes me to avoid using the word "equal" when addressing Christian gender issues. The word simply is not a perfect fit, and it has the potential to be misused by the devil to produce misunderstanding and fuel feelings of rivalry and controversy between males and females who feel they are not being treated "equally." In other words, if the broad idea of being equal is used as the touchstone for measuring or evaluating the propriety of the treatment of women, things can quickly deteriorate.

After studying the matter, I have decided to speak about Christian gender issues in terms of freedom rather than in terms of equality. I believe that men and women are both identically free in Christ. They both have the freedom to have their own relationship with Christ and to follow Him as He leads, regardless of their gender. They are free to make their own decisions about following Him and are not subject to other believers who might try to control or direct their spiritual or practical lives or block a path with which they disagree. There should always be mutual respect for each person's freedom, male or female—freedom which was given to them by God within moral boundaries, so that they could follow the Lord in the way He would lead them, without gender consideration or confusion.

In order to have a healthy Christian marriage, husbands and wives must give each other this kind of freedom. In order to have a healthy church experience, Christian men and women must give each other this kind of freedom. This works when both genders put their full trust in God. The truth is that male and female believers alike should always vie with one another in showing honor and humility and in yielding and submitting to one another. They should not want to rule over each other, but should trust one another to God. They should always keep the benefit of the other in mind and always respect and honor the freedom of the other to make personal decisions and choices before God within the moral boundaries God has set for them in His Word.

As for the matter of authority, all authority is God's and is expressed through His words. Every believer, male or female, has access to God's authority, but it is God who is the source of the power that backs up His words. No man controls that. God backs up His Word with the power of the Holy Spirit for those who are living and walking according to His Word and His Spirit—those who are holy ones, not hypocrites.

With these things in mind, I have endeavored in the material that follows to emphasize the matter of mutual freedom rather than the equality of males and females, even though some of the quotes I use from others speak about gender issues in terms of equality.

Early Centuries (Second, Third, and Fourth)

Chapters 4 through 7 of Hyatt's book, *In the Spirit We're Equal*, provide an in-depth look at what happened during the early centuries of the church with respect to the Spirit and with respect to the treatment of women. In brief, Hyatt's information shows how Satan used male Christian leaders, early church fathers, to produce conditions that shut down two things in the church: the manifest presence of the Spirit and the freedom of Christian women. The following quotes from Hyatt give us some perspective on this time period (footnote numbers in quotes have been omitted):

> As the first generation of believers passed away and as Christianity spread rapidly, two very different movements arose within Christendom: one was a move of God; the other, a move of man. The move of man gained precedence manifesting itself in what is known as institutionalism. Institutionalism is an emphasis on organization at the expense of other factors. It is a mode of organization whereby human control displaces the leadership of the Holy Spirit. In the early Church, institutionalism crept in at the expense of Spirit-life.
>
> One symptom of institutionalism was (and is) the division of Christians into two classes: a ruling class called *clergy (kleros)* and a subservient class called laity *(laos)*. This is a misuse of these two New Testament terms since both are consistently used to refer to all the people of God. All believers are both the "called ones" *(kleros)* and "the people of God" *(laos)*. Nevertheless, the institutional trend prevailed and this move of man defined the term clergy as "called ones" who ruled and laity as "the masses" who were ruled. (Hyatt, *In the Spirit*, 39–40)
>
> Subsequently, the Church moved rapidly toward a highly developed patriarchal system of government identical in structure to the political empire. (Hyatt, *In the Spirit*, 40)
>
> Virtually all church historians agree that the institutionalization of the early Church was accompanied by the demise of the charismatic gifts. The loss of spiritual power was accompanied by the marginalization and

subjugation of its female members. (Hyatt, *In the Spirit,* 42)

With organizational structure and religious ritual replacing the dynamic presence of the Spirit, women found themselves pushed down and under. It was clear that the developing clerical class would be for men only. (Hyatt, *In the Spirit,* 46)

These developments would necessitate the formulation of theologies to justify both the absence of Spiritual power in the Church and the secondary status of women. (Hyatt, *In the Spirit,* 47)

Throughout the centuries, the Holy Spirit has continued to renew true believers, and with these renewals have come efforts by the Spirit to democratize the Church and to reinstate the egalitarian status of women. However, the rejection of Montanism, the first renewal movement, was pivotal in the life of the Church. In fact, it has been said that the Church has never fully recovered from this early rejection of the Holy Spirit. It could also be said that women have never fully recovered. (Hyatt, *In the Spirit,* 47)

These early church fathers' prejudices concerning women and the political culture of their day influenced Bible translations and interpretations. The following quotes reveal some of their negative perceptions.

Clement of Alexandria ... said, "Nothing for men is shameful, for man is endowed with reason; but for woman it brings shame even to reflect on what her nature is." (Hyatt, *In the Spirit,* 51)

Tertullian ... called women "the Devil's gateway." Among many other derogatory statements about women, he said, "On account of your desert [i.e., punishment], that is, death—even the Son of God had to die." (Hyatt, *In the Spirit*, 51–52)

Origen ... expressed ... "Men should not listen to a woman ... even if she says admirable things, or even saintly things, that is of little consequence, since they come from the mouth of a woman." He also said, "What is seen with the eyes of the creator is masculine, and not feminine, for God does not stoop to look upon what is feminine and of the flesh." (Hyatt, *In the Spirit*, 52)

Ambrose of Milan believed that Eve was seductive and was the origin of all evil and lies.... He said, "Even though man was created outside Paradise (i.e., in an inferior place), he is found to be superior, while woman, though created in a better place (i.e., inside Paradise) is found inferior."... He also wrote, "A man may marry again if he has divorced his sinful wife, because he is not restricted in his rights as is the woman, because he is her head." (Hyatt, *In the Spirit*, 52–53)

Augustine .... wrote, "The woman herself alone is not the image of God whereas the man alone is the image of God as fully and completely as when the woman is joined with him." He said, "We should look upon the female state as being as it were a deformity." ... he said, "She [Eve] was the first to be deceived and was responsible for deceiving the man." He also said, "She [Eve] ... made her husband a partaker of the evil of which she was conscious." (Hyatt, *In the Spirit*, 53)

Chrysostom .... said, "The woman [Eve] taught once, and ruined all." He says that for a man to go to a woman for advice is like going to "irrational animals of the lower kind." ... Ruth Tucker and Walter Liefeld note,

> The man is "skilled at the greater things"
> but he is "downright inept and useless in
> the performance of the less important
> ones, so the woman's service is
> necessary... God maintained the order of
> each sex by dividing the business of
> human life into two parts and assigned
> the more necessary and beneficial
> aspects to the man and the less
> important, inferior matters to the
> woman." (Hyatt, *In the Spirit*, 54–55)

> Jerome .... said, "It is contrary to the order of
> nature and of the law that women should speak
> in a gathering of men." He also said that "women,
> especially those who assumed leadership roles in
> religion were 'miserable, sin-ridden wenches.'" It
> was his opinion that if a woman wanted to serve
> Christ, "she will cease to be a woman and will be
> called a man." (Hyatt, *In the Spirit*, 55–56) (Refer
> to Hyatt's book for bibliographic information.
> Footnote numbers have been omitted.)

Concerning Iranaeus and Tertullian of Carthage,
Bushnell wrote:

> Irenaeus, Bishop of Lyons in 177 A.D., following
> the teaching of Ben Sira and other Jews, says of
> Eve: "Having become disobedient, she was made
> the cause of death, both to herself and to the
> entire human race." But Tertullian of Carthage, a
> few years later, is particularly severe, and visits
> Eve's sin on all Christian women, in the following
> language: "Do you not know that you are an Eve?
> God's verdict on the sex still holds good, and the
> sex's guilt must still hold also. YOU ARE THE
> DEVIL'S GATEWAY, you are the avenue to the
> forbidden tree. You are the first deserter from the
> law divine. It was you who persuaded him [Adam]
> whom the devil himself had not strength to
> assail. So lightly did you esteem God's image. For
> your deceit, for death, the very Son of God had to
> perish." (Bushnell, para. 88)

Many of the theological views of the present day show the shaping of Tertullian's hand upon them, for, to use the concise statement of Lippincott's Biographical Dictionary, "He acquired great influence among the Christians of his time." Not a few of his literary works remain to this day. With such a view of woman, to start with (shut out by perpetual "guilt" from participation in the merits of Christ's atonement), it is small wonder that the next Scripture verse that we shall consider (Gen. 3:16), has been construed, in accordance with the teaching of the Talmud and Tertullian, as God's perpetual curse upon the entire female sex. (Bushnell, para. 89)

Penance has no purpose excepting to expiate guilt. When women are taught that they must take a specially lowly position; that they must meet their husbands' sensual demands with unquestioning obedience (see Lesson 14); that they must be silent in Church; that they must go veiled; must not teach or preach; that they must have no part in Church government,—and all because Eve sinned, they are taught to do penance, and they are taught thereby that in some sense guilt adheres to them. The teaching of all these things (whether acknowledged or not), is precisely what Tertullian dared to say, namely,—"God's verdict on the sex still holds good, and the sex's *guilt* must still hold also." (Bushnell, para. 732)

Dark Ages (Fifth through Fifteenth Centuries)

Women during the period of the Middle Ages were:

... valued only as 'wombs,' 'workers,' and objects of male gratification in a highly patriarchal society. The attitude of the institutional Church contributed to this hardship. (Hyatt, *In the Spirit*, 57)

The Beguines, for example were religious women in a movement that originated in the Netherlands in the twelfth century.... Not having the sanction of the papacy, however, they were condemned by the Church. They were charged with a number of deviations from orthodoxy including refusal to make confessions to a priest and to respect "the host." They were also "guilty" of preaching and theologizing, but their greatest "crime" was their translating of the Bible! As victims of the Inquisition they were among those who were burned at the stake. (Hyatt, *In the Spirit*, 57–58) (footnote numbers have been omitted)

Here are some quotes from church leaders of this period:

Thomas Aquinas .... said, "Woman is defective and misbegotten." He also said, "Woman is naturally subject to man because in man the discernment of wisdom predominates." (Hyatt, *In the Spirit*, 58)

Odo of Cluny ... wrote "To embrace a woman is to embrace a sack of manure."

Bonaventura was willing to concede that woman is "man's equal in nature, grace, and glory," but he agreed with Aristotle in saying,

> Woman is an embarrassment to man, a beast in his quarters, a continual worry, a never-ending trouble, a daily annoyance, the destruction of the household, a hindrance to solitude, the undoing of a virtuous man, an oppressive burden, an insatiable bee, man's property and possession. (Hyatt, *In the Spirit*, 59)

The Decretum of 1140 said, "It is right that he whom woman led into wrongdoing should have her under his direction so that he may not fail a second time through female levity." Friar Cherubino's 15th century *Rule of Marriage* said,

> Scold her sharply, bully and terrify her.
> And if this still doesn't work ... take up a
> stick and beat her soundly, for it is
> better to punish the body and correct the
> soul than to damage the soul and spare
> the body.... Then readily beat her, not in
> rage but out of charity and concern for
> her soul, so that the beating will
> redound to your merit.
> (Hyatt, *In the Spirit*, 59)

Such negative attitudes of church leaders produced horrendous abuse of women:

> The Medieval Church sanctioned the beating of wives, calling it "chastisement" and basing it on the "headship" supposedly espoused by I Corinthians 11:3. Because it was believed that woman had sinned more than man, it was taught that men were doing God's will when they made women suffer. "Men were exhorted from the pulpit to beat their wives and wives to kiss the rod that beat them." In the 13th century, the Laws and Customs of Beauvais advised men to beat their wives "only within reason" since an excessive number of women were dying of marital chastisement. (Hyatt, *In the Spirit*, 59)

> The Roman Church had been struggling from the fourth to the twelfth centuries to impose celibacy on the clergy. In its bid, it increasingly demonized female sexuality by attributing the power of sexuality to demons. "When sexuality was defined as demonic, a new concept of woman was invented—the medieval witch." The resulting persecution, "the witchcraft frenzy of the late Middle Ages, was one of the most sexist atrocities to have occurred in all of history." (Hyatt, *In the Spirit*, 60)

The absolute hatred of women, fear of female sexuality, and disdain for marriage can hardly be imagined in our minds. It is most clearly articulated, however, in a volume called The Witches' Hammer (1486). Written by ... two German theologians, it is a landmark document about witches, womanhood, and the unspeakable torture that was ordered to be used against them. In it, female sexuality is portrayed as demonic and women, in general, as evil, inferior, and deceitful. It alleges that the word describing woman, *femina*, came from *fe minus* or *fides minus* meaning "less in faith." As a result of this document and the persecution that it inflamed, it has been estimated that more than a million women were tried for the heresy of witchcraft and were burned at the stake. (Hyatt, *In the Spirit*, 61) (footnote numbers have been omitted)

Reformation (Sixteenth Century Forward)

During the Reformation period, things continued basically the same for women, but some rays of light began to break through the darkness:

Although during the Reformation era, women continued to be repressed, individual women gained a degree of prominence. Argula von Grumback (1492–1563), for example, was a highly intelligent and gifted woman who debated the Catholic theologians at the University of Ingolstadt. Rather than being applauded, however, she was condemned "an insolent daughter of Eve, a heretical bitch and confounded rogue." She was persecuted by the Church as well as by her husband who locked her up so that he would not be locked out of his job. (Hyatt, *In the Spirit*, 71)

For women, the period of Reformation continued to be a time of great darkness. They remained at the bottom of the chain-of-command in the thoroughly hierarchical mindset of the Church. A slight ray of light pierced the darkness with the formulation of the doctrine of the priesthood of all believers. Another ray of light flickered with the Anabaptist recognition of the prophethood of all believers. Nevertheless, these doctrines were not espoused on behalf of women. Consequently, they served primarily the purposes of a patriarchal culture. (Hyatt, *In the Spirit*, 74)

The belief in women's inferiority can be seen in statements by a well-known reformer of that day:

John Calvin (1509–1564), too, inherited the prevailing view of women derived from the Church fathers and common in the medieval church. It is not surprising, then, that he would say, "Let the woman be satisfied with her state of subjection, and not take it amiss that she is made inferior to the more distinguished sex." He wrote,

As the woman derives her origin from the
man, she is therefore inferior in rank ...
as the woman was created for the sake of
the man, she is therefore subject to him
... God's eternal law ... has made the
female subject to him ... God's eternal
law ... has made the female subject to
the authority of men. On this account all
women are born, that they may
acknowledge themselves as inferior in
consequence of the superiority of the
male sex. (Hyatt, *In the Spirit*, 67)

Bushnell provides revealing quotes from a number of male church leaders of that time. Concerning Martin Luther, she wrote:

And yet, amazing as it seems, Luther, as well as others, seems never to have grasped the idea of "free grace" for women. It is recorded of him that he said: "If a woman becomes weary and at last dead from bearing, that matters not. Let her only die from bearing; she is there to do it." Luther made much of "liberty of conscience," yet as regards women he said: "She must neither begin nor complete anything without man: where he is, there she must be, and bend before him as before a master, whom she shall fear and to whom she shall be subject and obedient." He left no place for "liberty of conscience" for women. (Bushnell, para. 831)

This period of time in history and the prevailing views about women had an impact on the translation of the King James Bible and on women.

> The low estate of women was further entrenched as the cultural norm through Puritan and Anglican efforts to bring order out of chaos. As both groups attempted to force their perspectives on society, the rulers increased their political power over the masses by using the power of religion in their personal lives. In this, both Anglicans and Puritans contributed to the notion that the home was to be considered a little church where patriarchal rule was to be enforced.

> An additional irritant that both groups were attempting to eradicate, especially between 1640 and 1660, was the host of powerful women preachers who had arisen among groups such as the Friends. Thus, they reasserted with great intensity the idea of authoritative male headship in the home. The man was called upon to manage his wife, his children, and his workers. His authority was sanctioned with enthusiasm and urgency by both the state and the church. A family was, in fact, described as a "little church and a little commonwealth," and was to serve as a school for training servants and women in subjugation." (Hyatt, *In the Spirit*, 78–79)

> According to this teaching, the home was to be seen as a little kingdom where the man was to rule as king of "his castle" in the same way as the King of England was to rule the state. Furthermore, the home was also to be seen as a little church were the man was to rule as high

priest in the same way that the King was to rule the Church of England. So the man was now king and priest of the home with woman as subject both politically and religiously. (Hyatt, *In the Spirit*, 80)

Hyatt presents a long record of moves of the Spirit that began at the time of the Reformation and that have continued to the present time. She traces the matching change in the status of women. In the following, she provides a high-level overview of this time period:

It is expedient for us to understand that the formulators of the prevailing, traditional theology about women maintained the pagan ideas that women are evil, inferior, unclean, and unequal. It is equally important to realize that Jesus taught by precept and example, a theology of womanhood that was totally opposite to this. It is, however, exciting to observe an elevation of women by the Holy Spirit beginning with great force among the Friends in the 1600s and continuing in recognizable dimensions among the early Methodists (1700s), the Holiness people (1800s) and the early Pentecostals (1900s), indeed, in the midst of great darkness, the Light would shine. (Hyatt, *In the Spirit*, 80)

Chapter 7
The Bad: Seven New Testament Lemon Translations

WITH THE BACKGROUND of some of the history of suppression of Christian women freshly in our view, we now come to the small bunch of misfit lemon passages in the New Testament that served as the basis for this suppression. Subjugation of women is totally against the character and purpose of God; it is totally in line with the character and purpose of Satan. God's estimation of woman is evident in the New Testament grape passages. These show Jesus' excellent treatment of women and also show Paul's proper valuation of them, as we covered in chapter 5.

Unfortunately, the seven New Testament lemons have received the greatest amount of attention, both historically and traditionally. As a result, they hang prominently in the biblical vineyard of verses about women. The purpose of this chapter is to "de-lemonize" these lemons, that is, to turn them into the grapes that they really are.

The first step in de-lemonizing a lemon passage is to evaluate it in the light of God's character. Whenever a lemon translation is read with the proper definition and understanding of true authority in mind, one cannot miss the obvious: The lemon translations promote the idea and practice of top-down hierarchical authority. They promote the satanic application of authority—that which readily exists in fallen human thought and is evident everywhere in fallen human culture. They promote the antithesis of God's self-sacrificing, humbling, and bottom-up supportive authority, which always operates in a gracious, as well as righteous and just way (as explained in "Authority and Freedom" in Chapter 3).

I hope that, at a very minimum, when these passages are considered in the light of a proper understanding of God's authority, sober-minded people will realize that something is seriously wrong with the message of the lemons. The existence of such an extreme disconnect between their message and the character of God demands that the lemons be re-studied, re-evaluated, and re-translated so as to conform to the practice of true authority which matches God's character and nature. These passages must not continue to stand as they are, representing God in a way that contradicts His character.

Some Foundational Information

Before addressing the New Testament lemon verses, we will briefly review some of what we have covered already and then discuss some translation principles.

Paul and Peter Not Sour Misogynists; Satan Lemonized Some of Their Grapes

None of the New Testament lemons were given to us directly by Jesus. Six of them are attributed to Paul and one of them to Peter. The six Pauline lemons have caused some people to label Paul as a misogynist. Peter has fallen victim to the same label because of one lemon passage. The truth is that Satan is responsible for the mischaracterization of Paul and Peter, because he is the one who lemonized their grapes through poor translations. As we saw in the history of Christian women in chapters 6 and 7, Satan began his work to adulterate the gospel message, especially with respect to women, in the newly formed church that was filled with young and inexperienced believers. He continued his corrupting activities in the centuries that followed, with the biggest push taking place during the second, third, and fourth centuries, when the Bible was translated into Latin and canonized by men who were under the influence of their own gender bias.

The following passages contain the six lemons found in Paul's writings:

- 1st Corinthians 11:2–16

- 1st Corinthians 14:29–40

- Ephesians 5:22–24

- Colossians 3:18

- 1st Timothy 2:8–15

- Titus 2:3–5

And, here is the one lemon passage by Peter: 1st Peter 3:1–2

An Enemy Grew Lemons in God's Vineyard

An enemy did this. As we have seen, Satan planned, for a very good reason, since the time of the Garden of Eden, to suppress and subdue woman and disrupt the role God has for her to play in His eternal purpose. Satan accomplished his goal by the gradual changing and misusing of God's words about women through translations. He was able to do this because the initial translators of the Bible were males. Females were not on translation committees until more recent times, and still only a few women participate. Because of the centuries of absence of female perspective and insight, the door was left wide open for translations of verses that were about women to be influenced by male bias. Thus, Satan managed to alter the message of certain verses pertaining to women. In the sixteenth century, he was the influence behind a Bible translation that altered God's very important words to Eve in Genesis 3:16.

I do not claim that any male translator purposefully introduced mistranslations; however, considering God's enemy and his schemes, and also the fallen nature of man, it is possible that some translators knew what they were doing. I leave the evaluation and judgment of translators' motives to God. My basic assumption is that Bible translators have worked in good faith to the best of their abilities to translate the Bible accurately. Nevertheless, it can be evidentially demonstrated that male bias in the translation of verses about women has played a definitive role in shaping for almost two millennia the prevailing view of Christian women.

After so many centuries, it is difficult for those men and women who hold traditional concepts about women to acknowledge and address the idea that Bible translations could have been responsible for cultivating wrong notions concerning God's view of women. It is even more difficult to make the decision to examine the Scripture for evidence of this. However, those who seek to know the truth and who want truth to govern their lives can overcome these difficulties. Jesus proclaimed that knowing the truth sets us free and also declared that he who seeks shall find. All who desire to know truth should be willing to examine evidence that clearly exposes male bias in translations of passages about women.

Furthermore, if the reason that women were not on translation committees in centuries past is that they were not educated and, therefore, not qualified, shouldn't men now allow educated women to ask questions? Shouldn't they expect, even encourage, women to study and set forth their findings? Shouldn't they then be willing to evaluate the results of such labor in a fair and scholarly manner? Where is there any harm in this? Will not truth be found and prevail? As Bushnell pointed out, if women had been the sole translators of the Bible for almost two millennia and men were the ones who found themselves limited by restrictive beliefs and practices that resulted from women's translations of passages about men, shouldn't women translators be willing for men to test and question their translations (Bushnell, para. 272)? Would not men expect women to fairly consider their findings, especially if there was evidence that female bias had played a role in translations?

Today, poor translations about women have produced a sickness in the body of Christ, a spiritual infection if you will. Satan introduced this chronic infection, and it has remained undiagnosed for centuries. This illness is debilitating and has produced great harm and disunity among believers in the body of Christ. Its presenting symptom is the suppression and devaluation of female believers by male believers who believe that, when they hold women in check, using lemon translations, they are serving God and protecting the body of Christ. By producing this terrible gender-based disunity of heart and mind among members of the body of Christ, Satan has effectively hindered the moving of the Spirit of God on this earth. He knows that God's Spirit will not work in power where disharmony and ongoing offenses and sins exist among believers.

The church is to be a light, a city set on a hill for all to see. Its practice should demonstrate the truth concerning males and females and their relationships with one another. Its light-bearing presence should serve to restrict the activities of the devil on the earth. Instead, the church's malpractice with respect to male and female relationships has become a bushel covering its light and giving a way for Satan's evil works to proceed unchecked. He has been free to saturate society with hideous gender-based sins.

The church's repentance and course correction with respect to the truth concerning males and females has the potential to bring in revival and a manifestation of the power of God, the like of which has not been seen since the time of the early church. Such repentance must come. It can only be accomplished by the declaration of biblical truth, which the Spirit will bless and use to convict and change believers' hearts. It is my prayer that God will bless every attempt to address this topic and that the Spirit of God will grant repentance to the acknowledging of the truth, so that we, who have been taken captive by the enemy's trickery, may be recovered out of his snare (2 Tim. 2:25–26).

What You Need To Know about Bible Translation

> But when we speak of the Bible as inspired, infallible and inviolable, we do not refer to our English version, or any mere version, but to the original text. Prof. Deissmann has well said, "*All translation implies some, if only a slight, alteration of the sense of the original.*" (Bushnell, para. 5)

Before tackling the lemon translations in depth, we need to spend a little time considering a few basics about translation: (1) the difficulties and complexities of translating from Hebrew and from Greek, (2) some of the methodologies employed in translation, (3) the impact on translations by the gender of translation committee members, and (4) a method Bushnell employed to evaluate the viability of any given translation.

Hebrew and Greek

The following comment, which is found in a section of *Vine's Complete Expository Dictionary of Old and New Testament Words,* explains that translating from Hebrew is more difficult and challenging than translating from Greek.

> While the books of the New Testament reflect a Greek dialect as it was used over a span of about 75 years, the Old Testament draws upon various forms of the Hebrew language as it evolved over nearly 2,000 years. Therefore, certain texts—such as the early narrative of the Book of Exodus and the last of the Psalms—are virtually written in two different dialects and should be studied with this in mind. (Vine, "Introduction," "The Hebrew of the Old Testament")

Making correct translations from the complex Hebrew language necessitates studying all occurrences of a particular Hebrew word in the Old Testament. The following quote by Archdeacon Wilberforce on the word, "rib," as it occurs in Genesis 2:22, reveals some of the methodology employed in determining proper word translations in Hebrew:

> ... the 'rib' [taken from Adam] seems to be a mistranslation. The Hebrew word translated 'rib' in both the Authorized and Revised versions, occurs forty-two times in the O. T., and in this instance alone is it translated 'rib.' In the majority of cases it is translated 'side' or 'sides,' in other places 'corners' or, 'chambers,' but never 'rib' or 'ribs,' except in these two verses describing the separation of Eve from Adam. In the Septuagint version, which was the Scripture quoted by our Lord, the word is *pleura,* which in Homer, Hesiod and Herodotus is used for 'side,' not 'rib,' and in the Greek of the N. T. is invariably translated 'side.' There is a word in the

O. T. the true translation of which is 'rib' and
nothing else, and it occurs in Dan. 7:5, but this is
a totally different word from the word translated
'rib' in the passage before us. (Bushnell, para. 39)

In the above statement, Wilberforce demonstrates a
technique employed to find or isolate errant translations.
His finding indicates that the translation should reflect
that a "side," not a "rib," was taken from Adam and used
to form Eve.

Bushnell explains the importance of women being
able to examine the original languages (Hebrew, Greek,
and Aramaic):

We are mistaken when we think we can get along
on a slovenly and incomplete knowledge of the
Bible. No amount of spiritual experience, or even
the Spirit's help and instruction will take the
place of the *study* God requires us to put upon
His Word. The world, the Church and women are
suffering sadly from woman's lack of ability to
read the Word of God in its original languages.
There are truths therein that speak to the deepest
needs of a woman's heart, and that give light
upon problems that women alone are called upon
to solve. Without knowledge of the original, on
the part of a sufficient number of women to
influence the translation of the Bible in
accordance with their perception of the meaning
of these truths, these needed passages will
remain uninterpreted, or misinterpreted.
(Bushnell, para. 13)

Such truths man is not equipped to understand,
much less to set forth to the understanding of
women, for, as the very learned Canon Payne-
Smith has said: "Men never do understand
anything [he refers to Bible translation] unless
already in their minds they have some kindred
ideas." And such truths as are messages to
women, women without knowledge of the original
languages, even if having the spiritual experience,
cannot discover. They find such a message often

an inexplicable mystery, or even distorted into meaning something painful. (Bushnell, para. 14)

An excellent example of both the difficulty and importance of proper translation is seen in 1st Corinthians 11:14. In King James, it is translated:

Doth not even nature itself teach you, that, if a man have long hair, it is a shame unto him?

Firstly, the answer to this supposed question should be, "No, nature does not teach us this!" (For more explanation, see Bushnell, para. 230.) So, what is going on here? In Greek, there is no punctuation, so the determination as to what kind of punctuation should be used becomes a contextual and interpretive matter. If the translators had decided that, in context, this was a statement and not a question, it would have been translated:

Nature itself does not teach you that if a man have long hair it is a shame unto him.

As you can see, translating this statement as a question totally changes the meaning. It is like the difference a comma makes in the following: "Let us eat children" and "Let us eat, children."

Gender Bias in Translation

The absence of women on Bible translation committees has resulted in verses which pertain to woman being interpreted and translated by males who were subject to their own natural male bias—a bias which came from Adam's fall and from the experience of generations of men after Adam—men who followed his fallen pattern of blaming women and blaming God for their ills. Mistranslations of these verses were an unavoidable outcome. The exclusion of women from Bible translation was clearly part of the devil's scheme to develop and promote religious beliefs about women that would lead to their suppression. Bushnell pointed out:

We must recall that every translator of the Bible, throughout Church history has been a male;* and gender bias came into existence very early in human history. In fact the sin in the garden at once affected the love between the sexes, and Adam sought to show excellence beyond Eve. Says the German divine, Dr. Lange, in his Commentary on Genesis: "The guilt proper is rolled upon woman [by Adam], and indirectly upon God Himself .... The loss of love that comes out in this interposing of his wife is, moreover, particularly denoted in this, that he grudges to call her Eve or my wife .... 'That woman by my side, *she* who was given to [be with] me of God as a trusty counsellor, *she* gave me the fruit.'" ... "An acknowledgement of sin by Adam, but not true and sincere." Secondly, Adam generated, by his unholy ambition, a desire to be *"as God"* which will never cease to exist in human nature until that Wicked One "*sets himself forth as God*," in the very Temple of God, and is destroyed by Christ's second coming. And since gender bias is of old, and also the masculine desire to rule, every version of the Bible, beginning with the first one—the Septuagint Greek version—reflects from its pages the sinful nature, in this regard, of those who have made the translation. It is beyond our province, however, to enter upon all the versions,—only upon the English.

* This statement is not absolute; women (a few) have translated a part of the Bible, or the whole. But their work is ignored, and allowed to perish. But we refer here to those translators who have been on Translation Committees, or whose work has been allowed a place of influence in the Church. (Bushnell, para. 377)

A few examples of gender bias in the translation of Hebrew words follow.

The Hebrew Word, "Chayil"

I have already provided an explanation about the gender bias shown in the translation of the word, "chayil," in Chapter 1, under the heading, "A Pivotal Moment."

The Greek Words, "Diakonos," "Prostatis," "Oikodespotes"

Another strong evidence of gender bias is seen in the translation of verses containing these words: *diakonos* (deacon, minister), *prostatis* (ruler), and *oikodespotes* (master of the house). Such words are translated one way when they refer to men and another way when they refer to women. Bushnell explains this in depth (Bushnell, paras. 364–370). The thrust of her argument is illustrated in this: If the translations of words concerning women had been *consistent* with the translations of those same words concerning men, then we would be reading the following in our Bibles:

> I will that the younger women marry, bear children, *rule* [not "guide"] the household, give none occasion to the adversary to speak reproachfully (1 Tim. 5:14).

> I commend unto you Phoebe our sister, *minister [or deacon]* [not "servant"] of the church which is at Cenchrea; for she hath been a *ruler* [not "succourer"] of many and of myself also (Rom. 16:1).

The Hebrew Word, "Aman"

Isaiah 60:4 says, referring to God, "thy daughters shall be nursed at thy side." This, however, is a strange translation because the word translated "nursed" is the Hebrew word *"aman,"* which is typically translated with meanings such as: "believe," "be faithful," "endure." The word "nursed" seems to be a stretch. Why was this not translated something like "thy daughters shall stand fast (or 'believe,' 'be faithful,' or 'endure,') at thy side" or "on thy side" (as against an adversary), since the Hebrew word for "side" also means figuratively "adversary"?

All of these evidences of male bias in translation are a very brief mention of material found in Bushnell's "Lesson 48," paragraphs 363–370, except for the comment about *"aman,"* which is mine. Bushnell ends her lesson with this evaluation of the problem of male bias:

The lesson is this: Expositors having once convinced themselves that Nature (they would not own to doing it themselves), has outlined a certain "sphere" for woman, whereas man is at liberty, under God, to outline his own "sphere;" and having convinced themselves that the Apostle Paul places teaching, preaching and governing outside women's "sphere,"—whatever supports this view as to woman's "sphere" is slightly (and sometimes more) exaggerated in our English translation [KJV]; and what would stand out as proof against this masculine preconception, is toned down in translation. This making use of *"divers weights and measures"* is an abomination in the sight of God. (Bushnell, para. 370)

Bushnell's Misfit Principle

Bushnell's starting point for questioning problematic Bible verses about women was their fit or misfit with the whole body of Scripture. She determined that any interpretation of a verse that did not fit all around in the whole body of Scripture was a misfit. If it did not fit with the whole, this pointed to something being wrong with the interpretation and possibly the translation. She illustrated this misfit principle as follows:

A clock needs a most careful fitting of all its parts. It is quite conceivable that a typewriter wheel might be used for other purposes, but it could never be fitted into a clock, to take the place of a broken clock wheel. It would be too heavy or too light; the rim too thick or too thin; the hub too big or too little, and the cogs too many or too few. It would prove to be a misfit all around; the clock would not keep proper time. So it is with Scripture: *"Every word of God is tried,"* and if we attempt to insinuate a false interpretation into it, it proves, on close inspection, a misfit all around. We shall demonstrate, by the misfit all around, that the usual interpretation of Genesis 3:16 is not correct. It bears a *resemblance* to the correct interpretation as a typewriter wheel may resemble a clock wheel, but it does not fit accurately anywhere. (Bushnell, para. 114)

As we have said before, a misinterpretation of a passage of Scripture can be proved by the misfit. ...the correct interpretation fits all around. (Bushnell, para. 124)

She carefully examined all such misfit verses concerning women for errors in translation due to interpretive bias. She found that these troublesome verses could be interpreted or translated, with interpretive male bias removed, in a way that was true to the original language and was a "fit all around" with the rest of the body of Scripture. (Let us pray that all demonstrable mistranslations concerning women will be acknowledged by the Bible translation powers that be and that they will do whatever is needed to correct them in our Bibles!)

De-lemonizing the Lemon Translations

It is noteworthy that all of the lemon translations, as commonly understood, give the same two basic messages: woman must bow down to man, and woman must stop talking. Seriously, is this the good news? Is this the gospel of Jesus Christ? Not at all! Remember that it was a woman who preached the first gospel message, and she delivered it to a male audience, no less. Was giving this message to men her bright idea? No. Jesus gave her the message and sent her to preach to her Jewish brothers the good news of His resurrection.

The clearest basis for repudiating all of the woman-subduing lemon translations, every last one of them, is found in this passage:

25 But Jesus called them to Himself and said, "You know that the rulers of the Gentiles lord it over them, and [their] great men exercise authority over them. 26 It is not this way among you, but whoever wishes to become great among you shall be your servant, 27 and whoever wishes

to be first among you shall be your slave; 28 just
as the Son of Man did not come to be served, but
to serve, and to give His life a ransom for many."
(Matt. 20:25–28, NASB)

Jesus said it shall not be like *this* among you. In
other words: It shall not be that one Christian lords it
over another. It shall not be that a Christian man lords it
over his wife. It shall not be that a Christian man tells a
Christian woman she cannot speak publicly or speak to
men about the Lord. God has given believers, male and
female, authority over themselves and their own choices,
not over fellow believers (excepting for children). In fact,
each one of us is independently accountable and will give
account to God for what we choose to do. It is our choice
to acknowledge the lordship of Jesus or not, and it is our
choice to submit to one another or not. God tells us what
He expects of us, but He leaves us with the choice to obey
Him. The only beings that we have a right to exercise
absolute authority over, as holy believers, other than our
children (in a just and right way), are the devil and his
minions.

When you look at each lemon translation in the light
of Matthew 20:25–28, there is no question you are
looking at a lemon—a misfit in light of Christ's teaching
about, and practice of, authority. Whenever you read a
lemon translation, the thing you must do first is stop and
remember the true God-definition of any "authoritative"
sounding words that are found in the lemon translations.
Remember that true authority is humble, self-sacrificing,
serving, loving, and righteous according to God's Word. It
is not top-down, hierarchical, lording-it-over-others
authority.

So, now we come to the explanation of the seven
lemons. Each lemon opens with four subheadings: "The
Passage," "The Misfit," "The Fit," and "The De-
lemonization." "The Passage" is typically a quote from the
King James Version. If the quote is from a different Bible
version, it is because that version's translation requires
less modification to turn it from a lemon into a grape.
"The Misfit" contains a summary of the way that the
passage is commonly understood. "The Fit" contains a
summary of the way that the passage can rightfully be

understood and, thereby, fit well in the context of the whole Bible. "The De-lemonization" provides a detailed explanation of how to change the lemon from a misfit to a fit, or I should say, from a lemon to a grape. I am covering the lemon passages in order of their appearance in the Bible. Each section also suggests a possible retranslation of the passage with some minor changes that turn it from a lemon into a grape.

Lemon One: 1st Corinthians 11:1–16

The Passage

Please read the following passage, the first of the lemon translations; and, when you finish, try to state aloud in your own words what you just read.

1 Be ye followers of me, even as I also [am] of Christ.

2 Now I praise you, brethren, that ye remember me in all things, and keep the ordinances, as I delivered [them] to you.

3 But I would have you know, that the head of every man is Christ; and the head of the woman [is] the man; and the head of Christ [is] God.

4 Every man praying or prophesying, having [his] head covered, dishonoureth his head.

5 But every woman that prayeth or prophesieth with [her] head uncovered dishonoureth her head: for that is even all one as if she were shaven.

6 For if the woman be not covered, let her also be shorn: but if it be a shame for a woman to be shorn or shaven, let her be covered.

7 For a man indeed ought not to cover [his] head, forasmuch as he is the image and glory of God: but the woman is the glory of the man.

8 For the man is not of the woman; but the woman of the man.

9 Neither was the man created for the woman; but the woman for the man.

10 For this cause ought the woman to have power on [her] head because of the angels.

11 Nevertheless neither is the man without the woman, neither the woman without the man, in the Lord.

12 For as the woman [is] of the man, even so [is] the man also by the woman; but all things of God.

13 Judge in yourselves: is it comely that a woman pray unto God uncovered?

14 Doth not even nature itself teach you, that, if a man have long hair, it is a shame unto him?

15 But if a woman have long hair, it is a glory to her: for [her] hair is given her for a covering.

16 But if any man seem to be contentious, we have no such custom, neither the churches of God. (1 Cor. 11:1–16, KJV)

I would have liked to have heard your recap of this passage! In my opinion, it is the most difficult to understand of all the lemon translations. First of all, its language is confusing. I have read this passage again and again in various translations of the Bible; and, each time, have been left with the feeling that it is impossible to understand. Its intended message, for surely Paul had an intent, is lost in the fog hanging over this swamp of words.

The Misfit

This passage is used to prove that woman is under the hierarchical control of man—that man is her head (understood to mean boss). The proof offered is that God is the head (boss) of Christ, and Christ is the head (boss) of man. This passage is also used to show that woman should be submissive to man and demonstrate proper regard for God's hierarchical order. Although there are other things covered in this passage, in modern times, they are overlooked or minimized. That man is the head of woman is never forgotten, however. It is maximized and used as necessary to keep women in their place.

The Fit

Paul was correcting the Corinthians for wrong teachings and beliefs that had been brought in among them by Judaizers. This passage sits in the middle of a number of other corrections by Paul. He was not *advocating* the things stated in this passage but was *repeating* or *quoting* what he had been told by the Corinthians. His purpose was to refute errant teachings, which he did.

The De-lemonization

First, we will go through this passage verse by verse as it stands in the King James Version of the Bible and make some observations and pose some questions.

Paul opens by telling them that he wants them to follow his example. He praises them for having remembered him and his teaching:

1 Be ye followers of me, even as I also [am] of Christ. 2 Now I praise you, brethren, that ye remember me in all things, and keep the ordinances, as I delivered [them] to you. (1 Cor. 11:1–2, KJV)

He begins his next sentence with "But." Why does Paul use a word which tells us that he is about to introduce something that contrasts with what he has just mentioned?

3 But I would have you know, that the head of every man is Christ; and the head of the woman

[is] the man; and the head of Christ [is] God. (1 Cor. 11:3)

Also, what does Paul mean by "head" here? The Greek word is *kephale,* a word which refers to the literal head of a physical body. If Paul is using it metaphorically to mean what we understand today to be "boss" or "leader," then why would Paul write that he would have us know that the Godhead is a hierarchy in which God is the boss of Christ, since the Bible reveals that the Godhead is not a hierarchy? Also, since the Greeks did not use the word *kephale* to refer to authority (Bristow), why would Paul do so?

> 4 Every man praying or prophesying, having [his] head covered, dishonoureth his head. 5 But every woman that prayeth or prophesieth with [her] head uncovered dishonoureth her head: for that is even all one as if she were shaven. 6 For if the woman be not covered, let her also be shorn: but if it be a shame for a woman to be shorn or shaven, let her be covered. (1 Cor. 11:4–6, KJV)

Here Paul appears to be saying that he thinks any woman who will not cover her head when she prays or prophesies needs to have her head shaved because she is dishonoring her head, who, according to prior verses, is man. Shaving a woman's head seems quite extreme as a form of punishment, and it has no precedent anywhere in the Bible.

> 7 For a man indeed ought not to cover [his] head, forasmuch as he is the image and glory of God: but the woman is the glory of the man. 8 For the man is not of the woman; but the woman of the man. 9 Neither was the man created for the woman; but the woman for the man. 10 For this cause ought the woman to have power on [her] head because of the angels. (1 Cor. 11:7–10, KJV)

Logically, if man shouldn't cover his head because he is the glory of God, the woman shouldn't cover her head because she is the glory of man! Instead, Paul seems to be arguing against himself and his own logic. And, what does it mean for a woman to have "power" on her head because of the angels? Paul's words about head-covering make me do some serious head-scratching.

> 11 Nevertheless neither is the man without the woman, neither the woman without the man, in the Lord. 12 For as the woman [is] of the man, even so [is] the man also by the woman; but all things of God. 13 Judge in yourselves: is it comely that a woman pray unto God uncovered? 14 Doth not even nature itself teach you, that, if a man have long hair, it is a shame unto him? 15 But if a woman have long hair, it is a glory to her: for [her] hair is given her for a covering. (1 Cor. 11:11–15, KJV)

Is Paul arguing for or against, his earlier argument? I have never been taught by nature that it is a shame for man to have long hair or that it is a glory for woman to have long hair. This whole passage is downright confusing, yet one verse in it (verse 3) has been lifted out and held high for centuries as justification for man having God-ordained authority over woman. This use has continued even when the practice of head-covering for Christian women has almost faded away. What a puzzling set of statements!

> But if any man seem to be contentious, we have no such custom, neither the churches of God. (1 Cor. 11:16, KJV)

What custom: that of covering or uncovering, or that of being contentious?

Something is dreadfully wrong with this passage! Would a man with the high intelligence and education of Paul have written something so confusing and illogical? The explanation for this confusing passage appears to be poor translation. It seems evident that the translators weren't really sure what Paul was saying here to the Corinthians. The way that they translated his words suggests they were under the influence of their male bias.

I recently made a discovery about the two letters Paul wrote to the Corinthians that gave me a key to understanding 1st Corinthians 11:1–16. Before I made this discovery, I had read some explanations about this passage that had helped me understand that there was something wrong with its translation, but I still found myself in a fog whenever I read it. After my discovery about Paul's letters, I saw how a few minor and justifiable (so it seemed to me) translation changes to this passage would line it up with Paul's purpose in writing these letters and remove the fog.

Here is what I discovered about Paul's two long letters to the Church in Corinth: Paul was not only exposing the corruption that was among them, he was targeting the cause of it. There were sectarian parties in the church that had been produced by the false teachings of various teachers that were among them. The Corinthians had been eating leavened bread (Matt. 16:6, 12). Paul's letters were unleavened bread, reminding the Corinthian believers of the truth that God was holy and that there should be no sin among His people (2 Cor. 4:1–2). He contended with them for the truth of the gospel by arguing against the numerous false teachings among them, including one lengthy argument in which he had to contend for the truth of Christ's literal resurrection from the dead (2 Cor. 15).

Paul declared that he had not come to them with the wisdom of words, like their teachers had done, but with the message of the cross. He proclaimed the truth in the Spirit and in power, exposing one after another of their wrong beliefs so that they might be rescued from the snare of the devil (2 Tim. 2:26). The Jews appreciated miracles, and the Greeks valued wisdom; but Paul preached only Christ as the power of God and the wisdom of God (1 Cor. 1:23–24). He was determined to know nothing among them but Christ and Him crucified. He was in fear and trembling, depending on the Spirit so that their faith would stand in the power of God, not in the wisdom of men (1 Cor. 2:1–5, 4:19–20). He fed them with the unleavened bread of sincerity and truth and warned them from his clear perspective of the judgment seat of Christ (1 Cor. 5:8, 2 Cor. 1:12, 2:17, 4:2–8, 5:10–11).

Under numerous leavened teachings, the Corinthians had become a leavened lump. The only way for them to become a new lump was to purge out all the leavened teachings from among them. Paul had sown spiritual truth, the truth of the gospel, and he expected to harvest spiritual fruit (2 Cor. 11:2–3). Others had sown false teachings, and carnal fruit had grown up among them (1 Cor. 9:11). Now the Corinthians needed to give due diligence to examine what they believed because of the leavened bread they had eaten, so they could clear themselves of the sins into which they had fallen. In summary, Paul's overall discourse in his first letter to the Corinthians could be simplified to something like this:

When you believed in Christ through what I taught you, you were espoused to Christ so that one day you might be presented to him as a chaste virgin. Now, through false teaching of others you have become corrupted! This is evidenced by all the evil fruit among you. The false teachers that you love may look and sound like ministers of Christ, but their fruit exposes them. They have brought you another gospel and another spirit. Just like in the Garden of Eden, your minds have been corrupted. You now have unholy relationships with one another, and your relationship with God is not right. You use the name of Jesus, but your lives are not according to the Holy Spirit! I want you to do what is right and repent for your own sake!

So, in summary, the key that I discovered is that, in chapters 5 through 15, Paul was at work purging out leaven by systematically addressing the false teachings that were among the Corinthians—teachings that were evidenced by their ungodly behavior. In chapter 5, he corrected their belief that it was right to continue to have fellowship with an unrepentant fornicating Christian. In chapter 6, he corrected them for believing it was right to go to law before the unbelievers and for misapplying a belief that all things were lawful as believers. In chapter 7, he clarified what was true about such things as circumcision, marriage, divorce, and separation—again purging out their leavened beliefs about these things. In chapter 8, he addressed eating meat sacrificed to idols, making the point that they should behave in a way to take care of the conscience of others, not themselves. In chapter 9, he poured out his heart of love for them and for all people, declaring that he gave up his own rights so others could benefit, further exposing by his example their self-centered focus. In chapter 10, he warned them of the danger they were in, comparing them to the disobedient children of Israel in the wilderness. Then he opened chapter 11 encouraging them to continue following his example. He then began reasoning with them about the false teachings among them that promoted male dominance. Immediately after this passage, he said he did not praise them for this, nor for the contentions and divisions among them, nor for stuffing their bellies in feast times and not caring for the poor among them that needed food. All these things were causing them to be judged by God when they came together.

So, with the idea of Paul purging leaven in view, I suggest that this first lemon passage, 1st Corinthians 11:1–16, be restated with a few minor changes, mostly punctuation, so that its message:

- Is clarified to show Paul was correcting and removing leavened teaching related to women and male dominance

- Does not appear to have Paul promoting the idea of a hierarchical relationship in the Godhead

- Does not appear to refute its own argument

- Does not contradict the practice of Paul or Jesus with respect to women

- Wins the argument that Paul is making against false teaching that was among the Corinthians

In the following, I present verses 3–6 in the form of questions regarding what the Corinthians were being taught about authority and women. I accomplish this by changing "I would" to "would I" in the opening phrase of verse 3, so that it reads, "but would I have you know that ...." This modification is followed by a long quote which contains a series of teachings from the false teachers. I conclude the quote with a question mark. So, by simply reversing the order of two words and changing some punctuation, Paul is no longer making statements about his own teaching, but is asking the Corinthians if he would teach such things.

1 Be ye followers of me, even as I also [am] of Christ. 2 Now I praise you, brethren, that ye remember me in all things, and keep the ordinances, as I delivered [them] to you. 3 But would I have you know that, "the head of every man is Christ and the head of the woman [is] the man and the head of Christ [is] God; 4 every man praying or prophesying, having [his] head covered, dishonoureth his head, 5 but every woman that prayeth or prophesieth with [her] head uncovered dishonoureth her head, for that is even all one as if she were shaven; 6 if the woman be not covered, let her also be shorn, but if it be a shame for a woman to be shorn or shaven, let her be covered"? (1 Cor. 11:1–6)

I am not a Bible translator, but my hope is that these suggested changes will stimulate some new thought and inspire some who are translators to do the scholarly work so greatly needed to de-lemonize this and other lemon translations. The changes that I have suggested are primarily determined by context. Note that the word, "but," which opens verse 3, fits better when it is followed by a question. As a question, Paul would be using the Socratic method[11] to persuade rather than to dictate to the Corinthians. First, he praises them for having accepted what he has taught them before. Then he asks them if they thought he would want them to believe certain false things. He then restates the false things which he had heard from them—things that misrepresent the relationship among the Godhead, the relationship between men and women, and also how fellow, female believers in Christ should be treated. These small changes cause this passage to fit with Paul's purpose of purging out leavened teachings that the Corinthians had accepted.

---

[11] The method of inquiry and instruction employed by Socrates especially as represented in the dialogues of Plato and consisting of a series of questions, the object of which is to elicit a clear and consistent expression of something supposed to be implicitly known by all rational beings (Merriam Webster, online). The intellectual Greeks highly valued Socrates' method of teaching;

and, in using his method, Paul would have been practicing what he preached about becoming all things to all men (1 Cor. 9:22).

Bushnell and other Bible scholars support the idea that some of Paul's words in his letters were a restatement or quotation of things that he had learned from the letter or letters written to him by the Corinthians. After providing a more detailed explanation about this, Bushnell wrote:

> ... We merely wish to show that this idea that Paul makes quotations from the letter he has received and is answering, is no novel idea, invented by us to suit a prejudiced view. Prof. Sir. Wm. Ramsay says, on this subject: "We should be ready to suspect Paul is making a quotation from the letter addressed to him by the Corinthians whenever he alludes to their knowledge, or when any statement stands in marked contrast either with the immediate context or with Paul's known views." (Bushnell, para. 205)

Verse 6 has clear evidence that Paul was referring to a leavened teaching, because it contains a reference to what could be done to women who unveiled that matched with what the Judaizers would expect to be done to such a woman:

> ... as to what would be done with the woman who unveiled, and thus furnished sufficient proof of "adultery" to compel her husband to repudiate her, we learn from Dr. Edersheim's Sketches of Jewish Social Life, p. 155: "It was the custom in case of a woman accused of adultery to have her hair shorn or shaven," at the same time using this formula: "Because thou hast departed from the manner of the daughters of Israel, who go with their heads covered .... therefore that hath befallen thee which thou hast chosen." An unveiled Jewish wife might, then, be tried for adultery; and when so tried, be "shorn or shaven." (Bushnell, para. 243)

In light of Paul's co-laboring with women and his obvious respect for their ministry, these statements about women do not appear to be something Paul believed or would recommend. Rather, he seems to be referring to leavened teachings the Corinthians had been given that reflected the influence of Judaizers who were pushing the Oral Law among new believers. Because of such teachings, the Corinthians were holding wrong beliefs about authority with respect to women and their place in the church. So, instead of Paul setting forth doctrinal statements for all time about hierarchical authority in the Godhead and about women being under man's authority, it makes more sense that he was seeking to persuade them to purge out this leaven.

Paul's message and attitude toward the Corinthians in chapters 1 through 4 is diametrically opposed to the message and attitude presented in this 1st Corinthians 11 passage as it stands in our Bibles today. In those early chapters, we see a man who was in fear and trembling, not wanting to speak in man's wisdom but rather in demonstration of the Spirit and power. We see a man who bemoaned having to speak to them as carnal, not spiritual, because of their condition. We see a man who was warning them about the seriousness of building with wood, hay, and stubble teachings that would be burned up. We see a man who was almost beside himself as he described his and Apollos' suffering and their humble manner of living on behalf of the Corinthians and others, a man who appealed to them to be like him, one who had toward them the heart of a father, not an instructor.

This was a man who in the chapter immediately following this chapter 11 lemon translation begged them to see themselves as members of the body of Christ who should realize they needed the more feeble members, who should bestow more abundant honor on those among them whom they thought to be less honorable (12:23). Is such a man one who could have told them to shave the heads of weaker female vessels among them if they wouldn't cover their heads? Surely Paul did not have two faces. In no way could the real Paul of the New Testament declare that such humiliating punishment of women was in order!

Now we move on to verse 7:

> For a man indeed ought not to cover [his] head, forasmuch as he is the image and glory of God: (1 Cor. 11:7a, KJV)

The word "indeed" used here is a Greek affirmative word, so Paul appears to be affirming that this part of what the Corinthians had been taught was true: a man should not cover his head. In the next part of verse 7, the word, "but," in the King James Version can be rendered "and," so I make this suggested change:

> and the woman is the glory of the man. (1 Cor. 11:7b)

If we use the word, "and," it makes it more apparent that Paul was pointing at their faulty logic. He was pointing to the statement that woman was the glory of the man (which these teachers had stated), and he was showing the Corinthians that it logically followed that, if a man should not cover his head because he is the image and glory of God, neither should a woman cover her head if she is the glory of man. This is valid logic, not faulty, self-defeating logic.

In verse 9, Paul states that the woman was created *for* the man. The word that is translated "for" in the King James Version occurs two times in verse 9, and both times it is rendered "on account of" in the interlinear text on the Bible Hub website (Nestle). Verses 8 and 9 are alluding to the creation story in Genesis 3 and 4 in which woman was taken out of man. This was done because something had changed with Adam such that it was no longer good for him to be alone (explained in Chapter 3, "Adam: Stumbled Before Falling"). It seems, therefore, that the interlinear rendering "on account of" would be a better fit:

> 8 For the man is not of the woman; but the woman of the man. 9 Neither was the man created on account of the woman; but the woman on account of the man. (1 Cor. 11:8–9)

Now we come to verse 10. After the Fall, it was the woman who exposed the serpent's involvement and received the promise that her seed would crush the serpent's head. Woman needs power or authority to be able to stand against the fallen angels, who hate her because of God's promise. Paul appears to be alluding to this in verse 10. The Greek word, *exousia,* which is translated "power" in verse 10, can also be translated "authority."

> For this cause ought the woman to have [G2192, hold, possess] authority [G1849, *exousia]* over [G1909, "over" with genitive case] her head because of the angels. (1 Cor. 11:10)

Without *exousia* (authority) over her head, woman is left to be ruled over by others—men and the devil—to the detriment of God fulfilling His purpose. With *exousia* over her head, she has the authority to stand in the battle against the devil and fight against him spiritually in order to help bring forth many godly men. Having authority over her own head, she is free to make decisions toward that end, just like Eve was free to make decisions in the Garden of Eden. The following are some other translations of verse 10. Some confirm the understanding just presented. Others indicate that woman does not have her own authority:

> It is for this reason that a woman ought to have authority over her own head, because of the angels. (NIV)

> For this reason, and because the angels are watching, a woman should wear a covering on her head to show she is under authority. (NLT)

> Therefore the woman ought to have [a symbol] of authority on her head, because of the angels. (NASB)

> This is why a woman should have authority over her own head: because of the angels. (ISV)

> Therefore, a woman should wear something on her head to show she is under [someone's] authority, out of respect for the angels. (GWT)

By changing Genesis 3:16 as he did, Satan misrepresented God and how His authority works, making it sound like God mandated that the husband was supposed to rule over the wife. This poor translation concealed the fact that God gives His creatures a measure of authority to evaluate and choose. The poor translation of 1st Corinthians 11:3–16 similarly misrepresents God's authority. It presents the Godhead as if Christ and God are in a hierarchical relationship and man and woman are in the same kind of relationship. These translations result in the suppression of women and hinder their effectiveness with respect to Satan's final demise.

In verses 11–13, another punctuation change (from a question mark to a period) brings clarity.

> 11 Nevertheless neither is the man without the woman, nor the woman without the man, in the Lord. 12 For as the woman is of the man, even so is the man also by the woman; but all things of God. 13 Judge in yourselves: it is comely that a woman pray unto God uncovered. (1 Cor. 11:11–13)

By pointing out the equity in the male/female relationship, Paul tells the Corinthians to judge rightly the logical conclusion of his argument: It *is* comely that a woman pray to God uncovered.

In verses 14–15, punctuation changes (a question mark to a comma and the addition of quotation marks) cause this passage to change from being an inane question to a statement that makes perfect sense.

> 14 Even nature itself does not teach you that "if a man have long hair, it is a shame unto him, 15 but if a woman have long hair, it is a glory to her: for her hair is given her for a covering." (1 Cor. 11:14–15)

Paul is not asking them to agree with him that nature teaches that if a man has long hair it is a shame to him, because nature clearly does not teach this. Instead, he is refuting a "nature" argument that others were making. Among the Greeks, who greatly influenced Jewish thought during the days of mingling, there existed a "nature" argument for male superiority as seen in what Aristotle wrote:

It is the best for all tame animals to be ruled by human beings. For this is how they are kept alive. In the same way, the relationship between the male and the female is by nature such that the male is higher, the female lower, that the male rules and the female is ruled. (Wijngaards quoted from Aristotle)

Nature also does not teach that long hair on a female is a glory to her and is given as a covering. Paul's argument is that man and woman are the same with respect to long hair and also with respect to head covering.

Finally, the Greek word that has been translated "contentious" in verse 16 literally means "fond to conquer" *(Greek Interlinear)*. So this verse could be translated:

But if any man seem to be fond of dominating we have no such custom, neither the churches of God. (1 Cor. 11:16)

Paul appears to be saying that if some seemed to be fond of conquering (or dominating), there was no such custom of lording it over or conquering in the churches of God. In this case, there was no such custom of males lording it over females in the churches of God.

The surface issues in this 1st Corinthians 11 passage are women and head-covering. Paul was refuting the intent that was behind these surface issues. The Judaizers intended to promote hierarchical domination, in particular, men over women. Their teaching was in line with Satan's desire to subdue woman. Their argument was that Christ was the head of the male, the male was the head of the female, and God was the head of Christ. Paul didn't let their argument go unchallenged. It defined the Godhead in terms of a hierarchy, and it also obscured the new-creation relationship between male and female. We will see what Paul really believed about Christ being the head when we cover the lemon passage, Ephesians 5:23–25.

Verse 3 of the 1st Corinthians 11 lemon passage has been used for centuries to support the idea that God ordained man to be in hierarchical authority over woman. It has been taught as if Paul's purpose in 1st Corinthians 11:3–16 was to set forth doctrine about women that was to govern their behavior for all time. Instead, his purpose was to correct the Corinthians' errant beliefs about male superiority and authority. He follows his correction with a pronouncement that their behavior (as a result of their wrong beliefs) was affecting them for the worse whenever they came together. He states that he does not praise them for this. Their mistreatment of women was one more sinful behavior among them that was displeasing to God. Thus, when they came together to partake of the Lord's supper, they were bringing judgment on themselves (1 Cor. 11:17–22).

So, here is a restatement of the whole passage with my changes, with verse numbers omitted:

> Be ye followers of me, even as I also am of Christ. Now I praise you, brethren, that ye remember me in all things, and keep the ordinances, as I delivered them to you.

> But would I have you know that, "the head of every man is Christ and the head of the woman is the man and the head of Christ is God; 4 every man praying or prophesying, having his head covered, dishonoureth his head, but every woman that prayeth or prophesieth with her head uncovered dishonoureth her head, for that is even all one as if she were shaven; if the woman be not covered, let her also be shorn, but if it be a shame for a woman to be shorn or shaven, let her be covered"?

> For a man indeed ought not to cover his head, forasmuch as he is the image and glory of God: and the woman is the glory of the man. For the man is not of the woman; but the woman of the man. Neither was the man created on account of the woman; but the woman on account of the man. For this cause ought the woman to have authority over her head because of the angels.

Nevertheless neither is the man without the woman, nor the woman without the man, in the Lord. For as the woman is of the man, even so is the man also by the woman; but all things of God.

Judge in yourselves: it is comely that a woman pray unto God uncovered. Even nature itself does not teach you that "if a man have long hair, it is a shame unto him, but if a woman have long hair, it is a glory to her: for her hair is given her for a covering." But if any man seem to be fond of dominating, we have no such custom, neither the churches of God. (1 Cor. 11:1–16)

Those who would continue to insist that 1st Corinthians 11:1–16 teaches that man is to be the authority over woman should be asked some serious questions:

- Are single females to be under the authority of males? If so, which males?

- Should men practice dominance over women as if the word, "kephale" (head), meant "boss" or "leader" or "authority over" when the Greeks of Paul's day did not attribute such a meaning to this word?

- If God is on the top of a hierarchical authority ladder and Christ is set on a rung below Him, what does one do with the fact that Christ is God?

- If Christ is the head of woman only indirectly through man, then what does one do with the verse that says Christ is the only mediator between God and each human being (1 Tim. 2:5)?

- Would it not go against God's nature to require a woman who did not have authority over her own actions to give account at the judgment seat of Christ for choices that her husband made for her? Wouldn't this mean that God should have stated somewhere in His Word that males would have to give full account, not only for themselves, but also for the women who were under their headship? What is to be done with the verse that says plainly that each one will give account (2 Cor. 5:10)?

More such questions can be asked, but these are sufficient to make the point that there is something wrong with believing that 1st Corinthians 11:3 is Paul's doctrinal presentation on authority and headship.

It is significant that the only New Testament Bible references to man as the head of woman are found in 1st Corinthians 11:3 and Ephesians 5:23 (which we will be addressing). Those who would insist that Paul wrote these verses to show that woman is subservient to man, and would use them to subdue women, should be true to the rest of the passage. They should demand that any woman who does not have her head covered when she prays or prophesies must have her head shaved! Christian practices today show that Paul's apparent mandate for shaving the heads of unveiled women has been set aside, while the part of this passage used to justify subduing women under men has been kept front and center.

Lemon Two: 1st Corinthians 14:29-40

The Passage

> 29 Let the prophets speak two or three, and let the other judge. 30 If [any thing] be revealed to another that sitteth by, let the first hold his peace. 31 For ye may all prophesy one by one, that all may learn, and all may be comforted. 32 And the spirits of the prophets are subject to the prophets. 33 For God is not [the author] of confusion, but of peace, as in all churches of the saints.

34 Let your women keep silence in the churches: for it is not permitted unto them to speak; but [they are commanded] to be under obedience, as also saith the law. 35 And if they will learn any thing, let them ask their husbands at home: for it is a shame for women to speak in the church. 36 What? came the word of God out from you? or came it unto you only? 37 If any man think himself to be a prophet, or spiritual, let him acknowledge that the things that I write unto you are the commandments of the Lord. 38 But if any man be ignorant, let him be ignorant. 39 Wherefore, brethren, covet to prophesy, and forbid not to speak with tongues. 40 Let all things be done decently and in order. (1 Cor. 14:29–40, KJV)

The Misfit

This passage is employed to say that women should be silent in the churches and that Paul did not allow them to speak. No doubt, due to the difficulty this imposed in all aspects of church practice, traditions have evolved that allow women to speak under certain situations, as permitted by various church polities. However, the verses have remained set in stone as originally translated.

The Fit

Paul was correcting the Corinthians for wrong teachings and beliefs that had been brought in among them by Judaizers. This passage sits in the middle of a number of other corrections by Paul. He was not advocating that women be silent and not be permitted to speak in the church, but was repeating, or quoting, what he had been told by the Corinthians. His purpose was to refute this belief, which he did.

The De-lemonization

In chapter 12 of Corinthians, Paul pleaded with the Corinthians concerning their being proud of having spiritual gifts, implying that this was causing them to abuse or neglect the less gifted among them. He showed them the more excellent way of love in chapter 13, again exposing their hypocritical situation. If they were truly spiritual they would love as he described in 1st Corinthians 13. Then, he exhorted them that if they wanted a spiritual gift, they should pursue the gift of prophecy—of speaking divine counsels—because it would produce good fruit. I believe Paul prescribed this because he knew that when people learned and spoke God's words for themselves, this would be a strong antidote against leaven finding a place among them. If they were all involved in learning and speaking God's words and in evaluating them with one another to confirm or refute the truth of what was spoken, the door would close on the leaven distributors.

> 29 Let the prophets speak two or three, and let the other judge. 30 If [any thing] be revealed to another that sitteth by, let the first hold his peace. 31 For ye may all prophesy one by one, that all may learn, and all may be comforted. 32 And the spirits of the prophets are subject to the prophets. 33 For God is not [the author] of confusion, but of peace, as in all churches of the saints. (1 Cor. 14:29–33, KJV)

Here Paul says plainly that all may speak. Then suddenly, right in the middle of his exhortation, we find two verses that stop us in our tracks:

> 34 Let your women keep silence in the churches: for it is not permitted unto them to speak; but [they are commanded] to be under obedience, as also saith the law. 35 And if they will learn any thing, let them ask their husbands at home: for it is a shame for women to speak in the church. (1 Cor. 14:34–35, KJV)

Regarding these verses, Charles Trombley wrote:

> Would the apostle permit the women to pray and prophesy in chapter 11:5 and then reverse himself and tell them to be silent in chapter 14:34–35? (Trombley, 15)

These stellar women-shut-your-mouths verses jump out as an anti-message in the middle of Paul's statement that all can speak (verse 31). Where did this idea of silencing women in the church come from? Verse 34 says it comes from "the law." This sounds like, all of a sudden, Paul remembered that the law said for women to be silent, so he corrected himself and began to write as if God had given man dominion over woman in order to silence her. In light of God's character and ways, this cannot be the correct understanding of this verse. Paul knew he was not to lord it over brethren, including female brethren. Paul was following Christ and His way of exercising authority, not the devil!

So, now we have to stop and look more closely at verses 34–35. These verses bear the earmarks of a problematic translation. For one thing, other Scriptures show Paul in practice encouraging women, converting women, working with women—not silencing them. Neither did Jesus silence women; He told them to speak (John 20:17). Secondly, and most glaringly, there is no place in the Old Testament law that says women are not permitted to speak! So, here we have identified a definite problem: The only "law" that taught as these verses do was the Oral Law of the Jews. If we continue to verse 36, we see that Paul recognized the source of these statements which were apparently circulating among the Corinthians. It would make sense that he exclaimed to those who were saying such things:

> 36 What? came the word of God out from you? or came it unto you only? 37 If any man think himself to be a prophet, or spiritual, let him acknowledge that the things that I write unto you are the commandments of the Lord. 38 But if any man be ignorant, let him be ignorant. (1 Cor. 14:36–38, KJV)

He was rebuking any who would try to shut the mouth of a female believer using dictates of the Oral Law. Such ones needed to acknowledge that the things Paul taught were the commandments of the Lord. He taught that all could prophesy one by one. He then continued with his appeal:

> 39 Wherefore, brethren, covet to prophesy, and
> forbid not to speak with tongues. 40 Let all things
> be done decently and in order. (1 Cor. 14:39–40,
> KJV)

I suggest that verses 34–35 be punctuated with quotation marks as follows to show that Paul was repeating the wrong statements that he was going to correct:

> 34 "Let your women keep silence in the churches:
> for it is not permitted unto them to speak; but
> they are commanded to be under obedience, as
> also saith the law. 35 And if they will learn any
> thing, let them ask their husbands at home: for it
> is a shame for women to speak in the church." 36
> What? came the word of God out from you? or
> came it unto you only? 37 If any man think
> himself to be a prophet, or spiritual, let him
> acknowledge that the things that I write unto you
> are the commandments of the Lord. 38 But if any
> man be ignorant, let him be ignorant. 39
> Wherefore, brethren, covet to prophesy, and
> forbid not to speak with tongues. 40 Let all things
> be done decently and in order. (1 Cor. 14:34–40)

Two quotation marks end the idea that Paul dictated that women had to keep silent and that it was shameful for them to speak in the church. (See Bushnell, lessons 25–28, for more about women and silence.)

Lemon Three: Ephesians 5:22–24

The Passage

> 22 Wives, [be subject] to your own husbands, as
> to the Lord. 23 For the husband is the head of

the wife, as Christ also is the head of the church, He Himself [being] the Savior of the body. 24 But as the church is subject to Christ, so also the wives [ought to be] to their husbands in everything (Eph. 5:22–24, NASB)

The Misfit

These verses, Ephesians 5:22–24, are used as the main support in the New Testament for the belief that wives are to be under the headship of their husbands and that they need to submit (understood to mean "obey") in everything.

The Fit

When Christ came, He rescued us from the devil by sacrificing himself for us. In so doing, He also demonstrated how husbands should love their wives and how they could make it possible for their wives to respect them: by loving their wives to the extent of laying down themselves for them. Christ, as the "head," did not demand submission, but won it by His self-sacrificing love. As a new creation, as a new man in Christ, according to Paul, man is to love his wife in the same way Christ did when He laid down his life for the church (Eph. 5:25).

The De-lemonization

To de-lemonize this lemon passage, we will need to spend some time understanding the meaning and use of two Greek words, *hupotasso* ("be subject" in v. 22) and *kephale* ("head" in v. 23).

Hupotasso (Submit, Be Subject)

The following helpful explanation of the Greek word *hupotasso* is taken from a paper written by my husband, which was his summary of Bushnell's and Penn-Lewis's works:

Paul wrote about subjection in the sense that we as Christians are to be subject one to another.

This is a New Testament revelation. The Judaizers took this truth and reshaped it to fit with their Oral Law and tradition, applying it to women to be obedient to men as if they were servants.

> The women are to keep silent in the churches; for they are not permitted to speak, but are to subject themselves, just as the Law also says. (1 Cor. 14:34, NASB)

The verb translated "to subject" is from two Greek words: *hupo,* meaning "next after" or "under" and *tasso* meaning "arrange." Therefore, the verb Paul used meant "to arrange after" or "arrange under." (Interestingly, the noun form of the word *[subjection]* does not appear in Greek writings before Paul's time. We might infer, then, that New Testament writers coined this word to describe a new posture that would be particular to those who are believers in Christ—a posture of yielding one's preferences to another rather than asserting one's rights.)

Paul used this word to express how we should comport ourselves with one another:

> *Hupotasso* yourselves one to another in the fear of God. (Eph. 5:21)

Paul told the Corinthians to submit to those who helped him; and, by the way, some of the ones who helped him were women (see Rom. 16:3, 12). Therefore, Paul would have the Corinthian men to subject themselves to some women:

> That ye *hupotasso* yourselves unto such, and to every one that helpeth with us, and laboureth. (1 Cor. 16:16)

Also, to the wives, Paul wrote the same thing:

> Wives, *hupotasso* yourselves unto your own husbands, as unto the Lord. (Eph. 5:22)

As we can see, Paul uses the same word with the wives that he uses for everyone else in the body of Christ. Therefore, we know that he does not expect a mere servile obedience from the wives with regard to their husbands. If Paul had intended to convey the meaning "obey," he could have used the Greek word, *hupakouo,* which does mean "to obey." When Paul described slaves who were to be in subjection to their masters (Col. 3:22) and children who were to obey their parents (Eph. 6:1), he did use the word *hupakouo.*

Another observation about the word *subjection* in the New Testament is this: When it is used regarding relationships between men, it is never understood to refer to a servile obedience of one man to another. Thus, it should be interpreted the same way for women.

The New Testament meaning of *hupotasso*—to yield one's preferences rather than assert one's rights—is different from the kind of rule God foretold that Adam would exercise over Eve in Genesis 3. In other words, Christian wives are not to be forced to obey or to be ruled over by their husbands. Forceful ruling of husbands over wives was a consequence of the Fall because Eve turned from God to her husband. In the New Testament, *hupotasso* describes a different kind of marriage relationship where there is mutual yielding. To the extent that grace works in a husband's heart, he does not want to lord it over his wife (nor does she want to control him).

For more information about the word, "subjection," in the New Testament (Gk: *hupotasso*), see paragraphs 293, 295, 303, 304, and 305 of Bushnell's book. This word is found in Ephesians 5:24, 1st Peter 3:1, and Titus 2:5.

Understanding Active, Middle, and Passive Voices of Greek Verbs

Finally, in order to get to the correct meaning of this Ephesians lemon, it is critical to understand the voice of the verb form of *hupotasso* that is used in it. Greek verbs have active, middle, and passive voices. The following explanation of Greek voices is quoted from the "Resources for Learning New Testament Greek" website (Resources).

Active Voice

... If the subject of the sentence is executing the action, then the verb is referred to as being in the active voice.

For example: "Jesus *was baptizing* the people" (paraphrase of John 3:22; 4:1, 2). "Jesus" is the subject of the sentence and is the one that is performing the action of the verb; therefore the verb is said to be in the "Active Voice".

Passive Voice

... If the subject of the sentence is being acted upon, then the verb is referred to as being in the passive voice.

For example: "Jesus ... *was baptized* by John in the Jordan" (Mark 1:9). "Jesus" is the subject of the sentence, but in this case He is being acted upon (i.e. He is the recipient of the action), therefore the verb is said to be in the "Passive Voice".

Middle Voice

The Greek middle voice shows the subject acting in his own interest or on his own behalf, or participating in the results of the verbal action. In overly simplistic terms, sometimes the middle form of the verb could be translated as "the performer of the action actually acting upon himself" (reflexive action).

For example: "I *am washing myself.*" "I" is the subject of the sentence (performing the action of the verb) and yet "I" am also receiving the action of the verb. This is said to be in the "Middle Voice". Many instances in the Greek are not this obvious and cannot be translated this literally.

It is more difficult for English speakers to understand the definition of middle voice because English grammar does not define a middle voice.

Paul *never* used the word *hupotasso* in the active voice. He used *hupotasso* in Ephesians 5:21–24 in the passive voice or the middle voice. Remember that the voice of *hupotasso* determines its meaning. First, we will consider its meaning in these Ephesians verses:

> 21 Submitting yourselves *(hupotasso)* one to another in the fear of God. 22 Wives, submit yourselves *(hupotasso)* unto your own husbands, as unto the Lord. 23 For the husband is the head of the wife, even as Christ is the head of the church: and he is the saviour of the body. 24 Therefore as the church is subject *(hupotasso)* unto Christ, so [let] the wives [be] to their own husbands in every thing. (Eph. 5:21–24, KJV)

The words, "submit yourselves," in verse 22, or words with similar meanings, appear as added words in some translations. For example, in the New American Standard Bible, the words that are shown to be added are "be subject," indicating that they are not in the Greek manuscript that was used.[12] It was inserted by the translators because it is implied by verse 21. Also, the words "let" and "be" in verse 24 are also supplied by the translators.

---

[12] The Greek word occurs in some manuscripts but not in others. For example, it is not in the Westcott and Hort of 1881 or the Nestle GNT of 1904; however, it does show up in Scrivener's Textus Receptus of 1894 and RP Byzantine Majority Text of 2005 (Greek Texts).

The following shows how these Ephesians verses would be understood if *hupotasso* were in the active voice:

> 21 Subordinate one another in the fear of God.

> 22 Wives subordinate your own husbands, as to the Lord....

24 Therefore as the church subordinates Christ, so let the wives subordinate their own husbands in everything.

A passive voice meaning of *hupotasso* in these verses would be understood this way:

21 Subordinated by one another in the fear of God.

22 Wives subordinated by your own husbands, as to the Lord....

24 Therefore as the church is subordinated by Christ, so let the wives be subordinated by their own husbands in everything.

Most of the commentaries and articles that I read concerning the meaning of *hupotasso* in these verses show that the meaning of *hupotasso* in verses 21, 22, and 24 tends toward the middle voice. The middle voice meaning would be understood as follows:

21 (Willingly) submitting yourselves one to another in the fear of God.

22 Wives (willingly) submitting to your own husbands, as to the Lord....

24 Therefore as the church is willingly submitted to Christ, so let the wives willingly submit to their own husbands in everything.

The important thing we learn from the voice of *hupotasso* is that Paul had in mind mutual submission, one to another, as a Christian grace and virtue. He did not expect wives to be submissive like children or slaves. He did not expect husbands to subordinate their wives.

So, in simple terms, verse 22 says that wives are to relate to their husbands in the same way that they relate to the Lord. How do believers relate to the Lord? They make the decision to willingly submit to Him when they see the demonstration of His love for them on the cross. Such love persuades them to choose to believe and to submit to Christ as their Lord.

Kephale (Head)

Now we come to verse 23 and the meaning of the word that is translated "head."

> For the husband is the head of the wife, as Christ also is the head of the church, He Himself [being] the Savior of the body. (Eph. 5:23, NASB)

To an English speaker, the word "head" brings to mind two things: the physical head of a body and the figurative head or leader of a group of people. In Greek, however, two different Greek words designate each of these things. The Greek word for the head of a body is *kephale*. The Greek word for leader or ruler is *arche*. *Arche* also has these other meanings: beginning, as in point of origin, and first, as first in importance and power. Paul was familiar with the word *arche* because he used it in the New Testament when he referred to rulers, princes, and other such leaders. However, when he wrote that the husband was *head* of the wife in Ephesians 5:23, he did not use the word *arche*. Instead, he used the word *kephale* (Bristow).

In addition to meaning head of a body, *kephale* also meant "foremost" in terms of position, like a capstone over a door, or a cornerstone in a foundation—but it was never used to convey the meaning of "leader," "boss," "chief," or "ruler." It was, however, used to refer to someone who led in battle—but not like a "general" or "captain" who ordered his troops from a safe distance. A *kephale* was one who went before military troops as a leader in the sense of being the first one into battle (Bristow).

One way to prove that *kephale* and *arche* were very different in meaning and usage and that *kephale* was not used to mean "boss" or "ruler" is to note the usage of these two words in the Septuagint. (The Septuagint is the Greek translation of the Hebrew Old Testament.) Just like the English word "head," the Hebrew word for head *(rosh)* had two meanings: "physical head" and "ruler." The seventy scholars who wrote the Septuagint carefully translated the word *"rosh"* by determining how it was used. If it referred to a "physical head," they translated it *kephale.* If it referred to the first soldier leading others into battle with him, they also translated it *kephale.* When *rosh* meant "chief" or "ruler," they translated it *arche* or some form of that word. This distinction held true for every translation of *rosh* in the Septuagint. The difference between the two words would have been very obvious to Paul, as a highly educated man, so his choice would have been purposeful. Unfortunately, the difference is not obvious to the average, modern-day reader (Bristow).

In Paul's time, most Hellenized people thought that the husband was an *arche* to his wife—a head of the household and ruler over all his family; so, it is noteworthy that Paul chose *kephale.* Understanding these clear distinctions between the meanings a*rche* and *kephale* is necessary in order to properly interpret Paul's meaning in Ephesians 5:23 (Bristow).

With the information about these two Greek words, *kephale* and *arche,* in mind, here is what I believe to be the proper understanding of Ephesians 5:23: Both of the meanings of *kephale* fit perfectly to describe how Christ is the head of the church. On one hand, just as the physical *kephale* of the body directly takes particular care of each cell of the physical body and directs every function of the whole body to that end, so does Christ directly take particular care of each member of His body, and so does He direct the whole of His body to take loving care of every member of His body, the church. On the other hand, just as a military *kephale* goes first into battle against the enemy, Christ also went first into battle with the devil and defeated him on the cross. As the *kephale* of the church, he laid down His life for her.

Now we can understand what Paul meant by man being the head of the wife. In verses 25–27, Paul further applied the meaning of *kephale* being one who goes into battle by telling the husbands that, just as Christ battled the devil on our behalf to the point of giving up His life, so should husbands battle the devil on behalf of their wives, even to the point of giving up their own lives. In verses 28–30, he further applied the meaning of *kephale* being the head of a physical body by saying that a man was not to hate his wife but to love her in the same way that he loved his own body—by nourishing and cherishing it.

Furthermore, the picture given in Ephesians 5:23–29 is profound in light of what happened in the Garden of Eden. The Greek root of *kephale* has the sense of "seizing" as the part most readily laid hold of *(KJV Exhaustive)*. You could say that in the garden after the Fall, Adam was the *kephale*—the first one God laid hold of—the first one to whom God spoke after what had happened. Like the role of a *kephale,* God held Adam responsible for what happened, no doubt, because God formed him first and because God directly commanded him not to eat of the tree of knowledge of good and evil. When God questioned him, Adam blamed Eve for the Fall. In other words, he loved himself and sacrificed her. That was the same as hating her. As a result, Eve, no doubt, lost respect for him.

When Christ came, He rescued us from the devil by sacrificing Himself for us. He cared for us as Adam should have cared for Eve. In so doing, He also demonstrated how husbands should love their wives and how they could make it possible for their wives to respect them: by loving their wives to the extent of giving up themselves for them. Christ, as the head, did not demand submission, but won it by His self-sacrificing love. Adam failed to love Eve in this way in the Garden of Eden; but, as a new creation, as a new man in Christ, according to Paul, man is to love his wife just as Christ did when He laid down his life for the church (Eph. 5:25). As a new-creation in Christ, a husband who chooses to give himself for his wife will be supplied by the Spirit to love her as Christ loved us. Wives will respond to such as they do to the Lord's love.

What a picture! When a man loves his wife in this way, the woman spontaneously will have great respect for him, and she will easily *hupotasso* to him in everything just as the church does in response to the sacrificial love of Christ:

> But as the church is subject to Christ, so also the wives [ought to be] to their husbands in everything. (Eph. 5:24, NASB)

The words "ought to be" were added by the translators. If the husband behaves as a new creation man, this verse makes better, if not perfect sense, without the added words "ought to be." With their removal, the verse becomes a statement of a resultant fact: "But as the church is subject to Christ, so also the wives to their husbands [new men in Christ!] in everything."

So, to sum up the de-lemonizing of Ephesians 5:22–24, a de-lemonized version would be something like this:

22 Wives to your own husbands, as to the Lord.

23 For the husband is the head of the wife, as Christ also is the head[13] of the church, He Himself [being] the Savior of the body.

24 Therefore as the church is willingly submitted to Christ, so let the wives willingly submit to their own husbands in everything.[14] (Eph. 5:22–24)

---

[13] In a version such as this, the words "head" in verse 23 and "willingly submitted" in verse 24 should have one or more footnotes that provide a clear explanation of the meaning and usage of *kephale* in this passage, along with its distinction from the word *arche*.

[14] Further discussion of verse 33 regarding a wife reverencing her husband is found in the de-lemonizing of the seventh lemon (1 Pet. 3:1–2).

Lemon Four: Colossians 3:18

The Passage

Wives, be subject to your husbands, as is fitting in the Lord. (Col. 3:18, NASB)

The Misfit

This is a sister passage to Ephesians 5:22–24 and is used as secondary support in the New Testament for the belief that wives are to be under the headship of their husbands.

The Fit

A wife's willing submission is tied to its propriety or its appropriateness in the Lord. In other words, there may be times that it would not be proper or fitting for a wife to willingly submit; therefore, in such times, she is free to choose not to do so. For example, if the husband tells her to do something that violates holiness as defined by God's Word, she will not do so because that would not be fitting in the Lord.

The De-lemonization

Colossians 3:18 is another instance of Paul giving a word that qualifies a wife's submission to her husband. In Ephesians 5:22, Paul wrote for wives to willingly submit to their own husbands as to the Lord. "As to the Lord" is a qualification, clarifying the kind of submission required. The meaning of "as to the Lord" is not that a wife should obey her husband as if he was her absolute ruler. It means that she should submit to her husband willingly—the same way that she submits to the Lord. She is persuaded to do so by his love and righteous behavior.

Here, in Colossians 3:18, Paul made this understanding even clearer when he wrote that a wife is to submit *(hupotasso)* to her husband "as is fitting in the Lord." The phrase, "as is fitting," also means "as is proper." This implies that her willing submission is tied to its propriety or its appropriateness in the Lord. In other words, there may be times that it would not be proper or fitting for a wife to willingly submit; therefore, in such times, she is free to choose not to do so. For example, if the husband tells her to do something that violates holiness, she will not do so because that would not be fitting in the Lord.

Bushnell wrote:

An *unqualified* subjection of one to another has never been enjoined upon man or woman Christian, by the Bible. (Bushnell, para. 359)

This understanding also sheds some light on the next verse, Colossians 3:19, which says, "Husbands love your wives and be not bitter against them." A husband might become embittered toward a wife who refuses to do everything he says, especially in a Greco-Roman culture where men were considered to be superior and rulers *(arche)* in the hierarchical family structure.

Lemon Five: 1st Timothy 2:8–15

The Passage

8 I will therefore that men pray every where, lifting up holy hands, without wrath and doubting. 9 In like manner also, that women adorn themselves in modest apparel, with shamefacedness and sobriety; not with broided hair, or gold, or pearls, or costly array; 10 But (which becometh women professing godliness) with good works. 11 Let the woman learn in silence with all subjection. 12 But I suffer not a woman to teach, nor to usurp authority over the man, but to be in silence. 13 For Adam was first formed, then Eve. 14 And Adam was not deceived, but the woman being deceived was in the transgression. 15 Notwithstanding she shall be saved in childbearing, if they continue in faith and charity and holiness with sobriety. (1 Tim. 2:8–15, KJV)

The Misfit

This passage is mainly used to prevent women from teaching in the church, the reason being that if a woman teaches a man, she is usurping authority over him. It is also used to say that women are to be silent in the church, to remain in subjection, and to learn in silence. (As explained earlier, the difficulties this causes in church function have made it necessary to explain it in ways that allow a woman to speak in certain situations.) It is also used to remind women that they were the ones who were deceived and tell them that this is why they must be submissive. Further, it is used to say that a woman's place is in the home bearing children, so that she can be saved, and also to control how women dress.

The Fit

All of these instructions were written by Paul to Timothy because of a situation in the church there that was due to the Ephesian culture. It was greatly under the influence of the worship of the Roman goddess Diana (same as Greek goddess, Artemis). Every sentence that Paul wrote concerning women (and men) in this lemon passage can be understood in light of certain temple practices in that worship. There were newly converted women in the church in Ephesus who were still very much under the influence of their old idolatrous worship of Diana. Paul was telling Timothy how to educate them in Christian truth.

The De-lemonization

I found this lemon translation to be the most difficult one to resolve. Even though I had studied it, prayed over it, thought about it—every which way—and researched others' thoughts about it, I always was left with the feeling that I was missing something important. I could find partial explanations for what Paul wrote, but none that really fit the puzzling compilation of the ideas he presented in this passage. What was Paul thinking? On top of Paul talking about men's praying and women's dressing and women's talking and women's childbearing, he even went back to the Garden of Eden and talked about Eve being deceived. One morning, I begged the Lord to show me why these verses were in the Bible and what they meant. Why did Paul write them? Why were they misfits with other parts of Scripture and with Paul's own practice?

A Letter to One Person

This troubling lemon translation is found in a letter from Paul that was written to one person: Timothy. It is not a letter to a church that Paul would necessarily have expected to be passed around to other churches establishing doctrine for all time. For all that Paul knew, after Timothy read this letter, and maybe after he shared it with others locally, he might dispose of it. It is a far stretch to think that Paul considered he was writing a statement of doctrine concerning Christian women that would be used in centuries to come to:

- Demand that they be in silent subjection to men

- Prohibit them from ever teaching anything to a man

- Dictate how they should dress

- Declare that they would be saved through bearing children if they met certain conditions

Could the man that wrote this passage really be the man whom Jesus called on the road to Damascus, the man who preached the gospel of salvation through faith in Christ? Could he really be the man who determined to know nothing but Christ and Him crucified? Could he really believe, as this passage seems to say, that women were to be saved a different way than men—that women had to bear children in order to be saved? Surely not! Whatever was Paul doing when he wrote this part of his letter?

In addition to all this, Paul's doctrine here and his manner of delivering it does not line up with the understanding of how true authority, God's authority, works. Instead of persuading, Paul appears to be dictating matters concerning female believers as if God had given him the authority to lord it over them. Paul certainly knew it was wrong to lord it over brethren, including female brethren, so why write like this? Paul also told us in Galatians 3:28 that there was no male or female in Christ. In light of God's character and ways, and in light of Paul's own teaching and practice, I knew that there had to be an explanation for what he wrote about women to Timothy.

The Key to the Passage

The morning after my prayer, I began to reconsider one of the explanations that I had read about—that Paul was addressing a situation that was specific to the Greek culture of the time. I wondered about that culture—how did its women treat its men? Were the women domineering, overbearing? That morning, I found an article by a Christian pastor named Wade Burleson. He provided a clear explanation that answered every question I had. He pulled together every piece of these puzzling verses into a cohesive explanation that made perfect sense. I highly recommend reading this article in its entirety. In what follows, I have provided highlights from it that completely succeed in de-lemonizing this lemon!

According to Burleson, understanding Paul's meaning is dependent upon a number of things:

- Understanding the historical culture of Ephesus, the place where Timothy was living

- Having a working knowledge of warrior women (Amazons) that the ancient Greeks believe founded Ephesus

- Grasping the influence that the cult and Temple of Artemis (known as Diana by the Romans), one of today's seven wonders of the world, had over those in Ephesus

  - The temple was dedicated to the power, beauty, and strength of women.

  - Carvings of Amazon women are in its base.

  - The cult taught that women were superior to men because the goddess Artemis was born first before the god Apollo and was, therefore, superior to Apollo.

- Understanding the nature and worship of Artemis

  - Artemis was the Greek goddess of women and war, called by Homer "the Queen of the Wild Beasts."

  - She was also the goddess of phosphorous or light. It was believed that she would deliver women from death if they prayed to her during childbirth.

  - Greek women worshipped Artemis in the temple, not with sacrifices, but with their apparel and their words. They wore hair braids, jewels, and ornate clothes.

  - Greek men worshipped raising their hands above their waist to pray to Artemis for victory in war.

- Understanding Paul's and Timothy's involvement in Ephesus:

  - Paul and Timothy spent three years in Ephesus (Acts 18:24–Acts 20:1).

  - Paul and Timothy caused a riot there because the gospel was causing the silversmiths to lose income from the sale of statues of Artemis.

  - Paul "fought the wild beasts at Ephesus" (1 Cor. 15:32). (This makes sense knowing that Artemis was referred to as the Queen of the Wild Beasts.)

  - Paul predicted shortly after leaving Ephesus that wolves would come among the flock that would distort the truth in order to draw disciples away (Acts 20:29–30).

Just from these few facts, one can already begin to see rays of light falling on this passage in 1st Timothy.

The following is my synopsis of the conclusions Burleson reached about this Timothy lemon translation.

I will therefore that men pray everywhere, lifting up holy hands, without wrath and doubting. (1 Tim. 2:8, KJV)

Paul's point here was that, whereas Greek men lifted up hands in prayer to Artemis for help in winning wars, converted men should lift up holy hands in prayer, believing in the true God, and not praying to win wars but to live peaceful lives, referring back to 1st Timothy 2:2.

9 In like manner also, that women adorn themselves in modest apparel, with shamefacedness and sobriety; not with broided hair, or gold, or pearls, or costly array; 10 But (which becometh women professing godliness) with good works. (1 Tim. 2:9–10, KJV)

The language about women's dress can be understood as a reference to the unbelieving women who worshipped the goddess Artemis. Paul's appeal was that women who had now believed in Christ did not need to dress in finery as they did to appear before Artemis, but that they needed to dress themselves in good works to appear before the only true God.

Let the woman learn in silence with all subjection. (1 Tim. 2:11, KJV)

In verses 9–10, the Greek word for women is in the plural, however, in verse 11, the word "woman" that Paul uses is singular, possibly indicating that he was speaking about a particular one that Timothy had told him about who was causing trouble among the believers in Ephesus by her practice and teaching.

The Greek word translated "silence" in this verse can better be translated "quietness." (Also, note that according to Thayer, the word [G2271] does not mean "speechlessness.") Burleson wrote concerning the woman that was causing trouble:

This woman in Ephesus, coming out of a society saturated with the power, strength, abilities and even domination of women through the Artemis cult, needed to realize that she had a great deal to learn about Christ and His kingdom.

She needed to learn in quietness, humility.

> But I suffer not a woman to teach, nor to usurp authority over the man, but to be in silence. (1 Tim. 2:12, KJV)

Concerning the phrase, "I suffer not a woman to teach," Burleson said:

> First, the phrase translated "I suffer not a woman to teach" is literally in the tense of "I am not now permitting a woman to teach." Again, the woman not now permitted to teach is in the singular. It is the same woman of verse 11. This woman needs to learn in quiet humility before she ever presumes to teach, because she is still too influenced by Artemis cultic beliefs.

Concerning the phrase, "usurp authority," Burleson wrote:

> This phrase *"usurp authority"* translates one Greek word *authentein.* This word is used only one time in all of Scripture—let me repeat that again—this word *authentein* is used only once in the entire Bible, right here in I Timothy 2:12. This word was used, however, in classical Greek literature and it meant "to murder someone." Paul could have chosen nearly fifty Greek words to speak of the ordinary exercise of authority, but he chose a word that more represents someone "dominating, controlling, or subjecting one to harm." Of course, this is precisely what the Artemis cult taught women to do. Artemis was the female goddess of fertility and war. Women in Ephesus were taught to use their voices, their charm, their sexuality and their beauty to dominate, control and subjugate men. It seems that this woman in Ephesus was causing trouble in the church by behavior in the assembly of Christ that was way too similar to the ways of the Artemis cult from whence she came.

Now, light is shining more brightly on this lemon. In the next verse, Paul wrote:

> For Adam was first formed, then Eve. (1 Tim. 2:13, KJV)

This is Paul's response to the cultic belief that woman came first and man came second. The truth according to Genesis is that God created man first and then He formed woman.

> And Adam was not deceived, but the woman being deceived was in the transgression. (1 Tim. 2:14, KJV)

In these explanations, we can see valid reasons for Paul bringing up Eve in his letter to Timothy. The words about Adam being formed first and Eve being deceived into the transgression have been used to blame women for the Fall and put them in their place. With Burleson's explanation, these verses suddenly make more sense. Paul was telling Timothy to warn a particular woman in Ephesus who was a new convert that, just as the young Eve in the garden was deceived, she too could be deceived. She should learn from others in Christ, even males, who were older in the Lord than her, like Adam was older than Eve. She needed to set aside her old cultic belief in female superiority and learn, even from males.

Thanks to an Unknown Woman

I cannot help but note that the behavior of an unidentified, troublesome woman in Ephesus has turned out to be somewhat of a blessing to women, because it resulted in Paul writing a very revealing piece of information about Adam and Eve (1 Tim. 2:14). Eve was deceived; Adam was not. This information gives more clarity as to why Paul wrote to the Romans that the sin of one man, Adam, was responsible for death entering the world (Rom. 5:12, 14). God held Adam responsible because Adam knew better. Adam was disobedient, *not deceived.* Eve, however, became involved in the first transgression because she was deceived (as covered in an earlier chapter). Of course, giving this piece of information about Adam and Eve was not Paul's purpose in writing to Timothy, but this one sentence has the power to silence the centuries-old, devil-instigated accusation against Eve as being the one who was responsible for the Fall!

Wrapping up the de-lemonizing of 1st Timothy 2:9–15, we come to the last verse:

> Notwithstanding she shall be saved in childbearing, if they continue in faith and charity and holiness with sobriety. (1 Tim. 2:15, KJV)

I offer this from Burleson about verse 15, the last verse in this greatly misused lemon translation. He elaborated the meaning of Paul's words to Timothy:

> Timothy, tell this woman that she will be okay during childbirth, even if she totally and fully renounces her trust in Artemis. Yes, she lives in a culture that teaches Artemis alone saves a woman from death during childbirth, but the truth is Christ holds the keys of life and death. When women continue in faith, hope and love—avoiding the sexual immodesty and looseness on display in the Temple of Artemis and the worship of the goddess of fertility and war—it will be the one true God who delivers them from death during childbirth, not Artemis.

With this understanding in mind, it seems that the word "notwithstanding" in verse 15 might be better translated by one of its other meanings, that is, "moreover." It seems Paul is adding a final thought about any fear women might have about dying in childbirth if they were to completely set aside their cultic beliefs and practices.

Another Consideration about the Childbearing Verse

I believe that it is possible there may be another aspect to what Paul wrote about women and childbearing. He may have also been making a positive statement about the role godly women play in bearing children. He may have been encouraging the Ephesian women that there was more to bearing children than just the act of physically giving birth. In other words, God had promised to crush the devil through the seed of woman. Therefore, strong women of God should not make their target men, but the devil! Women and men should be praying and working together in overcoming his evil works.

Bushnell wrote that she believes women will play a key role in bringing forth the man child of Revelation 12, meaning that women have a role to play in helping produce truly godly males—Christian men who have been transformed from living as men in the self-absorbed, old, serpentine nature, to godly men living as new creations in Christ. She did not believe, as some in her day did, that the man child in Revelation 12 was Jesus and the woman sign in the heavens was Mary, the mother of Jesus. She gives scriptural support for her belief that the Revelation 12 man child refers to a large number of overcoming male believers who will be involved in carrying out Christ's judgment of the devil on the earth in the end times (Bushnell, Lessons 98–99).

Also, according to Bushnell, the Greek word for "saved" that Paul used in the "saved through childbearing" phrase also means to "to deliver, protect." (Our understanding of the word, "saved," in this phrase is colored by our all-to-common use of the word "saved" with respect to Christian new birth.) If Bushnell's insights about this are correct, it would clarify the matter by translating the phrase in this way: "delivered through the childbearing." This would also allow for the possibility that Paul was referring to woman (and all mankind) being delivered from evil and the devil's oppression by the complete fulfillment of God's promise concerning the seed of woman. The promised seed of woman is not only Christ, but also those who believe in Him. This understanding is supported by Revelation's description of many believers overcoming the evil one, and also by the Bible's teaching that believers will reign on the earth with Christ, fully subduing and conquering the earth and its evil ruler, as God purposed in Genesis 1:26.

The note on 1st Timothy 2:14 in the NET Bible (Internet version) agrees with Bushnell's insight that "the childbearing" in verse 14 may refer to the seed of woman promised in Genesis. The meaning of the Greek word for "the childbearing" actually includes the *process of childbearing,* that is, rearing children, not just the initial act of giving birth. (Vine wrote concerning the Greek word for childbearing as follows: "denotes 'bearing children,' implying the duties of motherhood.") NET Notes mentions this meaning but proceeds to rule out its interpretive value because Christ, the seed of woman, had already come when Paul wrote Timothy. In other words, the NET Notes authors believe that the seed of woman refers to Christ alone; and, therefore, the idea of a process of childbearing is of no use in understanding 1st Timothy 2:14. If, however, Bushnell's understanding is correct—that the man child in Revelation 12 is male believers (the Greek word clearly refers to male) who are new creations in Christ, and that women have a role to play in bringing them forth, then the meaning that includes the whole process of child rearing, not just the act of giving birth, does fit and does help in interpreting this verse.

This suggests the possibility that Paul, when he wrote this phrase, might have had the seed of woman in mind and, therefore, might have meant to further encourage the strong women converts in Ephesus to forsake their old thought about subduing men and to press on with this new one. Now, they had a role to play in the final demise of the devil by living in a way of total dependence on and obedience to God that would help to turn disobedient and ungodly males back to God (1 Pet. 3:1–2).

Lemon Six: Titus 2:3–5

The Passage

3 The aged women likewise, that [they] be in behaviour as becometh holiness, not false

accusers, not given to much wine, teachers of good things; 4 That they may teach the young women to be sober, to love their husbands, to love their children, 5 [To be] discreet, chaste, keepers at home, good, obedient to their own husbands, that the word of God be not blasphemed. (Titus 2:3–5, KJV)

The Misfit

This passage is used to limit all women to teaching women only and to say that women should not work outside of the home.

The Fit

Actually this passage is specifically written to older women, not to restrict them, but to encourage them to teach the younger women how to be good wives and mothers. It does not logically follow that, just because the older women teach the younger women, they should be limited to teaching only younger women. Nor does it follow that, just because they are keepers at home, they cannot have work outside the home.

The De-lemonization

There are several difficulties with this passage that need clarification, since it has been wrongly applied. On the topic of women teaching, in addition to Bushnell's book (Lessons 40–47), I also recommend the book, *Who Said Women Can't Teach?*, by Charles Trombley. He masterfully covers the topic.

The bottom line is that the Bible *does* permit women to teach men. In one instance, in Paul's argument against the Judaizers in Galatia with respect to their bondage-producing perversion of the truth, Paul showed what he thought about women teaching men. He quoted a woman from the Old Testament, Sarah, Abraham's wife, and referred to her words as Scripture. Sarah told Abraham to "cast out the bondwoman and her son for the son of the bondwoman shall not be heir with the son of the free woman" (Gen. 21:10, Gal. 4:30). If Paul believed women could not teach men, he certainly would not have taught others by quoting the words of a woman who *taught her husband* the truth that the son of a bondwoman could not be heir with the son of a free woman! His exposition to the Judaizers on this topic (Gal. 4:21–30), which he supported by the quote from Sarah, indicates that he had received biblical revelation from her words! He was a man that appreciated her words, learned from them, and passed them on. He certainly knew what he was doing when he quoted the teaching of a woman to the women-suppressing Judaizers! It is clear that God had given Paul understanding about the meaning of Sarah's words and about their application to Paul's time. They meant that the period of bondage for the Jews had ended with Christ, and it should not continue. They also meant that the period of bondage for women had ended with Christ. (Bushnell, p. iv)

Another incorrect application of the Titus passage relates to women being only workers or keepers at home (G3626, *oikourgos*). Housekeeping is a necessary skill; but, again, it does not logically follow that this verse is intended to restrict women to the tasks of working at home and keeping house. Priscilla, one of Paul's co-workers, made tents with her husband, and Paul doesn't say that Priscilla should be restricted to being a housekeeper (or that she should not teach a man). Instead, he tells us that he made tents with the two of them and commends Priscilla and her husband for teaching Apollos the way of God more perfectly (Acts 18:26). Furthermore, 1st Timothy 5:14 shows that Paul considered woman's role in the home not to be that of a domestic servant but that of a ruler of the house. The word he chose to use in 1st Timothy 5:14, the one that is translated "guide the house," actually means *"rule a house."*

Finally, Titus 2:5 says that the young women are to be taught to be "obedient to their own husbands":

> [To be] discreet, chaste, keepers at home, good, obedient to their own husbands, that the word of God be not blasphemed. (Titus 2:5)

The Greek word that is translated "obedient" is once again, *hupotasso,* which is discussed at length in the de-lemonizing of Ephesians 5:22–24. The King James translators clouded the meaning of this verse when they chose to translate *hupotasso* as "obedient." The truth is that Titus 2:5 reflects wives willingly submitting to their husbands in the same way wives and husbands in Ephesians 5:21 willingly submit to one another (see Bushnell paras. 298–299).

Remember that the phrase in Ephesians 5:21, "submitting *(hupotasso)* to one another out of reverence for Christ," refers to all members of the body of Christ, without regard for gender. The idea of mutual submission means that there should never be a situation of domination or subjugation of females by males, or vice versa. Therefore, Titus 2:5 should not be understood to mean, as it appears to mean with the translators' use of the word "obedient," that aged women should teach younger women to be ruled over by their husbands.

We should also remember that this letter was not addressed to a church, but to Titus who was in Crete. In it, Paul wrote, referring to a Cretan, "One of themselves, a prophet of their own, said, Cretans are always liars, evil beasts, lazy gluttons" (Titus 1:12, NASB). This may be why Paul wrote as he did about the converts there. In verse 16, he wrote about some of the Cretans who professed to know God but denied Him by being abominable, disobedient, and reprobate with respect to good works. It was in the context of a very dysfunctional culture that Paul wrote Titus 2:2–6 concerning how aged Cretan men and women, and young Cretan men and women, should behave. This fact makes it highly doubtful that Paul was intending to define restrictive doctrine concerning women for all times and places.

Lemon Seven: 1 Peter 3:1–6

The Passage

1 Likewise, ye wives, [be] in subjection to your own husbands; that, if any obey not the word, they also may without the word be won by the conversation of the wives; 2 While they behold your chaste conversation [coupled] with fear.

3 Whose adorning let it not be that outward [adorning] of plaiting the hair, and of wearing of gold, or of putting on of apparel; 4 But [let it be] the hidden man of the heart, in that which is not corruptible, [even the ornament] of a meek and quiet spirit, which is in the sight of God of great price. 5 For after this manner in the old time the holy women also, who trusted in God, adorned themselves, being in subjection unto their own husbands: 6 Even as Sara obeyed Abraham, calling him lord: whose daughters ye are, as long as ye do well, and are not afraid with any amazement. (1 Pet. 3:1–6, KJV)

The Misfit

This passage has been understood to mean that a wife may win her disobedient husband to Christ by not saying a word about the things of God and, possibly, not saying anything, but just living a good, submissive life in front of him. It has also been used to support the idea that women are to be subject to their husbands as Sarah was and even that they should call their husbands, "lord."

The Fit

These verses do not mean that a woman must submit to her husband absolutely and not ever say a word back to him, or ever speak the Word of God to him. They mean, instead, that a woman should live out, or demonstrate, the truth of the Word of God in front of her husband. To do this, she will submit to him willingly, unless for conscience' sake she cannot. If he asks her to do something that violates the Word of God and His holiness, then she will not submit to him, but to Christ. She will tell her husband why she is unable to submit to him by using the Word of God to explain her action. Believers are commissioned to share the gospel with others, so she certainly is free to speak about her faith in Christ to her husband. As he watches her follow Christ and live righteously, he will begin to fear such a holy God, and this will help him be won to Christ. If she suffers for not submitting, this is well-pleasing to God.

The De-lemonization

In the process of de-lemonizing 1st Peter 3:1–6, I made a profound discovery. The first word in this lemon passage turned into a key that opened a fresh understanding of the whole book of 1st Peter for me. I marveled that a Galilean fisherman had written in such a wise way. As I looked backwards at my life history through the book's newly revealed prism and then looked forward through it to my eternal future, I was joyful to see how the two parts of my life in Christ fit perfectly and purposefully together. I actually had the thought that if this was the only book of the Bible I had, its words would give me the way to help people find the secret to a joyful Christian life. Yes, a book that is best known for its discourse on suffering holds the key to joy, both now and in the life that is to come. I hope that I will be able to give you a glimpse of this inspirational view of the whole book.

Without a Word

We'll start with the first two verses of the lemon translation of 1st Peter 3:

> 1 Likewise, ye wives, [be] in subjection to your own husbands; that, if any obey not the word, they also may without the word be won by the conversation of the wives; 2 While they behold your chaste conversation [coupled] with fear.

First, the word, "conversation," in Old English meant behavior or conduct, not just talking.

The New American Standard Bible says that the husband may be won by the wife without *a word*. This sounds as if the proper way for a wife to win her husband to Christ is not to say anything but just to live a good, Christian life in front of him. I heard this verse used in this way among Christians for many years, so I believed that this was what the verse actually said. I had wondered why Peter expected a woman to be silent, when Jesus commanded all believers not only to live the gospel, but also to preach it.

One day, while reading these verses for myself, I noticed that the King James Version said, "they also may without *the* word be won," instead of "without *a* word." I realized that "the word" (Gk. *logos*) might refer to the Word of God and not to the wife's words. I also realized that the phrase "without the word" made more sense if it modified the husband, instead of the wife. In this way, the verse would mean that a husband who did not obey, read, or believe the Word of God (was without the Word) could be won, even without it, by seeing the godly behavior of his wife. She would be a living demonstration of the Word of God, one that had the power to convict him.

Then it suddenly occurred to me that this new understanding turned the idea of woman's total submission to her husband on its head. If a wife lived her life according to the Word of God and took care of her conscience toward God, this would sometimes mean (such as in a case in which her husband asked her to do something illegal or unethical) that she would be right *not to do that thing, even though her husband asked her to do it!* It also could mean that God might use her "unsubmissiveness" in such a case to convict him. So, instead of these verses being understood as requiring absolute and silent submission, they can more fitly be understood to actually give a Christian wife the freedom to choose not to submit to her husband in certain situations in order to demonstrate the truth of the Word of God to him. This understanding goes perfectly with the meaning of *hupotasso* (choosing to submit oneself), which is found in verse 1.

This new understanding removes the need for the translator-supplied word "coupled" in the King James Version of verse 2:

> While they behold your chaste conversation [coupled] with fear. (1 Pet. 3:2, KJV)

It can be translated to make perfect sense without having to use this supplied word:

> While they behold with fear your chaste conduct.

This change causes the word, "fear," to modify the husband's behavior instead of the wife's. It is the husband who beholds with fear the holiness exhibited by his wife's chaste behavior.

Also of note in verse 2 is the choice of the word "chaste" by translators. The Greek word, *hagnos*, means "free from ceremonial defilement, holy, sacred." This meaning fits with the idea of the wife living a holy life according to the Word of God. The word "chaste" brings to mind the idea set forth by Pagnino's translation of Genesis 3:16 about woman's lust being the reason for man to rule over woman. A better translation of verse 2 might be:

> While they behold with fear your holy conduct.

With all these things in mind, a better translation of 1 Peter 3:1–2 might be:

> 1 Likewise, ye wives, in subjection to your own husbands; if any obey not the word, without the word they also may be won by the behavior of the wives, 2 while they behold with fear your holy conduct.

Not a Command

This lemon translation has been an especially problematic one for married women, in particular because of another word that is supplied by the translators in verse 1: "be." They apparently added this word to help clarify the meaning as they understood it. Unfortunately, for married women, this added word makes the verse appear to be a command that sentences them to silence and subjection to disobedient husbands. Such an incorrect understanding is dispelled by a close look at the grammatical voice of the Greek verb, *hupotasso,* which they have translated as "be in subjection."

Like many English students, I did not like the study of grammar; however, I have learned to greatly appreciate the rules of language after seeing the role they play in understanding the meaning of Greek words. I provided an explanation about a verb's voice earlier, however, knowing it is not easy to retain such information, here is a brief review: A verb's voice tells who (or what) is doing the action in a sentence or who (or what) is receiving the action in a sentence. There are three grammatical verb voices in Greek: active, passive, and middle. In active voice, the subject does the action; for example, John (the subject) loves (active voice verb) Jane. In passive voice, the subject is acted upon; for example, Jane (the subject) is loved (passive voice verb) by John. In middle voice, the subject acts upon, or for the benefit of, itself; for example Jane loves herself.

According to Greek dictionaries, the voice of *hupotasso* in 1st Peter 3:1 is either passive voice or middle voice. It is not active voice. If it was active voice, it would be understood to mean, "ye wives, subjugate, or rule over, your own husbands ...." In the passive voice, it would be "ye wives, ruled over by your own husbands ...." In the middle voice, it would be "ye wives, willingly submitting yourselves to your own husbands ...."

So, because the voice in 1st Peter 3:1 is either passive or middle, how do we determine which it is? The first word of this lemon passage, "likewise," points us back to the verses that seem to contain the answer to this question: It appears that, in context, both voice meanings of *hupotasso* can apply. The word, "likewise," refers back to prior verses which are about slaves. By his use of "likewise," Peter indicated that whatever he had written to slaves also applied to wives. So, in order to properly understand Peter's word to wives, we need to examine his word to slaves.

Peter's Word to Slaves

Peter wrote to slaves:

18 Servants, [be] subject to [your] masters with all fear; not only to the good and gentle, but also to the froward. 19 For this [is] thankworthy, if a man for conscience toward God endure grief, suffering wrongfully. 20 For what glory [is it], if, when ye be buffeted for your faults, ye shall take it patiently? but if, when ye do well, and suffer [for it], ye take it patiently, this [is] acceptable with God. 21 For even hereunto were ye called: because Christ also suffered for us, leaving us an example, that ye should follow his steps: 22 Who did no sin, neither was guile found in his mouth: 23 Who, when he was reviled, reviled not again; when he suffered, he threatened not; but committed [himself] to him that judgeth righteously: 24 Who his own self bare our sins in his own body on the tree, that we, being dead to sins, should live unto righteousness: by whose stripes ye were healed. 25 For ye were as sheep going astray; but are now returned unto the Shepherd and Bishop of your souls. (1 Pet. 2:18–25, KJV)

Bondslaves (G1401, *doulos*) were in a state of absolute servitude to earthly masters and were bound by civil law to do whatever the earthly master told them. In Ephesians 6:5 and Colossians 3:22, Paul wrote about this kind of slave—one who was a Christian—and used the word, *hupakouo,* which shows that a bondslave's relationship to his master was one of absolute obedience to the master's will. (Slavery was not something ordained or established by God, but was something that came into being as a result of the Fall. When man turned away from God and obeyed another, the devil, he became the slave of the devil. Subsequently, the practice of slavery became part of the human experience. In other words, slavery was a consequence of man's disobedience.)

So, such Greco-Roman slaves, who were in bondage to other men every moment of every day, faced a dilemma when they became believers. As believers, they had chosen to submit themselves (*hupotasso*) to another master, the Lord Jesus. The Bible says that one cannot faithfully serve two masters (Mark 6:24, Luke 16:13). Paul told these Christian bondslaves who were in a *hupakuou* relationship with their masters according to civil law that, as believers, they were now to be in a *hupotasso* relationship with their masters (Titus 2:9). This meant that they should willingly do what they were bound by civil law to do as slaves. At the same time, because they were believers and servants of the Lord Jesus, they were also supposed to live holy lives, because God is holy (1 Pet. 1:15). Thus, serving two masters could produce a dilemma: What would a slave do if a conscience conflict arose while serving these two masters?

Peter's words to Christians who were domestic servants (G3610, these had more rights than bondslaves) seem to be addressing this problem. He pointed them to Christ's example and told them to *hupotasso* to their masters. If for conscience toward God they had to disobey their earthly master, and if they were punished for this, then they were to take it patiently, like Christ did when He was crucified. They were not to threaten or fight back, but to commit their souls to Him who judges righteously. For example, if a master commanded a believing servant to kill someone, the believing servant, for conscience toward God, would not do so and might suffer punishment as a result. Patient suffering under such unjust punishment was acceptable to God (3:20).

So, interestingly, in these two passages (Titus 2:9 and 1st Peter 2:18), we can see both the passive and middle voice meanings of *hupotasso*. On one hand, slaves were subordinated to their earthly masters (passive voice meaning) because of civil law; and, on the other, they were willingly submitting themselves (middle voice meaning) to their earthly masters as good representatives of their heavenly master. In this way, both meanings (passive and middle voices) of *hupotasso* are a fit in Peter's passage about slaves.

Likewise, Wives

With Peter's passage about slaves in mind, we can now understand what Peter meant by "likewise wives." Both the passive and middle voice meanings of *hupotasso* also fit in the passage about wives. On one hand, wives are in a state of subordination, of being ruled over by their husbands (passive voice meaning) as a result of the Fall. As God explained to Eve:

> ... your trust is turning toward your husband,
> and he will dominate you. (Gen. 3:16, ISV).

Wives are in this state of subordination, being ruled over by their husbands, because they willingly look to them and put their trust in them, as Eve did with Adam. But now, as believing wives, ones who have willingly submitted (middle voice) themselves to Jesus as their Lord, they are to *willingly* submit (middle voice) themselves to their husbands who have been ruling over or dominating them. And, just as slaves don't have to submit if doing so causes them to sin against God, neither do wives. If they suffer for this, they are to take it patiently.

Peter expounds further on this by giving some additional words concerning wives. If they have husbands who don't obey the Word (of God), their husbands may be saved when they see their wives willingly submitting themselves to God and to them, and living holy lives.

In summary then, wives should submit to their husbands willingly unless conscience toward God requires them not to do so. For example, if a husband said, "Go with me to the idol temple and worship other gods," the wife's response would be, "No," in order to obey her heavenly master. She would worship the only true God and obey His Word, taking care to keep her walk with Him holy. If her husband were to ask or expect her to commit, to support, or to tolerate sin of any kind, again her answer would be, "No." Also, to be holy and right with God, if her husband was a believer, if he sinned against her, she would not be silent, but would obey God and speak the truth to him in love (Eph. 4:15) and, if necessary, would even rebuke him (Luke 17:3), seeking to "restore such an one in the spirit of meekness" (Gal. 6:1, KJV).

With this basic understanding, suddenly we have flipped on its head the common interpretation of 1st Peter 3:1–2. We have released married Christian women from the bondage generated by the misuse of these verses. They do not mean that a woman must submit to her husband absolutely and never say a word. They mean, instead, that a woman may, and even must, disobey her husband under certain conditions. If he asks her to do something that violates the Word of God and His holiness, or even if he tells her she cannot do something that God's Word requires of her, she must follow Christ and live righteously. In doing so, she may awaken her husband's proper fear of God and help him be won to Christ. If she suffers for this, this is well-pleasing to God.

The truth is that these verses, once properly interpreted, line up beautifully with the most fundamental truth of the gospel, because they focus on the salvation of the husband through the wife's experience of the cross of Christ. Christ spoke the truth in love and then suffered on our behalf as we killed Him. Actually, the whole book of 1st Peter accentuates the practical truth of Christ suffering in the flesh on our behalf, and of believers following in His footsteps and suffering likewise for the eternal benefit of others. When believers do what is right and patiently suffer the resulting mistreatment, they become a living demonstration of the righteousness and longsuffering love of God. In their suffering, the Spirit of God may lead them to share the gospel in meekness (strength with humility), even if only in a few words.

Suffering for doing well does not mean that a Christian woman, a weaker physical vessel, must suffer physical abuse at the hand of her husband. She is also under obligation to God to take care of her body as His temple, and also may have children who need protection. She would be in the right to separate herself from a husband who was violent. As for psychological abuse, this depends on the situation and is up to a wife to decide. If she is able to trust in God and look to him to meet her psychological needs and can find her joy in trusting Him, she may choose to suffer such abuse in hopes of becoming an instrument God uses for her husband's salvation. This is an individual decision for the woman to make with God's leading in light of her particular circumstances. Proper handling of this topic would require another book!

Sarah Trusted in God

The rest of this lemon translation says:

3 Whose adorning let it not be that outward [adorning] of plaiting the hair, and of wearing of gold, or of putting on of apparel; 4 But [let it be] the hidden man of the heart, in that which is not corruptible, [even the ornament] of a meek and quiet spirit, which is in the sight of God of great price. 5 For after this manner in the old time the holy women also, who trusted in God, adorned themselves, being in subjection unto their own husbands: 6 Even as Sarah obeyed Abraham, calling him lord: whose daughters ye are, as long as ye do well, and are not afraid with any amazement. (1 Pet. 3:3–6, KJV)

In light of the previous explanation, these verses do not need much explanation. The important thing is the wife's right relationship with Christ, the hidden man of the heart. Her outward behavior will match His. Meekness is not weakness; it is strength with humility. Peter referred to Sarah because she was such a woman. She was willingly subject to Abraham; however, she did not go along with him when he wanted to keep Ishmael. Sarah did the right thing when she told Abraham to cast out the bondwoman and her son, and God supported her. God used Sarah's words to convict Abraham that he was wrong and then told him to obey his wife. Abraham willingly submitted to Sarah's demand. At another time,

Abraham put Sarah in a terrifying situation by letting Pharaoh take her into his house, not telling him that she was his wife, knowing Pharaoh intended to take her into his bed. Sarah suffered through that mistreatment, trusted in God, and God protected her and delivered her. (It may appear that Sarah lied when she obeyed Abraham and said that she was his sister; however, because she actually was his half sister [Gen. 20:12], this was not a blatant lie. You might say it was a half truth.)

Likewise, Husbands

Just when I thought I was through with this lemon, I made another noteworthy discovery: There is another "likewise" in 1st Peter 3, one addressed to husbands:

> Likewise, ye husbands, dwell with [them] according to knowledge, giving honour to the wife, as unto the weaker vessel, and as being heirs together of the grace of life; that your prayers be not hindered. (1 Pet. 3:7)

"Likewise" means that husbands should live with their wives in the same way Peter had instructed wives to live with their husbands and slaves to live with their masters—willingly submissive to them (as in Eph. 5:21) unless it was not possible for conscience' sake, and then, likewise, accepting with joy any resultant suffering. This word to husbands also fits well in a situation in which there is a believing husband with a wife who does not obey the Word.

Then, Peter adds another word to the husbands. Peter tells them to dwell according to knowledge (a seeking to know, an enquiry, investigation of spiritual truth [Vine, G1108]) with wives as weaker vessels, giving them honor (respect) as joint heirs of the grace of life. In other words, husbands need to treat their believing wives as joint-heirs of the grace of life so that their prayers will not be hindered but answered! Peter understood, as should we all, especially Christian husbands, that our effectiveness in prayer—in warfare against the devil—is directly related to our having proper, mutually-submissive, and honoring relationships in marriage.

The translation of 1st Peter 3:7 seems to need improvement. Again, a Greek scholar would have to verify the possibility of something like the following, which makes more sense and seems to be justifiable when looking at Greek word helps and dictionaries:

> Likewise, ye husbands, dwell, according to knowledge with your wives, as weaker vessels, giving them honor also as joint-heirs of the grace of life, that your prayers be not hindered. (1 Pet. 3:7)

Peter Shows the Way into Joy

God's predictive warning to Eve came to pass:

> ... your trust is turning toward your husband, and he will dominate you. (Gen. 3:16, ISV)

Husbands have been ruling over wives for centuries. This state of affairs is bad for both husbands and wives. Wives have surrendered their freedom in the hope that safety, love, provision, etc. will come to them from their husbands. Men have lost their dignity and spiritual power by selfishly lording it over their counterparts, because they are stronger physically and can do so and because their wives let them. Wives have lost their dignity and spiritual power by selfishly enabling the bad behaviors of their husbands, all because of their own neediness and fearfulness. Both parties in marriage are thus locked in painful and debilitating relationship patterns, right where Satan wants them.

Then comes Jesus. Then comes believing.

Peter's message is to believers in various kinds of bondage: slaves, wives, and husbands. For wives, he points to the way out of their sad state of bondage when he tells them to live holy lives, pleasing to God, and, in so doing, demonstrate for their disobedient husbands the truth of the gospel. This is the way of escape God has made for them, the way to freedom from being ruled over by their disobedient husbands. As believers, they no longer need to look to their husbands for their happiness, neither do they need to rebel against them—they just need to yield fully to God, trust in Him, and always obey

Him. This means that they submit willingly to their husbands, unless for conscience' sake they cannot. God will protect them and take care of them, just as He did Sarah (when Abraham let Pharaoh take her), and He will bring their husbands to obey the gospel, just as He did Abraham (he had to obey Sarah and cast out Ishmael). Peter further points the way for husbands when he tells them to live with their wives, seeking to know spiritual truth, giving them honor as joint-heirs, so that their prayers won't be hindered. Living thus, wives and husbands will reap joy!

I find it noteworthy that Peter addresses wives before he addresses husbands. This fits with the new perspective of the role Eve played in helping Adam turn back to God that we covered in an earlier chapter. (See Chapter 3, "Eve: the First Woman Enabler," "Eve The First Woman of *Chayil*," and "Adam: The First Man to Repent, Be Transformed, and Father a Lineage of Godly Males.")

Peter also wrote that believers are not to be afraid or troubled by those who cause them to suffer, but to rejoice, so that when His glory is revealed, they will be glad with exceeding joy (1 Pet. 4:13). They are to sanctify the Lord God in their hearts, be ready to give a reason for their hope, and always keep a good conscience. Christ, the just one, suffered for the unjust, so they should be willing to do likewise (1 Pet. 3:15–16).

It also noteworthy that Peter wrote about joy through suffering near the beginning of his letter:

> 6 Wherein <u>ye greatly rejoice,</u> though now for a season, if need be, ye are in heaviness through manifold temptations: 7 That the trial of your faith, being much more precious than of gold that perisheth, though it be tried with fire, might be found unto praise and honour and glory at the appearing of Jesus Christ: 8 Whom having not seen, ye love; in whom, though now ye see [him] not, yet believing, <u>ye rejoice with joy unspeakable and full of glory:</u> 9 Receiving the end of your faith, [even] the salvation of [your] souls. (1 Pet. 1:6–8, KJV) [underline added]

And, near the end of his letter, he spoke again at some length about joy through suffering:

> 12 Beloved, think it not strange concerning the fiery trial which is to try you, as though some strange thing happened unto you: 13 But <u>rejoice</u>, inasmuch as ye are partakers of Christ's sufferings; that, when his glory shall be revealed, ye may <u>be glad also with exceeding joy</u>. 14 If ye be reproached for the name of Christ, <u>happy</u> [are ye]; for the spirit of glory and of God resteth upon you: on their part he is evil spoken of, but on your part he is glorified. 15 But let none of you suffer as a murderer, or [as] a thief, or [as] an evildoer, or as a busybody in other men's matters. 16 Yet if [any man suffer] as a Christian, let him not be ashamed; but let him glorify God on this behalf. 17 For the time [is come] that judgment must begin at the house of God: and if [it] first [begin] at us, what shall the end [be] of them that obey not the gospel of God? 18 And if the righteous scarcely be saved, where shall the ungodly and the sinner appear? 19 Wherefore let them that suffer according to the will of God commit the keeping of their souls [to him] in well doing, as unto a faithful Creator. (1 Pet. 4:12–19, KJV) [underline added]

This powerful and practical perspective of the gospel message permeates the whole book of 1st Peter. How very despicable it is that our enemy found the way to change Peter's encouraging words to wives into a lemon message—one that, instead of being used to further the gospel of Christ and the joy of it, has been used to fuel centuries of gender abuse in the body of Christ!

A Heavenly Perspective

We have reached the end of the de-lemonization of the seven New Testament lemons. Please remember that I do not claim to know Greek or to be qualified as a Bible translator. I believe, however, that with the help and insights I received while sitting at the feet of Jesus, I have been able to make a strong argument for qualified Bible translators to revisit the lemon translations.

The lemon translations have functioned like stealth weapons in Satan's warfare against mankind. The gender-based wounds resulting from wrong teaching set forth by them may be the single biggest reason for the existence of churches which have a form of godliness and very little, if any, power. Gender-based abuse that is perpetuated, tolerated, and even sanctioned by Christian leaders leaves the church weak and in a condition of powerlessness against the devil. The church's powerlessness has left the door open for him to produce an ever-deepening flood of horrendous gender-based sins on the earth.

With respect to the effect of the lemon translations on our world, you might say we are at a point in history of critical mass. The fissile material, the lemon translations, must be removed from the core message of the Bible, so that the church can begin to heal. When they are turned into the grapes that they really are, God will use the truth they convey to bring conviction and produce repentance! A huge relationship divide in the body of Christ will begin to heal. People will begin to see among God's people a model of proper relationships between male and female. Such light in the church, the family of God, will be like that of a city set on a hill that cannot be hidden.

Appendix C contains a chart with two columns that make it easy to compare side by side the seven lemon translations with their improved grape translations. For ease in writing about these troublesome Bible passages, I chose to use the metaphor of lemons in a grape vineyard; however, what these eight lemon passages really are is leaven, and what I might have called the passages in the New Testament is the "seven leavens." When the seven leavens in the New Testament and the one leaven in the Old Testament are purged, the whole Bible will become the unleavened bread that it truly is.

In the next chapter, we will take a closer look at the war between the two seeds and what the Bible has to say about it.

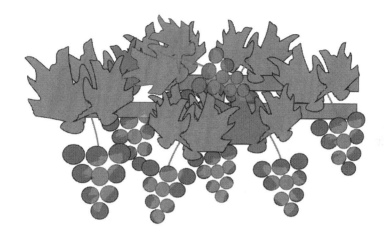

PART FOUR:
TODAY

Chapter 8
The Battle: Two Seeds at War

And there was war in heaven: Michael and his angels fought
against the dragon; and the dragon fought and his angels,
(Rev. 12:7)

One Woman Too Many

I T IS A MERE ILLUSION that things are better for modern
women as some might argue. Yes, women have more
societal rights, and things may appear to be better in
some ways; but, be assured, Satan's warfare against
Christian women hasn't lessened.

Just prior to leaving on a trip to the state of
Washington in 2014 to visit some friends, I was
considering the current status of Christian women. Even
though as a modern-day woman I had been a victim of
abuse because of my gender, and even though I was
personally aware of a good number of other such modern-
day cases, I was on the verge of convincing myself that,
overall, things were better in the present than in times
past. Then, while in Washington, maybe in order to
adjust my thinking about this, Jesus put me in an eye-
opening situation.

We attended a few Christian home meetings while
visiting our friends. Our friends told us that a new couple
had joined their home meeting some months before. The
husband of the couple was beginning to show that he had
an agenda. It seemed he wanted to persuade the men in
the group to silence the women in the group. His wife,
whom I met, was very quiet and subdued. Her sad face
carried the pain of the oppression she was under. Her
husband was in possession of two documents that
spelled out, using the lemon passages, what he believed
about the role of women in the church. He had told his
wife to give them to our friends. They passed the
documents to me. I was shocked to find that the message
in them was the complete antithesis of Bushnell's book. It
presented a contrary message up against hers almost

point by point. It shocked me to see the anti-argument spelled out in print so clearly and persuasively. It made me sad to learn that this man's wife agreed with his beliefs and agenda. She believed they were of God—but how could she do otherwise? The lemon passages supported her husband's dogma.

I learned that his papers were the product of some kind of new movement among Christian men designed, in the name of God, to help Christian women stay in their "biblical" place. My "this-work-is-of-the-devil" Geiger counter was clicking away as I read this man's papers. I also heard God's message to me, "Don't think the enemy has given up on this front and don't forget the countenance of this man's wife. If *only one woman* is oppressed by a man acting on false beliefs about Me, *that is one woman too many.*" Through my little God-opened Washington window, I understood that Satan's enmity would be at work to the bitter end, fueling his fight against godly women and their godly seed. I had to stay the course and follow the Lord wherever He led me in this battle.

The Enmity between the Two Seeds: The Unnamed Conflict

When God put enmity between the serpent and the woman and between their two seeds in the Garden of Eden, this was the beginning of the enmity between those who belong to God and those who belong to Satan. It also was the beginning of a conflict that would escalate over time into an all-out war. The pattern that has been repeated over and over is that of Satan gradually infiltrating, influencing, and corrupting God's people, and of God then coming to rescue His people and preserve godly seed for Himself. Noah's story is one example of this. There were only eight righteous persons left when God came, judged the ungodly seed of the serpent, rescued the righteous, and started over.

By the time of Abraham, Satan had gained the upper hand again. God then called Abraham to follow Him out of his idolatrous country. This time, God took new steps to protect His people and keep the devil from infiltrating and corrupting them. He told Abraham that he and all his male descendants must be circumcised. Circumcision was a mark, a sign, borne by the males among God's people that designated them as godly seed and that separated them from fleshly, ungodly seed (the seed of the serpent, the Gentiles).

God may well have instituted this ritual act performed upon males because of the male's disobedience at the time of the Fall. Adam disobeyed God when he ate the forbidden fruit that Eve gave him. He also sinned when he did not own up to the devil's presence and involvement in what had happened, and blamed the woman instead. Adam had not repented for the latter at the time that God drove him out of the garden.

When Christ came in the flesh, He came as a male. His first act was to humble himself, to empty himself, and become flesh. When sinful men decided to crucify Him, He didn't opt to save or protect Himself as Adam had done in the garden. Instead, He laid down his life to save us and make us new creations in Christ.

Christ's death was the reality of what circumcision signified. By it, the old Adam was crucified—cut off. At the same time, a new man was created in Christ—one that had a circumcised heart that could bring forth fruit unto God. A fundamental truth of the cross of Christ is that, with it, God ended the enmity (Eph. 2:15) and took down the wall of protection that had shut His people in and shut the Gentiles out. The cross ended the enmity that God put in place at the time of the Fall. It opened the way for the Gentiles to have access to God through the blood of Christ. On the cross, all things were put beneath the feet of Christ.

Today on the earth, we do not yet see the spiritual fact of Christ's victory with our physical eyes, but those who believe this truth see it by faith. They see Jesus, the one who authored their faith and who will finish it. The day is coming when all eyes will see the reality of what Christ accomplished on the cross. Until that day, we will continue to see evidence everywhere on the earth of the enmity between the woman and the serpent and their two seeds. Blinded by the devil's darkness, men who don't believe in Christ cannot recognize or call this enmity what it is. Can you imagine a news commentator saying, "What we are seeing in this turbulent world today is evidence of Satan's hatred against mankind and of his centuries-old war against the woman and the seed of woman. He wants mankind destroyed!" They would be reporting truth; but, in a short period of time, they probably would have a pink slip in hand or maybe a referral to a psychiatrist.

Instead, we see news commentators and pundits scratching their heads and asking questions day after day like, "What is happening to this country?" "What has brought about the downhill slide of our society?" "Who is responsible for this?" They voice things like, "I just can't understand why or how ..." followed by descriptions of the bizarre behavior of governments and citizens alike. Right-wing conservatives blame liberal progressives for everything and liberal progressives, likewise, blame right-wing conservatives. Black people blame white people. Jews and Christians blame Muslims. Muslims blame and kill Jews and Christians.

I want to tell all of them to read Genesis 3:14–15! The problem we are facing on this earth started in the Garden of Eden. There, God pronounced a judgment concerning Satan that still has standing today. God said to Satan:

> 14 ... Because you have done this,
> Cursed are you more than all cattle,
> And more than every beast of the field;
> On your belly you will go,
> And dust you will eat
> All the days of your life;
> 15 And I will put enmity
> Between you and the woman,
> And between your seed and her seed;
> He shall bruise you on the head,
> And you shall bruise him on the heel. (Gen. 3:14–15, NASB)

God made this pronouncement to a real being, Satan, not to some kind of fairy-tale or mythological character. Today, much to Satan's satisfaction, unbelievers (and sadly some believers) make jokes about the devil and laugh at the idea of his existence. Many picture him as a cartoon character with two tiny horns sticking out of his head and an evil smirk on his face. He wears red long-underwear, has an arrow-tipped tail curling up behind him, and has a pitchfork in his hand. He is thought of as being so small that he can sit on a man's shoulder and whisper in his ear. This pathetic fabrication is nothing more than a creation of man's devil-inspired imagination. Here is what the late Justice Antonin Scalia of the U.S. Supreme Court had to say about the existence of the devil to someone who did not believe:

> You're looking at me as though I'm weird. My God! Are you so out of touch with most of America, most of which believes in the Devil? I mean, Jesus Christ believed in the Devil! It's in the Gospels! You travel in circles that are so, so removed from mainstream America that you are appalled that anybody would believe in the Devil! Most of mankind has believed in the Devil, for all of history. Many more intelligent people than you or me have believed in the Devil (Senior).

If you want to have some idea of what the devil is really like, take all the characteristics of the worst rulers and warlords in all of earth's history (men like Genghis Khan, Alexander the Great, Charlemagne, Hitler, Caligula, Nero, Julius Caesar) along with all the worst criminals the world has known from Jack the Ripper to Geoffrey Dalmer and put them all together into one person. Even then, you won't scratch the surface of the evil that resides in, and comes out of, the devil. As the prince of this world, the devil has been the overlord and energizer of every wicked world ruler and every wicked person on this earth. Many such men are now dead and part of the past. Their power on earth is over, but the devil is still active, carrying out his very real and purposeful agenda through new pawns. You do not need to look far to see his evil fruit. He is driven by hatred—the hatred that God set in place in Genesis after his act of treachery against man. The devil thinks that he is in control; but, actually, he is under the control of this hatred.

When you look at the extreme hatred of the Muslims for the Jews, you are looking at enmity that has its roots in the Genesis pronouncement. When you look at the murderous hatred of terrorist groups, you are looking at the devil's hatred for man. No amount of bloody wars or of peaceful negotiations will remove the hatred that is between these two seeds. I repeat: The reason for earth's turmoil is the hatred that God put between Satan and woman and between their two seeds millennia ago.

Today, behind the scenes, Satan continues to plot, scheme, and attack God's people day and night. God's people continue to fight him by prayer and acts of faith. Even though human beings cannot see this spiritual war with their natural eyes, it exists. It is real, and it is fierce. Satan is at work using fallen men (his seed) to apply trickery, deceit, and malice of every kind against the godly seed of woman. A massive cloaking device, like the ones fictional spaceships use in battle, conceals Satan's presence. The Bible describes this cloak as gross darkness that covers the whole earth in order to blind peoples' minds to the light of the gospel (2 Cor. 4:4). Satan does everything he can to keep this shield up so he can work in stealth as he tries to prevent the light of the gospel of the glory of Christ from shining into his dark realm.

I pray that what I write in this chapter will bring to light more truth about the hidden war that is taking place upon the earth. I pray that God will open the spiritual eyes of every born-again heart to discern the devil's warring presence and his subtle, hidden ways of working. I pray that Christian warriors will stand up and become holy people standing against the enemy who has come in like a flood. I pray they will hasten the coming of the day when this long war is ended forever.

A Scale Model of the War: The First Family

In the account of what happened to the first family both in and outside the Garden of Eden, we find a small scale model of the massive, many-faceted battle on earth. We can learn much from that first, small battle about

Satan's strategy and his objectives, and also about the way of victory over him.

What happened to the first family? First, Adam and Eve's relationship with God was broken, and then their relationship with each other was broken. Satan was the first cause of this breach. He was also responsible for the breach that took place when Cain murdered Abel. We know this because Jesus attributed Abel's murder to the devil (John 8:44). This horrible murder widened the breach that already existed between Adam and Eve. No doubt, this was what Satan intended in his divide-and-conquer strategy. So, the first division on the earth took place between a male and a female, a husband and a wife. Then came a division between their two children that resulted in murder. Then, thankfully, after that murder, much to Satan's exasperation, Adam and Eve's relationship with God and with each other was restored and they birthed another son, Seth, who was a godly seed.

The Genesis account is the first evidence in the Bible of a broken relationship being healed. Two marriage counterparts, male and female, were restored to each other and began living together in harmonious, mutual submission to God and each other. Then, right in Satan's domain, they brought forth a godly seed—just as God had promised! After the devastating breaches that Satan had managed to create, Seth's appearance was a frightening glimpse for the devil of just what God was capable of accomplishing. It was evident that more such godly marriages would produce more godly men like Seth and like Seth's son, Enos, who called on the name of the Lord!

Thus grew Satan's determination to suppress and subdue the troublemaking woman whom he hated. Women had the potential to turn things completely around in their fallen marriages. Women could help heal broken families. Women could be instrumental in helping their backslidden husbands choose to turn back to God. Women were capable of stopping their own bad enabling behavior. Women had the power to turn a family crisis into a blessing and to facilitate the multiplication of godly families on earth. A prophecy by Jeremiah perfectly supports these ideas:

... for the LORD hath created a new thing in the earth, A woman shall compass a man (Jer. 31:22b, KJV)

According to Vine, the word compass [*cabab*, H5437] in this verse means "to turn, go around, turn around (change direction)." I suggest that, in line with the perspective of Eve that I am presenting in this book, the end of this verse would be better translated something like, "... a woman shall turn a man" or "... a woman shall turn a man around," meaning change his direction back to God.

There is evidence that this last part of Jeremiah 31:22 has puzzled translators of the Bible. *Cabab* is translated as "compass" or "encompass" in a number of Bible versions; however, it has also been translated in numerous other unique ways such as:

the woman will return to the man. (NIV)

Israel will embrace her God. (NLT)

a woman encircles a man. (ESV)

a female will shelter a man. (HCSB)

a woman will protect a man. (ISV)

something as unique as a woman protecting a man! (NET)

Such translations indicate how difficult it is for males to translate a verse in a way that does not match with their preconceptions about the role of a woman. It is interesting that the most obvious understanding of this verse in light of the straightforward meaning of *cabab*—"*a woman shall turn a man*"—does not appear in any of the translations, at least not in those I examined. I suggest that this is because it simply did not fit male translators' concepts.

History tells us that Satan has continued his Eden plan to divide male and female and to ruin families. It also shows us that, although he has been successful in using fleshly men, including fleshly Christian men, in his war against woman and her seed, he has not been able to stop the seed of woman.

The miniature battle that took place in the first family provides us with an understanding of what we are witnessing on a large scale in the present. Today, Satan has gone so far as to openly and blatantly target the very institutions of God-initiated and God-defined building blocks of human society: marriage and family. The lemon translations planted prominently in the Bible, as if they were God's words, may be considered as a master stroke in this endeavor. He has used them to produce an unhealthy dynamic in Christian marriages, one that is far from Christ's relationship with the church as seen in Ephesians 5. As a result, many Christian marriages and families have fractured. So, instead of a Christian marriage dynamic among believers that demonstrates the truth of the beautiful relationship that God intends to exist between male and female, it demonstrates the opposite and gives ground for Satan to slander and turn men and women away from one another and away from God. The load of sin resulting from the practice of the lemon passages is a heavy burden weighing on the church today, preventing God from pouring out His blessing on her and on society.

A Current Battle Report on the State of Society

The state of modern-day society testifies to the long-term success of Satan's plan to break down the family unit. There is much evidence of catastrophic forces at work to destroy the family unit, especially in the last fifty years. Among unbelievers and believers alike, adultery is rampant. The divorce rate is off the charts. Fathers routinely abandon their wives and children. Women are daily fighting to survive divorce and abandonment. They are forced to bring up their sons and daughters alone. Such women either struggle against the dark, forceful tide, hoping to save their sons, or they, and their daughters, succumb to it. Inmate populations in prisons are burgeoning, predominantly with males. Rape is commonplace. Out of wedlock pregnancy is rampant. Abortion is not only accepted, it is promoted. Tiny innocent human beings growing safely in their mothers' wombs are suddenly murdered. No doubt, rampant abortion is one of the most terrible byproducts of Satan's attack on the family. In light of Satan's hatred of the seed of woman, this hideous crime, which directly attacks woman's seed before it is born, can be seen clearly as part of Satan's plan to block God's purpose on earth.

Fatherless Fathers

On top of all this, fatherless sons who reach adulthood, without ending up in prison, marry and begin families of their own. They then usually fail at their attempt to father their own sons and daughters, because they were never themselves properly fathered. Such men are fatherless fathers.

With the breakdown of the family unit that was established by God for man's highest purpose and good, society looks like an out-of-control, supercharged race car with its gas pedal stuck to the floor. It is speeding down the devilish, steep incline straight into the mouth of Hell.

Wade Horn, Ph.D., President of the National Fatherhood Initiative, wrote an article entitled, "Of Elephants and Men" (Horn). His findings, well worth the read, describe the plight of young male elephants that were separated from their bull elephant fathers when they were relocated to another African game reserve. The young males became wild and violent and went about terrorizing, attacking, and killing other animals in the reserve. They exhibited behavior not observed before among elephants. Almost miraculously, when older male bull elephants were brought to the reserve where these violent young males were, their aggressive behavior soon disappeared. Horn gave scientific evidence to support his findings that young male elephants will go rogue if they do not have the influence of older bull elephants in their lives. Bull elephant fathers are responsible for keeping younger male elephants under control as they physically mature and as their ever-increasing levels of testosterone begin to drive them towards more and more aggressive behavior. The young males learn from their bull fathers to control themselves and to behave normally and properly.

The parallel between this and the situation of young male human beings who are deprived of fathers at an early age is obvious. What is even more serious about the human problem is that there is an ever-increasing shortage of "bull elephants." To date, there have been several generations of men who have grown up without fathers. Fatherless fathers have had sons and those sons have had sons. Properly fathered men—ones who could help normalize younger "rogue" human males—are decreasing in numbers as they die off. Such men are today's grandfathers and even great grandfathers.

My husband, who is now a grandfather, is a man who was un-fathered. His father abandoned his mother and him when he was a young boy. As a result, our two sons suffered and were hurt because they were the sons of a man who did not know how to father them, having never been fathered himself. I married an un-fathered man, having no idea that there was such a thing, or that this would have a detrimental impact on me and on my children. The problem was compounded by the fact that I also had a father who was un-fathered! I will say more about my husband and our family later and about how God Himself has fathered my husband and rescued our family from the devil's plot to destroy us.

In Eden, we see the first un-fathered man: Adam. He was in the process of being fathered by God when Satan took him captive, and he began living a life separated from His true Father, God. In the Fall, he became a son of the devil. As such, Adam did not properly father his first son, Cain, with the result that Cain became a proud and jealous man, one who ended up murdering his younger brother, Abel.

Unbridled Immorality

In his attack on the modern family, Satan has used the medium of movies and television to fill people's minds with pictures, stories, and themes. Over time these have become more and more degraded and immoral. This slow-drip input has been successful in stupefying men's consciences. Society-changing messages about sex now come daily through actors and actresses, and even commercials, and open the door wide to real people committing real sexual sins in real society, and doing so without fear of societal rejection. Now, via the Internet, Satan has provided instant access to filthy pornography. Using technology to promote and even glorify filth and filthy behavior, Satan has succeeded in producing a general societal acceptance of sex outside of marriage and of sexual deviances, to a degree that was unimaginable only a few decades before. Today, unmarried people no longer think twice about cohabiting, and they expect, even demand, that their behavior be accepted and treated as normal by others; and, for the most part, it is. Marriage is no longer a societal necessity, and sex outside marriage is no longer taboo. People joke about pornography as if it was some harmless form of visual entertainment. The truth is that it opens a door of immorality that leads to Hell.

Such acceptance of immorality has made it easy for Satan to attack the God-initiated institution of marriage. His objective is to redefine the marriage mandate that God conceptualized, instituted, and clearly defined in the Bible. He is pushing for his own definition of marriage to prevail, one which includes the sexual perversion of men having sex with men or of women having sex with women. Such blatant rebellion against God's natural law of creation and reproduction is nothing less than rebellion against God Himself, which the Bible says is the same as the sin of witchcraft (1 Sam. 15:23). What the Bible calls an abomination, some world governments now call a "human right."

Wave after wave of anti-God forces continue to roll onto our societal beaches and take aim at the family. At the time of this writing, the latest anti-God, anti-Christ wave to crash down upon us, no doubt, has a long-term, yet-to-be-announced goal of washing away all evidence of gender distinction. This wave is the government mandate that all restrooms in public schools be open to people who feel they are of a different gender than the one to which their body declares they belong. This requirement defies all logic; and, mind you, it is done in the name of personal rights and non-discrimination. Of course, the definitions being used for personal rights and non-discrimination are satanically-inspired ones.

The attempt to remove gender distinctions is just one more satanic counterfeit of God's truth. What else can we expect from the one who specializes in counterfeits? Here is God's truth about gender: In Christ, there are no *spiritual* gender distinctions. All believers are the same in Christ. All are new creations in which there are no males or females. This, however, does not mean there are no distinctions in the fallen flesh of males and females! Our fallen, earthly bodies definitely have gender distinctions and, according to the Bible, those are to be acknowledged and respected as long as we indwell these earthly tabernacles. Physical gender distinctions, along with God's directives about how to respect them, will remain as long as earth exists in its current fallen state. God will continue to expect that women will be modest, appropriately concealing their physical attractiveness, and that men will exercise self control over their eyes and their lust. The simple and most obvious fact is that men and women are physically different, and their physical differences define their gender! Even small children know this! It is madness born in darkness that says gender is determined by how a person feels, and that other parties have to abide by such feelings no matter what eyeballs declare!

According to God, people living in the flesh, male and female, are to view their bodies as temples for God to indwell. They are never to view their bodies as sexual objects or behave as if their bodies were pleasure machines run by unbridled passion that drives them to have sex like animals. Sex is for procreation and for pleasure, but only within the boundaries of biblically-defined marriage. Such marriage is for the protection and health of both individuals and society. God is holy and the male-to-female marriage bed is undefiled (Heb. 13:14). The Bible also says that the offspring of such marriages are holy (1 Cor. 7:14). Most importantly, procreation is for God's original purpose that man subdue and conquer the earth for God. Any and all sexual involvement outside of holy marriage is nothing but disobedience and defilement that produces bondage to the devil and locks man away from fellowship with God. Of course, this is just what the devil wants! When men are cut off from the presence of God and access to His power, they lose their power over the devil.

Satan's "no gender distinction" counterfeit is a pre-emptive strike which is designed to confuse and hide the emerging truth about the beautiful relationship that God has always intended to exist between male and female. In this relationship, there is no gender distinction in the spiritual usefulness of each person. Such a healthy relationship between male and female is exceedingly possible, actually inevitable, in all who follow Christ and seek to know Him in truth! Believers who accept a counterfeit, male-dominant, authoritarian model in marriage, and a similar leadership model in churches, have been deceived. When they repent for this and begin to preach and practice what is really true, Satan's days are numbered.

Be assured, as history teaches us, Satan's long-term battle strategy in free societies is to produce civil laws which he can use to persecute the godly seed of woman. Don't forget that much of the modern-day lingo about individual rights operates under satanic definitions which cry for equal rights only for those who define things as Satan does. This cry for equal rights has nothing to do with God's truth. It is a cry for something that is a counterfeit of true justice. It always excludes the topic of God from the conversation. It exalts and pushes perverted definitions of individual rights and freedom with the end result of destroying proper God honoring relationships, families, and society as a whole.

Satan has, and will, use his twisted definitions to persecute those who walk in the truth of God's Word. As you can see, when it comes to the truth about gender, there is a gaping chasm between Satan's counterfeits and God's truth. Satan's definitions promote attitudes that have no concern whatsoever for propriety and morality. He knows well that the removal of gender distinctions will open the door for even more rampant immorality and give him more ground to capture and hold people in bondage.

If I, or others like me, suffer for making these kinds of true statements, we can take comfort in remembering the apostle Peter's words. He told us that we can be happy when we suffer for doing what is right (1 Pet. 3:14).

Never forget that Satan's whole intent is to stop godly seed, in particular, godly male seed, from being produced. He did not want Adam and Eve to reproduce and fill the earth with godly seed; so, he captured them and damaged their relationship with God and with each other, and he brought about the murder of one of their sons by the other. I hope you will spend some time to consider this perspective of the first family and try to retain it in your thought. It is a microcosm of the broad societal destruction taking place on this earth through Satan's war against the seed of woman. When we can understand the problem and name the war that we are in, we can find and apply the solution, because there is a solution.

A Current Battle Report on the State of the Church

Most importantly, the problem in society is directly tied to the condition of the church. If Christians are a living testimony of truth, as they should be, the condition of society will reflect this. History testifies that whenever there has been a true revival by the Spirit of God, society has reaped the benefits. During the Welsh revival (1904–1905), so many people gave their lives to Christ that many taverns closed because of the lack of patrons. Instead of gathering to drink liquor, people were gathering to drink the Spirit of the living God. There was also a revival in the United States in the 1730s and 1740s referred to as the Great Awakening:

> It resulted from powerful preaching that gave listeners a sense of deep personal revelation of their need of salvation by Jesus Christ. The Great Awakening pulled away from ritual, ceremony, sacramentalism, and hierarchy, and made Christianity intensely personal to the average person by fostering a deep sense of spiritual conviction and redemption, and by encouraging introspection and a commitment to a new standard of personal morality. (Wikipedia)

This revival preceded and greatly influenced the formation of the constitutional form of American government.

Unfortunately, the church today, overall, is in poor condition, much like the church in Laodicea (Rev. 1:14–22), which God said was neither cold nor hot, but lukewarm. He was ready to spit her out of His mouth because of her claim that she was rich and increased with goods. The truth was that she was wretched and miserable and poor and blind and naked. She had an extreme case of hypocrisy, a disease which is rampant in many modern-day churches.

The Christian side of the war between the two seeds today can be summed up in two words: almost defeated. The enemy is overrunning the earth because truth has fallen in the street (Isa. 59:14). The stories about the children of Israel and their enemies in battles were given to us for our learning today. They teach us that if Christians are to turn the tide and be victorious on earth's battlefield, broken relationships (divisions), sexual immorality, and self-exalting idolatry in the body of Christ must end.

The Culmination of the War at the End of the Bible

At the end of the Bible in the book of Revelation, we are given God's perspective of two women on the earth, both of whom are involved in the great dragon's war. One woman is described in chapter 12. The other is described in chapter 17. These two chapters provide strong evidence of the long-term battle between the devil and the woman and between their two seeds. The enmity described in these two chapters is the ancient enmity that began at the time of the Fall and is today at the root of every conflict on this earth. Revelation shows that this war will end in a final, climatic battle, which Christ wins hands down, using the sword of His mouth, because He has already won the victory on Calvary.

A Great Red Dragon and a Pregnant Woman

Revelation 12 describes a wonder seen in heaven. Satan, described as a great red dragon with seven heads and ten horns, is standing before a sun-clad, pregnant woman. He is waiting, ready to devour her child as soon as it is born. In the following quote from Revelation 12, take note of the phrases that are underlined, which refer to war or acts of war directed towards the woman and her seed.

The Woman and the Dragon

1 And there appeared a great wonder in heaven; a woman clothed with the sun, and the moon under her feet, and on her head a crown of twelve stars: 2 And she being with child cried, travailing in birth, and pained to be delivered.

3 And there appeared another wonder in heaven; and behold a great red dragon, having seven heads and ten horns, and seven crowns on his heads. 4 And his tail drew the third part of the stars of heaven, and did cast them to the earth: and the dragon stood before the woman which was ready to be delivered, for to devour her child as soon as it was born.

5 And she brought forth a man child, who was to rule all nations with a rod of iron: and her child was caught up to God, and to his throne. 6 And the woman fled into the wilderness, where she has a place prepared of God, that they should feed her there a thousand two hundred and three score days.

The War in Heaven

7 And there was war in heaven: Michael and his angels fought against the dragon; and the dragon fought and his angels, 8 And prevailed not; neither was their place found any more in heaven. 9 And the great dragon was cast out, that old serpent, called the Devil, and Satan, which deceives the whole world: he was cast out into the

earth, and his angels were cast out with him. 10 And I heard a loud voice saying in heaven, Now is come salvation, and strength, and the kingdom of our God, and the power of his Christ: for the accuser of our brothers is cast down, which accused them before our God day and night. 11 And they overcame him by the blood of the Lamb, and by the word of their testimony; and they loved not their lives to the death. 12 Therefore rejoice, you heavens, and you that dwell in them. Woe to the inhabitants of the earth and of the sea! for the devil is come down to you, having great wrath, because he knows that he has but a short time.

The Dragon Persecutes the Woman

13 And when the dragon saw that he was cast to the earth, he persecuted the woman which brought forth the man child. 14 And to the woman were given two wings of a great eagle, that she might fly into the wilderness, into her place, where she is nourished for a time, and times, and half a time, from the face of the serpent. 15 And the serpent cast out of his mouth water as a flood after the woman, that he might cause her to be carried away of the flood. 16 And the earth helped the woman, and the earth opened her mouth, and swallowed up the flood which the dragon cast out of his mouth. 17 And the dragon was wroth with the woman, and went to make war with the remnant of her seed, which keep the commandments of God, and have the testimony of Jesus Christ. (Rev. 12:1–17, AKJV) [underline added]

A Red Beast and a Woman Sitting on It

The woman described in Revelation 17 sits astride a red beast, full of names of blasphemy, having seven heads and ten horns. She is described as a great whore. Again, note the underlined parts in the passage that refer to war or acts of war.

The Woman on the Beast

1 And there came one of the seven angels which had the seven vials, and talked with me, saying to me, Come here; I will show to you the judgment of the great whore that sits on many waters: 2 With whom the kings of the earth have committed fornication, and the inhabitants of the earth have been made drunk with the wine of her fornication. 3 So he carried me away in the spirit into the wilderness: and I saw a woman sit on a scarlet colored beast, full of names of blasphemy, having seven heads and ten horns. 4 And the woman was arrayed in purple and scarlet color, and decked with gold and precious stones and pearls, having a golden cup in her hand full of abominations and filthiness of her fornication: 5 And on her forehead was a name written, MYSTERY, BABYLON THE GREAT, THE MOTHER OF HARLOTS AND ABOMINATIONS OF THE EARTH. 6 <u>And I saw the woman drunken with the blood of the saints, and with the blood of the martyrs of Jesus</u>: and when I saw her, I wondered with great admiration.

The Mystery Explained

7 And the angel said to me, Why did you marvel? I will tell you the mystery of the woman, and of the beast that carries her, which has the seven heads and ten horns.

8 The beast that you saw was, and is not; and shall ascend out of the bottomless pit, and go into perdition: and they that dwell on the earth shall wonder, whose names were not written in the book of life from the foundation of the world, when they behold the beast that was, and is not, and yet is. 9 And here is the mind which has wisdom. The seven heads are seven mountains, on which the woman sits. 10 And there are seven kings: five are fallen, and one is, and the other is not yet come; and when he comes, he must continue a short space. 11 And the beast that

was, and is not, even he is the eighth, and is of the seven, and goes into perdition. 12 And the ten horns which you saw are ten kings, which have received no kingdom as yet; but receive power as kings one hour with the beast. 13 These have one mind, and shall give their power and strength to the beast.

The Victory of the Lamb

14 <u>These shall make war with the Lamb, and the Lamb shall overcome them: for he is Lord of lords, and King of kings: and they that are with him are called, and chosen, and faithful.</u>

15 And he said to me, The waters which you saw, where the whore sits, are peoples, and multitudes, and nations, and tongues. 16 <u>And the ten horns which you saw on the beast, these shall hate the whore, and shall make her desolate and naked, and shall eat her flesh, and burn her with fire.</u> 17 For God has put in their hearts to fulfill his will, and to agree, and give their kingdom to the beast, until the words of God shall be fulfilled. 18 And the woman which you saw is that great city, which reigns over the kings of the earth. (Revelation 17:1–18, AKJV) [underline added]

These two chapters, Revelation 12 and 17, provide a vivid description of the climax of the ancient conflict between the devil and woman. They put the significance of this war where it belongs: front and center at the end of time. These two chapters plainly call the conflict *war.* They name and describe many of those involved (such as the devil, his angels, the Lord, the remnant of the seed of the woman, the woman clothed with the sun, and the woman on the beast). They also tell us the final outcome of the war, which is the victory of the Lamb.

I will not attempt to interpret all that is written in these two chapters of Revelation, for that is not my purpose in quoting them. I will, however, make several interpretive observations about both chapters with respect to women, because I believe that there are practical applications and lessons to be learned from them. I do not claim my interpretive observations are foolproof or right in all aspects, for only God knows the true interpretations of prophecies about future events, and only time will reveal them. I am simply offering for your consideration what I have come to believe to date.

About the Revelation 12 Woman

Some interpreters believe the Revelation 12 woman is the virgin Mary and the man child is Jesus. I do not believe this simplistic interpretation because there are too many parts of this passage that do not match the Jesus and Mary story. A few examples are: Jesus was not caught up to the throne of God at the time of his birth. It could be said that Mary fled, but it was with Joseph and with Jesus, and the flight was to Egypt, not to a wilderness. Not only that, Revelation 12 clearly refers to the time of the great tribulation, because it specifically mentions the tribulation period of 1260 days. Also, there is no suggestion in the Bible that the devil was cast down to the earth at the time of Christ's birth, nor is there any suggestion or evidence that God had to open the earth to protect Mary from a flood produced by the devil. Neither is there any suggestion or evidence that the devil made war with something referred to in the Bible as the rest of Mary's seed.

I personally believe that the Revelation 12 woman represents God-fearing women throughout all time who have been involved in the fulfillment of God's promise concerning the seed of woman. I believe that the moon, which was the lesser light that God set in the heavens to rule during the night (Gen. 1:16), represents the law of the Lord given to Israel, which produced only a fading reflection (2 Cor. 3:12–13) of the true light. The sun, the greater light that God set in the heavens to rule during the day, represents the brilliant light of the new covenant, which does not fade. This woman is standing on the moon and clothed with the sun. She represents both Old and New Testament women in full accord with God's promises in the Old and New Testaments. She is clothed with the sun as a garment, meaning that she is bearing the glorious light of the full revelation of the truth of the gospel of Jesus Christ. She has passed through the night of the Old Testament, under the fading light of the law. She is no longer under the bondage of the old covenant which Paul referred to when he wrote that the earthly Jerusalem was in bondage with her children (Gal. 4:25). She is free and is standing strong, having been born of the Jerusalem above which is free and is the mother of us all (Gal. 4:25–26).

Twelve individual shining lights are a crown on her head. These stars represent the twelve male apostles—the first godly males of the New Testament era to reflect the glory of God in the face of Jesus Christ. She is crowned with these stars because she played a role in their appearance. They came into being as a result of the willing obedience and cooperation of a woman named Mary, who considered herself a humble handmaiden to God when she said, "Be it unto me according to Your word." Through Mary came the promised and long awaited seed of woman, Jesus Christ. Then, through Jesus, came these twelve stars, the first of many more godly male seed of the New Testament era.

The Revelation 12 woman, appearing as a sign in the heavens at the end of time, represents all godly Christian women who have found freedom from bondage, returned to God, and suffered a very long and difficult pregnancy on earth bringing forth fruit to God—the victorious seed of woman. The two groups of women included in this sign are the Old Testament God-fearing women of *chayil* and New Testament Christian women of *chayil*. Both groups are made up of spiritual warriors. The first group brought forth Christ. The second group, of which we are called to be a part, is in labor, travailing to bring forth a man child, a male seed that will rule all nations with a rod of iron (Rev. 2:26–27). A great red dragon is standing in front of her ready to devour her child. This bright woman suddenly gives birth, and her male child is caught up to God and to His throne. She then flees to a place God has prepared for her where He feeds her. War then takes place in heaven, and the dragon is cast down to the earth. He persecutes the woman, but she is protected by God. The dragon then goes and makes war with her remaining seed, who are still on earth keeping the commandments of God and holding the testimony of Jesus.

I will not offer my thoughts on what is meant by all the events that take place after she gives birth, because they are not relevant to my message. I will, however, comment on the idea of the *remnant of her seed*. According to this passage, the remnant of her seed is definitely God's people and definitely Christians because they bear the testimony of Jesus. They are named as the seed of the woman who are on earth and who appear to be different from the male child that was caught up to God and to His throne. Although it is not clear exactly who they are, I will make one point about them: The idea of a remaining seed who are God-fearing people on earth during the tribulation period does not line up well with the predominant Christian belief that all believers will be whisked away to heaven *before the tribulation* that is to come upon the earth. Again, I do not have a full and clear interpretation of the whole of Revelation 12, but I offer the following additional thoughts that I have about this passage:

• Beginning with the time of the revelation of the glorious gospel of Jesus Christ, Christian females who were made free in Christ were called to return to Him fully and play a significant role in bringing forth Christian males who are conformed to the image of Christ.

• Similar to Jesus' statement about laborers in His field that the last would be first and the first would be last, women—formed last in the Garden of Eden and also historically last in Christian ministry (having been held back throughout most of Christian history from laboring as free women)—near the end of time, become first in spiritual maturity. This happens when they discover their God-given freedom and enter the field in late centuries, near the close of the New Testament age. God will not treat them differently than Christian males laboring in His field and will give them equal pay. At the end of the age, males— created first in Genesis and in the forefront of

Christian ministry through most of the church age—
will be *last* at the close of time because of the devil's
full force attack against them with his massive family
destroying flood of societal filth and corruption.
Through the painful spiritual labor of females, many
males will be brought back to God and fully delivered
from the devil. Stated more simply: At the beginning
of the Bible, a young female comes out of a mature
male. At the end of the Bible, a young male comes out
of a mature female. In this picture, it seems that God
has made a clear statement of gender balance with
respect to His view of both males and females and His
purpose for them. This picture brings to mind the
equalizing words of Paul in 1st Corinthians:

> 11 In the Lord, however, woman is not
> independent of man, nor is man
> independent of woman. 12 For just as
> woman came from man, so also man is
> born of woman. But everything comes
> from God. (1 Cor. 11:11–12, BSB)

- At the close of the age, Christian females will play a
critical role, laboring in God's field to bring forth, on a
large scale, Christian males—godly seed of woman.
This will happen during a time in which the attack of
Satan against males in human society, in ways like
those described earlier in this chapter, is at its peak,
a time when godly males are on the decline. The godly
males brought forth by laboring women will be the
Revelation 12 man child: new creation beings who are
conformed to the image of Christ and who will fulfill
the subduing and conquering role over the devil (not
one another or woman) that God intended for man
from the beginning.

- When this biblically prophesied man child comes
forth and stands up against the devil and engages in
spiritual warfare against him, it will only be a short
time before the serpent's ancient war comes to its
end.

- The Revelation 12 man child will be born when, in the
last days, one by one, abusive Christian men come

under conviction by the Spirit for the centuries-old sin of setting themselves against Christian women. When they repent for this, put to death their old man, stop hiding their failures like Adam did in the garden (Job 31:33), stop blaming their wives, and end their friendship with the devil, the Spirit will come upon them, making them new godly men who are like Christ. The final fulfillment of the promise concerning the seed of woman will come to pass, and the final crushing of the head of the serpent will take place. Christ will set up His kingdom and reign on the earth.

About the Revelation 17 Woman

The woman in Revelation 17 is not standing. She is sitting. Her posture is passive. She is fully submitted to and dependent upon the devil, the great red dragon upon whom she sits, and on the kings and kingdoms of the earth that he rules over in darkness. She is a woman filled with darkness who is in bondage to the devil and has brought forth the seed of the serpent. She is not clothed in light, a symbol of purity, but clothed in earthly seductive clothing; and she is filthy. She is decorated with gold and precious stones and pearls, which according to Old Testament imagery (see Ezek. 16) may refer to her being decked with God's people. She may appear beautiful to the kings of the earth, but in God's eyes she is abominable. She has a golden cup in her hand that is filled with filth and abominations from which she drinks and gives others to drink. She has committed fornication with the kings of the earth and has intoxicated the inhabitants of the earth with her fornication. Her seed is just like her: harlots and abominations. Demons, foul spirits, and unclean and hateful birds dwell in her. She has drunk the blood of God's holy people. She is filled with delicacies that make merchants rich. She has glorified herself and boasted in her position. She is fully deceived and believes she will see no sorrow, even though her judgment is imminent.

At first blush, one might be inclined to think that the Revelation 12 woman refers to the people of God and the

Revelation 17 woman refers to those who are not the people of God. However, the underlined part of the following verse makes it crystal clear that some of God's people are found in the Revelation 17 woman. Otherwise, God would not call *His people* to come out of her:

> 1 And after these things I saw another angel come down from heaven, having great power; and the earth was lightened with his glory. 2 And he cried mightily with a strong voice, saying, Babylon the great is fallen, is fallen, and is become the habitation of devils, and the hold of every foul spirit, and a cage of every unclean and hateful bird. 3 For all nations have drunk of the wine of the wrath of her fornication, and the kings of the earth have committed fornication with her, and the merchants of the earth are waxed rich through the abundance of her delicacies.
>
> 4 <u>And I heard another voice from heaven, saying, Come out of her, my people, that you be not partakers of her sins, and that you receive not of her plagues.</u> 5 For her sins have reached to heaven, and God has remembered her iniquities. 6 Reward her even as she rewarded you, and double to her double according to her works: in the cup which she has filled fill to her double. 7 How much she has glorified herself, and lived deliciously, so much torment and sorrow give her: for she said in her heart, I sit a queen, and am no widow, and shall see no sorrow. 8 Therefore shall her plagues come in one day, death, and mourning, and famine; and she shall be utterly burned with fire: for strong is the Lord God who judges her. (Rev. 18:1–8, AKJV) [underline added]

What does it mean that God has to call His people out of this filthy woman, whom Revelation 17 also refers to as a great city? First of all, it means that some of His own people have been deceived to such an extent that they have become part of this great city. If they were not deceived, as God's people, they would not be a part of her. This tells us that Satan's war against the seed of

woman using filth and sexual perversions was so effective
that even God's people became filthy and intoxicated with
her fornications and other such abominations. If you
doubt that God's people could be in this condition, open
your Bibles to Ezekiel 16 and read God's description of
unfaithful Jerusalem. You will think at times that you are
reading chapter 17 of Revelation.

When God judges the Revelation 17 woman, He will
also judge all of His people that are part of her, unless
they heed His warning and come out of her. Her main
characteristic is defilement. This is how she is
identifiable. So, whenever Christians find themselves in
Christian settings where sexual sin is tolerated among
believers, even their own sexual sin, they should realize
they are in "her." If they are in Christian settings where
there is darkness, not light, due to infighting and division
among brethren—where conflict is not resolved biblically,
but is tolerated and glossed over with talk about love and
forgiveness, they are in "her." If they are in Christian
settings where any other name is exalted, where men, not
God, are served and followed, they are in "her." This last
condition is the hardest to recognize because the pattern
which most people living in the world naturally identify
with, and easily accept, is to follow other people and their
agendas. It is a situation where prestige, control over
others, and greed are at work in some form. Christians
that find themselves among Christians who practice or
tolerate such things need to respond to God's call to come
out of her fully, and to follow the Lamb of God only, or
they will share in her judgment.

> Therefore shall her plagues come in one day,
> death, and mourning, and famine; and she shall
> be utterly burned with fire: for strong is the Lord
> God who judges her. (Rev. 18:8, AKJV)

These verses are reminiscent of Paul's words to the
Corinthians believers who had become defiled:

> 13 Every man's work shall be made manifest: for
> the day shall declare it, because it shall be
> revealed by fire; and the fire shall try every man's
> work of what sort it is. 14 If any man's work
> abide which he hath built thereupon, he shall

receive a reward. 15 If any man's work shall be burned, he shall suffer loss: but he himself shall be saved; yet so as by fire. (1 Cor. 3:13–15, KJV)

There are others who are part of the Revelation 17 woman—those who are not God's people. They are like the Old Testament wife of Ahab whose name was Jezebel. Jezebel's character represents women who have been totally taken over by Satan and used for his evil purposes. Instead of helping men return to God, they have been used to enable men's evil ways and to ensnare them, usually sexually, and hold them captive to the devil.

After he is cast down to the earth, the devil is filled with rage, knowing that his time is short. Like a self-absorbed child, he lashes out against everything and everyone. God uses his rage to judge wicked people and even to discipline His own people who are defiled. Do not forget that God used the enemies of Israel to cruelly discipline her in Old Testament times. In the New Testament, many like to talk about God's love as if it has replaced God's discipline. These should not forget that it was in New Testament times that Paul prayed for God to deliver the sexually sinful Christian in Corinth to Satan for the destruction of his flesh so that his spirit might be saved in the day of the Lord. Also, the writer of Hebrews warns several times that the New Testament God of love is still one who disciplines, even scourges, His children to help them come to repentance.

Bushnell's View of the Man Child in Revelation 12

The following stellar comments by Katharine Bushnell about the promise concerning the seed of woman and the Revelation 12 man child speak for themselves. As you read them, keep in mind that she wrote from the perspective of a woman who lived in the last half of the 19th century and the first half of the 20th:

Now we ask, How did God *begin* to fulfill that Great Promise of Genesis 3:15 about the victory of woman's seed? Did He look about for some *body of people,* visible or invisible, who bore a name, appropriate, or inappropriate, of the *feminine gender,* and begin to fulfill that promise to them because of the *gender* of their name, when He had promised to fulfill it to woman? Did He think it sufficient, after He had made the promise concerning very real and very literal woman, in the presence of Eve, a woman, to fulfill that promise to a *sect?* Verily, He did not: that is not God's way of doing. He made that promise to woman, in the presence of a woman, Eve; and He began the fulfillment of that promise *to a woman,*—the Virgin Mary; and as He has begun so will He, in faithfulness to His word, continue.

God will not be satisfied to send an offspring to the apostate Christian church, merely because the word "church" *(ecclesia)* is of feminine gender. That offspring will be sent to a feminine *person* (or company of feminine persons), not to a feminine *word,* describing a masculine body,—for the visible church on earth, which excludes women, for the most part, from ministry at its altar, and shuts them out of its councils, and out of the fullness of Christ's atonement, cannot appropriate such a Great Promise as this, by merely masquerading in the garb of a female. God deals with realities, not with shams. Women belong, in large numbers, to the *mystical* Body of Christ, the *true* church; they do not actually belong to that body—the visible church—which merely enrolls their names on a list while it makes them irresponsible as regards its entire polity. Therefore this visible church will never grasp this Great Promise.

We are driven to the conclusion that, just as the covenant promise of Genesis 3:15 was fulfilled to a literal woman, up to a certain extent, in the birth of Jesus Christ of a virgin (no human male having any part in its realization), so will it be *to the end.* As Christ was born of a literal woman, so will this man child be born of that sex. The beginning of the fulfillment was to one woman;

but it seems more likely that the filling out to the full of the terms of that great covenant will be to many of that sex,—a body of women.

Since the only actual interpretation of prophecy must come after, not before its fulfillment, we can only form a conjecture as to the meaning of these things. Since the sign John saw was "in heaven," the events seem to refer to the spiritual world. The agony and travail of the Woman seem to signify some great spiritual travail of soul into which women will be plunged just before the Lord's second coming; and as a result a large body of men (the man child), of exceptional holiness and devotion will rise; this will be that bringing forth of a man child. The entire sign relates to spiritual transaction; and the man child will be the spiritual, not the physical, seed of the woman. (Bushnell, paras. 821–824.) [underline added]

I will make one further comment about Bushnell's last paragraph. It has occurred to me that many Christian women today in the Middle East are being plunged into great spiritual travail of soul as they watch their husbands, children, brothers, fathers, and even fellow women being tortured and beheaded by the seed of the serpent. It is not hard to imagine such women fleeing, especially during the time of even greater tribulation that lies ahead, to a place of safety that God has prepared for them in the wilderness. Neither is it hard to imagine the possibility that the reference to the woman being carried to the wilderness on the wings of an eagle might refer to aircraft from the United States, which has the eagle as its symbol, carrying persecuted women to America, a place which was a wilderness only a short time ago, relatively speaking. America's history shows that America certainly is a place prepared by God, and her history also shows her to have carried out humanitarian rescues by air. Again, I offer this as an educated speculation, not a prediction.

To Which Woman Do You Belong: Bond or Free?

The Bible sometimes refers to humanity in general (made up of both male and female) as a woman. We can see this in the description of the woman in Revelation 17. As a Christian, if you are having your needs met by trusting and depending on someone or something other than God, and if you are putting anyone or anything before Him, God sees you as part of the Revelation 17 woman. Though you may not feel like it, you are sitting on the great red dragon, and you are being used by him in some way to further his ends. You are not standing in the freedom you have been given by Christ. You are sitting in a situation subject to control by the devil. By fully turning your heart to God, giving yourself to Him without reservation, trusting in Him alone to meet your every need, standing up and taking off the bushel that is covering your light, you can escape from the scene described in Revelation 17.

As a Christian male, if you believe you have God-given authority over females and feel justified in subduing or subjugating them, God sees you as one in bondage to the devil. He sees you as part of the Revelation 17 woman. You are helping the great red dragon further his goal. By repenting for your male-dominant attitude and actions and taking off your light-blocking bushel, you can escape the scene described in Revelation 17.

In Revelation 12, we see a woman and her man child. This imagery specifically points to males and females. Those who are part of the woman are females who have learned to stand on their own feet by faith in His pure Word. They are clothed with the bright and shining Holy Spirit given through the new covenant. They are free from satanic control; and, of their own free will, they are submitted to God. They are heavenly light bearers to others. Those who are part of the man child are those who are strong, god-fearing, overcoming males who have been birthed by the spiritual labor of females.

The salient point of the imagery found in Revelation 12 and 17 is that there is no neutral ground. Male or female, God sees you as part of either one scene or the other. If you find yourself in the Revelation 17 scene, I hope you have been, or will soon be, persuaded to respond to God's call and come out of her! Many have responded to that call, and so can you! As a Christian woman or man living on earth in these perilous times, you are called to be a part of the scene in Revelation 12.

In case you are balking at the idea that a Christian could be in any kind of bondage to the devil, remember Paul's warning to the Galatians when some were coming among them seeking to bring them into bondage. His appeal to them was that they should stand firm in the freedom Christ had given them (Gal. 2:4–6). The whole book of Galatians shows a war taking place in the early church between the seed of woman (the believers) and the seed of the serpent (false brethren). Paul understood the seriousness of this battle and spoke about it in terms of a bondwoman and a free woman. This was covered in "A Fit with the Redemptive Message of the New Covenant" in chapter 3 in the subsection about Galatians.

The emphasis in this book is on the role of women, so my interpretation is necessarily geared toward them; however, please do not forget that all of God's holy people, male and female, are the seed of woman. All of His people are under attack by the seed of the serpent. Godly women are attacked in particular ways and for particular reasons, as are godly men. Likewise, the seed of the serpent is both male and female, and Satan uses both to attack the godly seed of woman. All of God's children, both male and female, are called to stand in freedom in Christ. Whether you are male or female, ask yourself if you are part of the bondwoman or the free woman. Your most fundamental assessment should be made, not by considering where you attend religious services, but by taking a good, honest look at yourself in the mirror and answering such questions as these:

- Is there sexual sin of any kind in your life (including pornography) for which you have not repented and from which you have not been fully delivered?

- Are there any relationships (husband, wife, father, mother, brothers, sisters, Christian brethren) in your life that are broken, for which you have not done (or are not doing) all the Bible requires of you in order to try and reconcile?

- Are there any sinful attitudes which you hold and nurture (pride, gender biases, racism, hatred, rebelliousness) toward others?

- Are you lording it over or subjugating anyone in your life?

- Where does your confidence really rest: in your bank account or in God?

- Do you love Him above everyone and everything else in your life, including yourself?

If you are unsure about the answers, ask Him to show you the truth about yourself. He will do this because He wants you to choose to be a part of the free woman. When you make that choice, He will help you walk according to it.

The Lord of the Armies Left Us a Seed

I will close this chapter with an unusual and enlightening verse about the seed of woman, one I only recently discovered. This verse highlights and confirms Satan's end game in his war against the seed of woman. In Romans chapter 9, Paul quotes Isaiah 1:9:

> And as Isaiah said before: "Unless the LORD of Sabaoth had left us a seed, We would have become like Sodom, And we would have been made like Gomorrah." (Rom. 9:29, NKJV)

This verse is found at the end of the description of a vision God gave Isaiah about Judah and Jerusalem:

> 2 Hear, O heavens, and give ear, O earth! For the LORD has spoken: "I have nourished and brought up children, And they have rebelled against Me; 3 The ox knows its owner And the donkey its master's crib; [But] Israel does not know, My people do not consider." 4 Alas, sinful nation, A people laden with iniquity, A brood of evildoers, Children who are corrupters! They have forsaken the LORD, They have provoked to anger The Holy

One of Israel, They have turned away backward. 5 Why should you be stricken again? You will revolt more and more. The whole head is sick, And the whole heart faints. 6 From the sole of the foot even to the head, [There is] no soundness in it, [But] wounds and bruises and putrefying sores; They have not been closed or bound up, Or soothed with ointment. 7 Your country [is] desolate, Your cities [are] burned with fire; Strangers devour your land in your presence; And [it is] desolate, as overthrown by strangers. 8 So the daughter of Zion is left as a booth in a vineyard, As a hut in a garden of cucumbers, As a besieged city. 9 Unless the LORD of hosts Had left to us a very small remnant, we would have become like Sodom, we would have been made like Gomorrah. (Isa. 1:2–9, NKJV) [underline added]

This description of God's people sounds much like that given of the woman in Revelation 17. This was the condition of Judah after a prolonged period of the devil's warring to corrupt them. Isaiah portrays Judah and Jerusalem as being in a state of almost complete destruction as far as God was concerned, but then Isaiah says that unless the Lord of the Sabaoth (which means the Lord of Armies) had left them a seed, they would have—note this—gone into a much worse condition and become like Sodom and Gomorrah! Sodom and Gomorrah symbolizes a situation in which Satan has fully possessed males and caused them to fully reject females. They no longer have any regard for God and His laws of creation, and they desire each other for sexual pleasure. This is the practical end game of Satan when it comes to men: take away their need for, and involvement with, woman—all the way to the most basic level in creation—sexual relations. This actually translates into stopping mankind's procreation. If society became such that men only had sex with men and did not need women at all, this would result in the end of the human race. Satan's strategy is to use males to abuse females, all the way to the point of a complete and total rejection of them. The desire for sex is what usually causes men to be willing to solve personal problems with their wives. When male sexual desire is met by a male partner, the devil has greatly advanced his plan to prevent godly male/female relationships.

But, thankfully, Isaiah (Isa. 1:9) and Paul (Rom. 9:29) tell us that, although Satan may try, he will never succeed in making God's people like Sodom and Gomorrah. God has left His people a devil-terminating seed, the seed of woman. These verses indicate that, without woman and her seed and God's promise concerning them, Satan would have won the war and would have already destroyed mankind.

Satan's battle through sexual perversion is a battle that women can win, not only by pouring the water of verbal truth on the fire of sexual perversions, but by also building a bigger fire of truth that shows the beautiful relationship that God intended to exist between male and female. This truth fire will bring light on the real behind-the-scenes war on the earth and the reason for it. It will bring us closer to God's war-ending move with the birth of the man child as seen in Revelation! I believe many women will speak this message at the close of the age.

"The Lord gives the word [of power]; the women who bear *and* publish [the news] are a great host." (Psalm 68:11, AMPC)

Chapter 9
The Blessing: Lost and Found

I call heaven and earth to record this day against you, that I have
set before you life and death, blessing and cursing: therefore
choose life, that both thou and thy seed may live:
(Deut. 30:19)

IN THE PREVIOUS CHAPTER, we covered the spiritual battle that is being waged on the earth. Satan's stealth weapon in that war has been and still is the lemon translations. In this chapter, we will see God's secret weapon, one which has the power to not only undo the effect of Satan's work, but to turn it into a situation of abounding blessing on the earth.

> 19 ... When the enemy comes in like a flood,
> The Spirit of the LORD will lift up a standard
> against him.
>
> 20 "The Redeemer will come to Zion,
> And to those who turn from transgression in
> Jacob,"
> Says the LORD. (Isa. 59:19b–20, NKJV)

What Does It Mean To Have God's Blessing?

In 1973, I had an experience which radically changed my understanding of what it means to have God's blessing. Before that experience, I thought of God's blessing as the prayer that my great-aunt Evie prayed before we ate a meal with her. The end of her "blessing" was the signal that we could finally pick up our forks.

Today, I understand that God's blessing refers to a state of affairs in which God is manifestly present and working without hindrance. He does unanticipated, wonderful things. He answers prayers. He defeats our enemies. He sets captives free. He fills our hearts with thankfulness, even when we are suffering in difficult circumstances. When God's blessing is absent, so are such manifestations of His presence. This simple explanation of God's blessing allows us to assess the state of affairs in Christendom today. Overall, God's blessing is missing. It has been lost. Before I say more about this, I am going to share about a personal experience which taught me something about what it means to have God's blessing. The following is a condensed version of what I wrote about that experience in my book, *The Thread of Gold:*

Don't Leave Me Out

The doctor who had repaired the rectal tear after the birth of my first son had told me I should never again have a normal episiotomy (an incision to aid in childbirth). If the rectal wall were to tear again, it could be very serious. He had instructed me to tell any new doctor about this during any future pregnancies so that he could prevent another tear by giving me a *lateral* episiotomy. I felt it was important to be fully awake in the delivery room to remind my new doctor of this, so I decided to go to natural childbirth classes. An added benefit was that John, if he went to the classes, could go with me into the delivery room. Acknowledging my fear, John agreed to attend the classes, albeit reluctantly.

At this time in my life, I was under Christian teaching that said it was wrong to enjoy things in life that were for, or about, me—not the Lord. Such things were considered to be "soulish" or "natural" and were, therefore, bad. I was supposed to deny myself daily. This meant that I always had to be on guard about loving things other than Jesus. Therefore, I believed it was wrong to enjoy my pregnancy and to look forward to having another baby.

I was several months pregnant when I read one day in my Bible:

A woman when she is in travail hath
sorrow, because her hour is come: but
as soon as she is delivered of the child,
she remembereth no more the anguish,

for joy that a man is born into the world. (John 16:21, KJV)

When I came to this verse, I became upset. I shoved my Bible across the table and said, "I know I'm not supposed to, but I want to enjoy having this baby!" The verse had made me think about the fact that I was secretly enjoying being pregnant. As soon as I said this, God calmed my heart saying, "There is nothing wrong with you enjoying having your baby—just don't leave Me out." I sank in relief, thanking Him, and telling Him that I would include Him.

Shortly after this, God showed me that I had been wrong in my approach to John about the natural childbirth classes. Deep down, I had known that if I had asked him for his real feeling, he would have told me he really didn't want to go to those classes. At the time the Lord showed me that I hadn't given John a choice about this, He asked me if I would rather have my way or have His blessing on the birth of this child. When I chose to have His blessing, the Lord told me to go to John and ask him what he really wanted to do. John made it clear to me that he did not want to be in the delivery room, and he wasn't interested in the classes. So I released him.

A few days later, Sandra Brown, a friend who was a natural childbirth expert, offered to help me prepare. She would also go to the hospital with me to assist me while I was in labor. My doctor didn't want me to have natural childbirth and told me it was better to use a painkiller. Actually, a painkiller was better for him, not me. I was determined to deliver without painkillers, even if he didn't want to help. I began happily preparing for the coming birth, knowing it was going to be a blessed event!

A few days before my due date, it occurred to me that if labor started during the middle of the night, Sandra would have difficulty making it to the hospital because she and her husband had moved about forty minutes across town. I called and asked her what to do if I went into labor at 2:00 a.m. She assured me she would be there. She then made arrangements for another sister to drive with her, even in the middle of the night. At about 6:00 p.m. that same evening, a sister called me to ask if Todd could spend the night with her child. This was a first. Todd had never before been invited to spend the night with a friend. I let him go.

During the night, I awoke with sharp labor pains. John called Sandra, and we were all on our way at 2:00 a.m.! At the hospital, I was surprised to find out that my doctor had been called out of town unexpectedly. The doctor who had taken his place was very much in favor of natural childbirth. He made sure I had a nurse who was trained in the method and would help me. Sandra and John took turns coming in and out of the labor room helping me with my natural childbirth breathing patterns. John located a place on my back where he could press and relieve some of my pain. He marked the area with a pen and wrote in it "O Lord Jesus." The nurse and Sandra also took turns pressing the "O Lord Jesus" spot. Several hours later, after a doctor's check, he asked me where my husband was and then left. They took me to the delivery room.

Once I was on the delivery table, I looked down at the end of the table to see John standing there with the doctor! Later, John told me that the doctor had asked him, "Would you like to see the birth?" Of course, this was entirely against the hospital rules, and the doctor knew it. John told me that to his own amazement, at that moment, he realized how much he wanted to be there and see our baby born. He said, "Yes." The doctor got him gowned, scrubbed, and into the delivery room. I was overjoyed! For John, it turned out to be what he considers one of the most amazing experiences of his life. Minutes later, Matt was born, and they let me touch him.

They asked me what the big (9 lbs. 6 oz.) boy's name was. They all laughed as I said, "Amy." (I had planned on having a girl.)

In the recovery room, tears kept filling my eyes as I replayed the events of the prior evening in my mind. The Lord had taken care of every detail of this birth. What kind of a God was this? Who was I that He would do this for me? I was just a little nobody, a woman having a baby like thousands of other women every day. How could the God of the whole universe have time to be so involved in such little things? He had prepared Sandra for the 2:00 a.m. call. He provided a place for Todd. He arranged for a different doctor to take care of the delivery and thus take care of my desire to have the baby naturally. In spite of the hospital rules, He had brought John into the delivery room with a changed heart, one that wanted to be there!

Lying there on the bed in the recovery room, I recalled my conversation with the Lord many months before when I had made the choice to have His blessing rather than my way. So this is what it meant to have His blessing! Why, it included everything, even having it my way but without any effort on my part to get it! I kept saying, "Lord, You are so wonderful." Then I thought of a song we sang and began singing it in my heart to Him, "Wonderful, wonderful, wonderful, wonderful, isn't Jesus our Lord wonderful?" Somehow that word wasn't adequate to describe what I was experiencing. I tried to find another one, but couldn't, so I just told Him, "Lord, I need a new word; 'wonderful' is too common for You!"

Children Who Are Not Breathing Well

Once in my hospital room, I fell asleep. The doctor awakened me with a very grave look on his face. Our baby was having difficulty breathing and had been put into a special incubator to supply him with extra oxygen. I froze. The first possible explanation was a birth trauma that would go away in a short amount of time. Unfortunately, I already knew the next possibility: underdeveloped lungs. Someone I knew had lost two babies as a result of this irreversible problem. The doctor left, and I started crying and praying, "Dear Lord, please don't take my baby from me. Please. I don't trust any of these doctors here. They'll do their best, but his life is not in their hands. It is in Yours. You are the only One who can help my baby. Please let him live!" As I prayed, the Lord spoke gently to my heart, "I have children who aren't breathing well, and I need you to help them." "I will, Lord, I will." Day one passed. No change.

Day two came. When the new mother in the bed next to me received her baby for feedings, I turned over and looked the other way, crying silently. I kept praying that my baby would be okay. They put me in a wheelchair and rolled me down to see him in his incubator. Through the incubator's thick glass, his chest appeared very large and deformed. I ached for him, and I felt like my heart was breaking. They took me back to my room to wait. Day two ended. Again, there was no change. I cried myself to sleep. In the middle of the night, however, I was suddenly wide awake. I heard a verse plainly spoken in my heart, "weeping may endure for a night, but joy cometh in the morning" (Psa. 30:5, KJV). I slipped into a quiet sleep.

The doctor awakened me several hours later. Matt's breathing had normalized. As the Lord had promised, weeping endured for a night, but joy came in the morning. This was the morning of the third day, and these words came to mind, "After two days will He revive us; in the third day He will raise us up" (Hos. 6:2, KJV). Symbolically, my son had been given back to me in resurrection after two dark nights.

I had sinned against my husband by not asking him if he wanted to be in the delivery room. I didn't see this, but God did. When he convicted me about it, I had to repent to my husband for thoughtlessly trapping him into doing what I wanted. The removal of this one small sin opened the way for God to bless, and bless He did. He not only blessed Matt's birth by taking care of all the details that surrounded it, it turned out that His blessing has also extended to all of Matt's life. Not only that, I later realized that God had further blessed the time of Matt's birth by using His breathing problem to ask me if I was willing to help His children who were not breathing well. My "yes" set me on the course He had planned for me (Eph. 2:10).

The biggest lesson I learned from this experience was that, although God's love for us is unconditional, His blessing is conditional. It depends on our being right with Him. God spelled this out plainly in the Old Testament when He told the children of Israel that He set before them two paths: one of blessing and one of cursing. He admonished them to choose the path of blessing. It was contingent upon their obedience. The only way back if they disobeyed was repentance.

The Dove Can Be Chased Away

Amy Carmichael, a well-known missionary to India, once told a story which shows how sensitive the Spirit is to sin among believers and how it impacts His blessing on them. A large number of missionaries were at a retreat for a time of recuperation from their demanding gospel labors in India. They had a series of meetings in which the Spirit of God was moving mightily. Then one day, they came together, and the atmosphere in the meeting was cold and dead. No one could do anything to change the situation. The spiritual air was so oppressive that they decided to stop the meeting. People went outside and began to talk together in groups of two and three under the trees on the surrounding grounds. After some time passed, they re-assembled and, immediately, according to

Amy, the presence and glory of the Lord filled the meeting. It was apparent to all that there had been at least two believers that needed to get right with one another. This story always reminds me that the Holy Spirit is like a dove that can be easily chased away, but genuine repentance will bring Him back.

When there are ongoing, unresolved offenses among believers, the Spirit's blessing upon them is lost. Amy Carmichael's story was about a small group of Christians in one meeting at one point in time. It may be that the hindering problem was only between two people. The children of Israel were defeated in the battle at Ai because of the sin of one person among them, and many died as a result. How about God's people today? Pause for a moment and think about the centuries-long suppression, even oppression, of untold numbers of Christian women by Christian men. What kind of blockage to the Holy Spirit's working do you think such a mountain of unresolved sin has produced? What kind of blessing has the earth lost because of this?

Iniquity and Unanswered Prayer

In the perilous times in which we live, more and more believers are gathering to pray and beg for God's help, yet the heavens do not appear to be responding as they should according to God's Word:

> Call to Me, and I will answer you, and show you great and mighty things, which you do not know (Jer. 33:3, NKJV).

Isaiah tells us that the sin of God's people causes God to hide His face and not answer their prayers:

> 1 Behold, the Lord's hand is not shortened, That it cannot save; Nor His ear heavy, That it cannot hear. 2 But your iniquities have separated you from your God; And your sins have hidden [His] face from you, So that He will not hear. (Isa. 59:1–2, NKJV)

Solomon's long prayer at the dedication of the temple (2 Chron. 6:14–42) shows that he understood the connection between iniquity, repentance, and answered prayer. For example:

> 26 When the heavens are shut up and there is no rain because they have sinned against You, when they pray toward this place and confess Your name, and turn from their sin because You afflict them, 27 then hear [in] heaven, and forgive the sin of Your servants, Your people Israel, that You may teach them the good way in which they should walk; and send rain on Your land which You have given to Your people as an inheritance. (2 Chron. 6:26–27, NKJV)

God heard Solomon's prayer and responded:

> 13 "If I shut up the heavens so that there is no rain, or if I command the locust to devour the land, or if I send pestilence among My people, 14 and My people who are called by My name humble themselves and pray and seek My face and turn from their wicked ways, then I will hear from heaven, will forgive their sin and will heal their land. (2 Chron. 7:13–14, NASB)

Verse 14 is a verse that is frequently quoted to encourage people to pray for the United States and today's world situation. This verse was quoted at the end of the movie entitled *The War Room* that came out in 2015.

God's answer to Solomon continues:

> 15 "Now My eyes will be open and My ears attentive to the prayer [offered] in this place. 16 For now I have chosen and consecrated this house that My name may be there forever, and My eyes and My heart will be there perpetually.... 19 But if you turn away and forsake My statutes and My commandments which I have set before you, and go and serve other gods and worship them, 20 then I will uproot you from My land which I have given you, and this house which I have consecrated for My name I will cast out of My sight and I will make it a proverb and a byword among all peoples. 21 As for this house,

which was exalted, everyone who passes by it will be astonished and say, 'Why has the Lord done thus to this land and to this house?' 22 And they will say, 'Because they forsook the Lord, the God of their fathers who brought them from the land of Egypt, and they adopted other gods and worshiped them and served them; therefore He has brought all this adversity on them.'" (2 Chron. 7:15–16, 19–22, NASB)

The place referred to in verses 15–16 is the temple. This was the place where God put His name in Old Testament times. In New Testament times, the place where God has put His name is in His people, His living spiritual temple, in those who worship Him in spirit and truth. Verses 19–22 are God's declaration of what will happen to His people if they sin and become defiled, profaning His holy name. They will bring judgment on themselves.

God's answer to Solomon's long prayer is still in effect today in the place where God has chosen to put His name: with His holy people. When God's people sin against Him, they lose His blessing—just as they did in Solomon's day—and they come under judgment. When they repent, God's blessing is restored.

When there are problems or needs, I often hear Christians say they will pray and that they will tell others to pray. I hear expressions of encouragement that God answers prayer. I rarely, if ever, hear one Christian tell another to ask God if there is any hindrance in their life to God answering their prayers. Is there sexual defilement in their life? Do they have broken relationships with others that they have not gone the required distance to reconcile? Do they love and serve themselves more than God? Have they overstepped others' boundaries or failed to perform duties for others that God requires. Christians today seem to have lost the connection between iniquity and unanswered prayers even though the Bible makes this connection very clear.

Hindrances in the Body of Christ

> 1 But realize this, that in the last days difficult times will come. 2 For men will be lovers of self, lovers of money, boastful, arrogant, revilers, disobedient to parents, ungrateful, unholy, 3 unloving, irreconcilable, malicious gossips, without self-control, brutal, haters of good, 4 treacherous, reckless, conceited, lovers of pleasure rather than lovers of God, 5 holding to a form of godliness, although they have denied its power; Avoid such men as these. (2 Tim. 3:1–5, NASB)

Do you find yourself in this list? We don't have to look far within the Christian community to find people who love themselves more than God, who love money, who brag and think they are better than others, who are verbally abusive, who don't obey their parents, who complain rather than give thanks in everything, who are defiled by sexual immoralities, including pornography. They do not show love to others, are never satisfied, repeat stories about others with the intention of hurting them, can't control themselves, are physically violent, hate those who do good, can't be trusted, and love worldly pleasures more than they love God. They spend the majority of their time on themselves and their purposes, while at the same time their mouths declare that they love God above all else. They religiously go to church on Sunday. They wring their hands over the bad things happening on the earth, never realizing that they could play a part in changing things if they repented!

Such offenses and iniquities cause God to withdraw His blessing. Left unprotected and unblessed, God's people come under debilitating attacks of the enemy. God's purpose in allowing His defiled people to suffer such consequences is to persuade them to repent and return to Him with all their hearts.

There is no question that believers today need to repent. Over a hundred years ago, a believer named William Booth made the following statements about what he feared for the church in the future:

1. Religion without the Holy Spirit

2. Christianity without Christ

3. Forgiveness without repentance

4. Salvation without regeneration

5. Politics without God

6. Heaven without Hell

A man named J. Meyers added to this list one more item: Bible information without revelation. All these things abound today, making all these statements prophetic. I will add one more: Worship without godliness, or worship in hypocrisy. Hypocritical believers are those who come to worship God at the same time that they are participants in sins that God abhors. They bring shame to the name of the Lord, and according to the Bible, they will not go unpunished by Him.

Things God Hates

The presence in the church of things which God hates guarantees that God will withdraw His blessing and His manifest presence. The things God finds abominable are:

1. Sexual immorality

    Sexually immoral believers defile their bodies, the temple of God. They practice sexual perversions, such as viewing pornography and committing adultery, fornication, and homosexual acts. Whenever believers are defiled by sexual sins and come to pray or worship, they do not worship God in spirit and in truth. They pray and contact the spiritual world; but, because their spirit is dirty through sin (2 Cor. 7:1), they cannot access the holy God. Unprotected by the cleansing blood of Christ, they open themselves up to evil spirits who can deceive and control them. They worship in ignorance (John 4:22). They don't drink the cup of the Lord but the cup of demons. The Bible calls this having fellowship with demons. God hates this. He withdraws from such ones, and they come under judgment. Evil beings can trick them with "spiritual" messages and experiences that are not from the Holy Spirit of God, and cause them to do terrible things. Some may even lose their minds. You can find many such people in mental institutions.

A believer's body is a temple of the Holy Spirit and must not be joined to a harlot. When believers allow and even voice tolerance for sexual sin and perversions in the church of the living God, they are involved in something God detests (1 Cor. 6:15–20).

Pulpits today are relatively silent on issues of sexual immorality—relative, that is, to the size of the sexual immorality problem in society that is also in the church. One reason for this silence is the ongoing "politically correct" dialogue that is becoming more and more dominant in society. An even greater reason is found in the spiritual condition of pastors and male members alike. A survey taken at a Promise Keepers rally twenty years ago revealed that over 50% of the men in attendance were involved with pornography within one week of attending the event (Lane). The statistics on pastors who are involved in Internet pornography today are staggering. It is not hard to understand why an addicted pastor would not speak against pornography from his pulpit on Sunday morning.

2. Ongoing offenses, discord, and division among Christians

Long-term discord is a result of not obeying Christ's instructions for problem resolution among believers (Lev. 19:17; Matt. 5:23–26, 18:15–17). The first quarrel or break after the Flood was between Noah and Ham. That offense was apparently not resolved because Noah cursed Ham's son, Canaan. The descendants of Canaan were the Canaanites who opposed the children of Israel when they went into the good land. The city that became Jeru-salem (a shortened word for

Jebusites plus the Hebrew word for peace) was the biggest stronghold in the land. It was where Jebusites (descendants of Canaan) lived. It was said that even the lame among the Jebusites could battle better than the strong soldiers who came against them. David, however, was able to conquer them, and Jerusalem became known as the city of David. The point is that long-term problems (generations of them) spring out of offenses that are not cleared up (by confronting and repenting). It appears that Ham never repented, but it could also be that Noah did not confront him and give him opportunity to repent; instead, he cursed Canaan out of anger.

Subordination of Christian women by Christian men fits under this category of sins. When men lord it over women in the name of God, they display a false and repelling message to an unbelieving world that greatly offends the Spirit of God. When believers excuse themselves and others for not biblically addressing offenses, divisions, and discord among believers, they are participating in furthering the work of the devil in the very house of God.

Satan has divided and nearly conquered God's people, just as he divided and conquered the first family. Division manifests itself between Christian men and women due to gender and authority issues. It manifests itself between Christian groups who divide over doctrinal matters that are not germane to the faith once delivered to the saints of God. Christian men kill one another verbally because of pride and jealously. The church is polluted with immorality and filthiness; such things are tolerated in the name of love.

For clarity's sake, when I say "church," I am referring to all persons who have chosen to accept Christ as their Lord and Savior. As for what we see in church organizations in Christendom today, there is an easily recognizable divide between charismatic or Pentecostal believers and fundamental or non-charismatic believers (to be referred to simply as charismatics and non-charismatics). This divide is like two halves of a broad valley split by a wide chasm. On one side of the chasm believers major on the Spirit of God (charismatics); and, on the other side, believers major on the Word of God (non-charismatics). Spirit-focused believers stress being Spirit-filled, having gifts of the Spirit such as prophesying and speaking in tongues, while placing less emphasis on the Word of God. Bible-focused believers stress the Bible as God's Word and minimize the Spirit (or don't even mention the Spirit at all). Spirit-focused believers can be easily deceived by false spiritual experiences coming to them from deceiving spirits. Word-focused believers can easily become lifeless legalists who think they are serving God when they cut other Christians to pieces with the letter of the Bible.

If the church was healthy, there would be no divide in God's field of believers. Believers would be filled with the Spirit and have all the gifts of the Spirit and, at the same time, they would be strong in knowing, obeying, and speaking the Word of God. Men's and women's lives, marriages, and families would bear testimony to the beautiful relationship God intended between man and woman.

3. Idolatry

Idolatry means to worship and serve other gods. A Christian who loves and serves anything more than they love and serve God, is an idolater. The Bible says that a covetous Christian is an idolater (Eph. 5:5). Idolaters will find themselves separated from God and under judgment.

The world, both secular and religious, abounds with idols—things and people that compete to take God's place in a person's heart. The best way for a Christian to know if he has an idol is first to want to know if he does, and next to ask God to show him. This is one prayer God will answer quickly, because God hates idolatry: You shall have no other gods (none) before Me. Suffice it to say the root of idolatry is self love. If you love yourself more than Him, you are an idolater. You put yourself in a place of greater importance than Him or others. Idolatrous self love is at the root of division and immorality.

Paul told us that Christ was to be the One who had preeminence in all things (Col. 1:18). An example of a Christian who loved himself more than Christ in the New Testament is Diotrephes. The apostle John pointed him out in 3rd John 1:9 as someone who wanted to have the preeminence, who not only slandered the apostle but also would not receive the brethren he recommended and put out of the church any who would receive them.

Evidence of Idolatry: False Teachings and Practices

Every false teaching and practice among believers is sourced in God's enemy. He deceives men who love themselves more than God and uses them for his own ends. Timothy warns:

> 1 But the Spirit explicitly says that in later times some will fall away from the faith, paying attention to deceitful spirits and doctrines of demons, 2 by means of the hypocrisy of liars seared in their own conscience as with a branding iron ... (1 Tim. 4:1–2, NASB)

False teachings may sound good on the surface, but if their fruit is examined, the source of the teaching will be exposed. The Bible says:

> Know ye not, that to whom ye yield yourselves servants to obey, his servants ye are to whom ye obey; whether of sin unto death, or of obedience unto righteousness? (Rom. 6:16, KJV)

If you obey what someone teaches you, and as a result you end up sinning against God (usually by breaking some other command of God), this is a strong indication that you are involved in idolatry. In other words, if there is someone else, usually a Christian teacher, that you are obeying in place of God, you have that person as an idol in your life. You are accepting what that person tells you rather than being responsible to check for yourself the truth of what you are being taught.

A False Teaching: Forgiveness without Repentance

Love, grace, and forgiveness teachings abound today without a balancing message about sin and the need for repentance. Messages about sin and repentance have almost disappeared. They are considered to be too condemning and discouraging for people to handle. This unbalanced teaching is a false one. It is another gospel, different from that delivered to us by the apostles, which is the true grace message. The result is that people believe all is well even when they are living in ways that are sinful. They believe God's love is so great that He overlooks their sin, having already paid the price for their forgiveness. They have confidence that they are going to heaven when they die and will get their mansion, no matter how they live in this life. They do not take sin seriously. They believe they can sin over and over again and be cleansed over and over again, because God loves them so. But Paul says this is using grace as a license to sin. The false grace message minimizes sin to the point of not even naming sins. Yet, the Bible says that if your brother sin, rebuke him; if he repents, forgive him (Luke 17:3). We obtain mercy when we confess and forsake our sins (Prov. 28:13).

Paul spoke the true grace message: Grace comes through faith. When we believe the truth (what God's Word says), agree with it, and obey it, then we receive grace that empowers us to walk daily in obedience. This is different than initial salvation. The Bible calls this kind of Spirit-empowered change sanctification. The moment we believe that Christ died for our sins and rose again, we are given the gift of salvation by His grace. Then, we begin to learn to walk in obedience, being sanctified by His

Spirit. Living in the light of God's desire to fully sanctify us, we choose to obey Him. When we do, we get more grace that helps us do so.

The false grace message produces people with tickets to heaven who sit happily in church on Sunday while their daily living is lacking in God's holiness. They don't spend time with God in His word to have their minds renewed and transformed. The false grace message produces people who believe that the main thing a believer should do after salvation is be happy that they have a ticket and tell others to get one, too. Of course, they will do good works at church when called upon by others to do so.

A False Practice: Lording It Over Others

Teachings about authority and obedience to one another as believers are misused by church leaders who practice authoritarianism and misuse the flock of God for their own ends. Authoritarian sins against women come under this category of sins.

Today, authoritarian, gender-based sin is one of the most damaging sins among believers, because it isn't recognized for what it is, and it isn't called what it is: sin. Many actually think that the suppression of Christian women is sanctioned and even expected by God. How can the church be a warrior (Eph. 6)—one who prevails in prayer, defeats the devil, and spreads the gospel on the earth—if some of her members are wounding, suppressing, and spiritually killing other members? If roughly half the body of Christ is suppressing the other half, what else can this be called but sin?

All the things that God abhors, when present in the church, produce a church which the Bible says has only a "form of godliness" (2 Tim. 3:5). Most of the church has been without God's blessing and manifestations of His presence and power for so long that she doesn't even know what blessing looks like. She believes, acts, and testifies as if her work, which is mostly the work of men's hands, is God's power at work. She is void of His power and doesn't know it! Leaders and members alike work and work and work, and then work some more. They justify their working so hard by saying they are exercising faith and trusting God to work. The work, work, work goes on because it must, or the church will wither. I did not say all, but it seems that most of the church is in this condition. Throughout history, there have been believers and churches here and there that have found the way to blessing through repentance and have experienced the manifest power of the Holy Spirit working among them. When the Spirit of God moves in power, there is no flavor of man's effort or work. How we need the mighty, powerful, and undeniable presence of God among us today!

God's Secret Weapon: Genuine Repentance

God's secret weapon brings healing and blessing. Do we really want to experience God's blessing and see the evidence of His manifest presence appear in the midst of the darkness that is swallowing the earth today? Then it's time for genuine repentance! Something at the core of the church has to change in a big way. The many breaches in God's family need to be closed by real, heart-changing, person-by-person repentances. The reason should be obvious as to why these three words are the most difficult for men and women to say: "I was wrong."

When the children of Israel went together up to Jerusalem to worship God, they sang songs of ascent as they climbed the high mountain to reach the city. Psalm 133 is a song of ascent. It says that it is "good and pleasant for brethren to dwell together in unity ... for there the Lord commanded the blessing, even life forevermore."

Travel time to Jerusalem for them served a purpose similar to the purpose of the trees in Amy Carmichael's account. If there were problems among them, they had to get right with one another before they reached Jerusalem and went to the House of the Lord to make their offerings and pray to God. Jesus spoke about the absolute necessity of getting right with one another before bringing offerings to God. He commanded that if anyone came to the altar to offer a gift to God and there remembered that one of his brethren had something against him, he should leave his offering at the altar and go and be reconciled with his brother (Matt. 5:23–24).

This was, and still is, the way of blessing. When there is no attempt to reconcile, consequences of this disobedience will follow—not the least of which is that prayers will not be answered. How many people today come to God's altar, knowing others are offended with them or that they have offended others, yet they have done nothing about this? How many come in a state of sexual defilement? How many come and declare they love God wholly but they don't keep his commandments? How many routinely slap on a confession band-aid for sins that they repeat week after week, believing that this is how they are supposed to live the Christian life and that all will be well?

According to the Bible, every believer is responsible to have his or her own relationship with God and His Word. However, people's natural tendency is to look to others and their words about God, instead of looking to God Himself and hearing His words for themselves. When Israel wanted a king to take care of and protect them, God said they had rejected Him. Satan uses this natural bent in man to cause him to follow other voices and obey them. Then, to bring whole flocks into bondage, all he has to do is to deceive their leaders. Christians must take up their responsibility to know the Word of God for themselves. They must learn to verify for themselves, using the Bible, whatever they are taught by leaders! This is definitely possible by the Holy Spirit.

As for knowing the Word, in the Old Testament, God commanded the kings in Israel to write out a copy of the book of the law for themselves. They had to handle it directly. So must we! In modern times, we are without excuse, having unhindered access to Bibles and even having many tremendous resources electronically.

When Christians don't have their own direct, personal relationship with God, they can easily become, and remain, dirty by participating in things God hates. This is a very serious situation. Satan is thrilled when he can bring Christians into a dirty state and, at the same time, have them convinced that they are serving God. When Christians come to pray and worship in an unclean state, they do not worship God in spirit and in truth. When they pray, their prayers will not be answered. They will have been rendered powerless and ineffective, yet don't realize it! They carry on with a form of godliness, all the while denying the power that is rightfully theirs in Christ (2 Tim. 3:5).

Repentance before the Blessing of the First Coming of Christ

Before Jesus came the first time, God's people were full of sin. God sent John the Baptist beforehand to preach the message of repentance. John's message was a voice crying in the wilderness that it was time to make straight the way of the Lord. His message paved the way for Christ to come. John's message was: "Repent, for the kingdom of heaven is at hand!"

> 1 In those days came John the Baptist, preaching in the wilderness of Judaea, 2 And saying, Repent ye: for the kingdom of heaven is at hand. 3 For this is he that was spoken of by the prophet Esaias, saying, The voice of one crying in the wilderness, Prepare ye the way of the Lord, make his paths straight. 4 And the same John had his raiment of camel's hair, and a leathern girdle about his loins; and his meat was locusts and wild honey. 5 Then went out to him Jerusalem, and all Judaea, and all the region round about Jordan, 6 And were baptized of him in Jordan, confessing their sins.

> 7 But when he saw many of the Pharisees and Sadducees come to his baptism, he said unto them, O generation of vipers, who hath warned you to flee from the wrath to come? 8 Bring forth therefore fruits meet for repentance: 9 And think not to say within yourselves, We have Abraham to [our] father: for I say unto you, that God is able of these stones to raise up children unto Abraham. 10 And now also the axe is laid unto the root of the trees: therefore every tree which bringeth not forth good fruit is hewn down, and cast into the fire. 11 I indeed baptize you with water unto repentance: but he that cometh after me is

mightier than I, whose shoes I am not worthy to bear: he shall baptize you with the Holy Ghost, and [with] fire: 12 Whose fan is in his hand, and he will thoroughly purge his floor, and gather his wheat into the garner; but he will burn up the chaff with unquenchable fire.

13 Then cometh Jesus from Galilee to Jordan unto John, to be baptized of him. 14 But John forbad him, saying, I have need to be baptized of thee, and comest thou to me? 15 And Jesus answering said unto him, Suffer [it to be so] now: for thus it becometh us to fulfil all righteousness. Then he suffered him. 16 And Jesus, when he was baptized, went up straightway out of the water: and, lo, the heavens were opened unto him, and he saw the Spirit of God descending like a dove, and lighting upon him: 17 And lo a voice from heaven, saying, This is my beloved Son, in whom I am well pleased. (Matt. 3:1–17, KJV)

The people were convicted and repented. They were blessed by the coming of the Messiah.

Repentance before the Blessing of the Second Coming of Christ

Today, as the day of Christ's second coming grows ever closer, society abounds with many messages, but the message of repentance is missing. There are appeals for people to take care of the environment and animals, even little fish. Some cry out for the right of people to be accepted by society even though they are sinning sexually in ways that God calls abominable. Some plead for able-bodied and mentally-capable people to be cared for without having to work. Some call for the right of foreign immigrants to come to America and live as next door neighbors to the very Christians that their religion commands them to kill! Some lobby for the secular government to dictate how its citizens live and think in all areas of their lives—as if the government was God.

In this mixed melee of societal messages, we also have an apostate message coming from the Christian community that cries love, love, love, while ignoring and even embracing what God calls sin! Even though Christ paid the highest price to remove these things from His people, they can only be removed by repentance. Pastors who avoid using words like sin, judgment, and eternal damnation, and who avoid speaking out against sexual sin, division, or idolatry, are among the first that need to repent.

Where is the voice that is crying out for this kind of repentance? Repent! Repent, for Christ is coming in His glory to judge the earth! Repent and close the breaches! Repent so that God can answer your many prayers for deliverance! Repent so He can pour out His convicting and saving Spirit on thirsty unbelievers! Where is such a voice? Who will sound the cry of repentance today? Who will proclaim that sexual immorality, division, and idolatry among God's people *have to go!* If a man's prayers are hindered by his not showing honor to his wife (1 Pet. 3:7), how much more, then, are the prayers of the church hindered by male believers who dishonor female believers by treating them as spiritually inferior members who need to be silenced and controlled? Who will make this case and call for repentance?

It is time for the latter rain to fall in abundance on God's people and on all the earth. It is time that the church's prayers for His blessing and for His kingdom to come on earth be answered. Repentance is a pre-requisite!

Repentance Is Overdue!

Repentance for such sins by Christians is long overdue. Christian women need to join together in a spiritual labor to learn the truth of God's Word about sexual immorality and impurity, about God's hatred for division and disharmony among brethren (especially between male and female), about counterfeit authority that mimics true authority, and about God's utter disgust with Christian hypocrisy. Christian women need to speak the truth about these things everywhere they can find an audience, be it in Christian meetings, among friends and family, or by using social media. They do not need salaries or titles to do this effectively. God will make a way where there is no way. John the Baptist preached a message of repentance in the wilderness, and women can do likewise.

When women repent and begin to speak the truth in love and call for repentance, the Spirit of God will speak and work through them and carry out His job of convicting Christians, both male and female, who are sinning against God in all the aforementioned ways. There is no doubt that the enemy will fight against women who stand up with the sword of truth to reclaim the turf the devil has been wrongfully holding for centuries, but that does not matter one bit, because he will not be able to stop them. Satan's spiritual fortresses will begin to crumble when women step forward by faith and expose the false stones upon which Satan has built sinful bulwarks right in the house of God—right before His face.

If ever there was a day that the church needed to experience the blessing of God on the earth, if ever there was a day that the prayers of the church needed to be heard and answered powerfully by God, this is it! This is the day for repentance!

In chapter 10, we will look at how God turns today's women into women of *chayil* whom He can use to sound this message.

Chapter 10
The Brave and the Bold: Today's Women of Chayil

For as the earth brings forth her bud, and the garden causes the
things that are sown in it to spring forth, so the Lord God will cause
righteousness and praise to spring forth before all the nations.
(Isa. 61:11, AKJV)

God Is Calling for Christian Women of Chayil

WHAT KIND OF CHRISTIAN WOMEN can call for
repentance? Women of *chayil*. These are women
who are brave and bold and who themselves
have repented and are right with God. God is seeking
such women, women who want to be what God intended
them to be.

In chapter one, I introduced the meaning of the word
chayil and explained that a woman of *chayil* is a woman
of strength, capability, and power. When her strength is
God-directed, she is a bold and fearless spiritual warrior.
Your first thought may be that she is a woman prayer-
warrior, and you would be right about that. She is a
prayer warrior—not just because she decided to pray—
but because of her strong faith, which comes from her
knowing the Bible and believing every word of it. Most
importantly, with God's ever present help, she obeys it,
and she speaks it to others. If she sins, she is quick to
repent. She expects that God will respond to her prayers
according to His promises. She bows to Jesus Christ
alone as her supreme Lord. She always walks with a
submissive attitude toward others. She is always ready to
yield her preference, that is, unless principle or truth is
at stake, and then she stands firmly and holds her
ground like the towering Rock of Gibraltar overlooking a
turbulent Mediterranean sea.

Recall the truth we learned from Peter regarding how
wives should behave. The kind of character and strength
with genuine humility that Peter described was that of a

woman of *chayil*. Such character does not come naturally to women and can only be acquired by walking on a narrow path with Jesus and learning hard lessons from Him in real life situations.

From Bushnell's time to the present, there has been an ever increasing call by the Spirit for women to repent for their silence and have courage—the courage to read the Bible for themselves and believe that God will speak to them directly; the courage to act according to the truth of the Bible; the courage to speak the truth, even hard truth, regardless of the gender of the hearers; and the courage to suffer any treatment that might come as a result of their doing so.

Who Me?

I must confess that this chapter on today's Christian women of *chayil* was the most difficult one for me to write. In my heart, I felt that this chapter was very important. Not only did it need to encourage Christian women to turn to God fully and follow Him when He called them to come forward and speak up bravely, it needed to provide a good explanation of what a Christian woman of *chayil* is, as well as how a woman becomes such a person. How could I exhort women to do what I myself still found difficult? How could I, someone who has spent much of her life as a Christian female coward, tell other women they should be bold and brave?

When, as an eleven-year old, I was born of God, the first words that I heard God speak to my heart were: "Have no fear; I am with you." He knew my fear and insecurity problem long before I recognized it. Only He knows how many times He has brought those same words to mind over the course of my life. They typically came when I was in a state of fearful anxiety.

I was born fearful; I grew up fearful; and I lived fearfully—even after my new birth experience—until the first time I saw God work in another person's life. That happened around age nineteen, when I traveled down a path of faith that ended with my then boyfriend (now husband) coming to Christ. His conversion was nothing short of miraculous to me because, for the first time, I saw evidence in another person's life of how real God was. That experience changed everything. I found new strength and confidence in my walk with Him. Fear no longer loomed large over me, and whenever it came around, verses like Philippians 4:6 would come to my rescue:

> 6 Be anxious for nothing, but in everything by prayer and supplication with thanksgiving let your requests be made known to God. 7 And the peace of God, which surpasses all comprehension, will guard your hearts and your minds in Christ Jesus. (Phil. 4:6–7, NASB)

Then, after a number of years of learning to trust and obey and see Him work, I was hit hard in the head with a hammer of church discipline swung at me by some zealous Christian men who felt it was their God-given responsibility to knock me into my "place" as a Christian woman. From that time forward, under their watchful eyes, I began living in fear again—tremendous fear. Their actions and words left me with the belief that I had been deceived by the devil and that I could become deceived again if I, as a woman, read the Bible for myself and expected to hear from God or to pray and have God hear me.

From that time forward, in one circumstance after another, I quickly grabbed hold of fear's hand when it reached out to me. I let it lead me to a corner, sit me down, and tell me to be quiet ("let your women keep silent in the church"). I let it remind me that I was to do only what others told me to do ("for the woman was first deceived"). I was not supposed to read my Bible and hear God speak to me because I had been told that women could not get their own revelation from the Bible—and for thirteen years after their hammer fell, I didn't. Ten years after the hammer hit, my husband moved us away from these men and from the reach of their "God-given" hierarchical authority. It took a few more years, but I finally was able to pick up my Bible again. However, I did so with great trepidation. The words the Lord used to speak to me at that time were from Zechariah's song:

74 That he would grant unto us, that we being delivered out of the hand of our enemies might serve him without fear, 75 In holiness and righteousness before him, all the days of our life. (Luke 1:74–75, KJV)

How good the words "without fear" sounded to me. Was it really possible I could read the Bible again without fear?

Have No Fear

One day, during the time I was struggling to write this chapter, as I was walking up the steps of a building to keep an appointment that I felt some anxiety about, I heard these all too familiar words in my heart again, "Have no fear; I am with you." It suddenly occurred to me that these words actually contained a *command,* not a request. It was my choice to obey this command or not, but nonetheless, it was a command. It also occurred to me that if God was commanding me not to be afraid, it was because He knew I did not need to be afraid. I decided in that moment that I did not ever have to allow myself again to entertain fear. I did not have to be afraid because God had commanded me not to be afraid. I AM is with me. He is the one who IS. That means He is the one in control of all things, the one who is able to take care of all things in all situations. It also occurred to me that when I accepted fear's hand, I was disobeying God.

That day, I took God's hand instead, and fearlessly proceeded to that appointment. I later returned home to work on this chapter, rejecting the fear that I was not going to be able to write it and that I would not be able to finish this book. God began to help me by giving me some new thoughts and a new writing approach. So, instead of delivering a big dose of exhortation in this chapter, I am going to take you on a trip through some parts of my life that show God changing me from a trembling, fearful child into a calm, confident (well, most of the time) woman of *chayil*. God has a unique purpose for each woman, and His training for each will be customized with that in view, just as mine has been. However, the basic lessons are similar for all. I hope to bring some of the basic ones into view.

My Customized Boot Camp

When my customized training by God began, I had no idea that, among other things, He was one day, many years in the future, going to arm me with a slingshot and some de-lemonized Word-stones and have me stand before Satan's lemon giant and challenge that Goliath in the name of the living God. God prepared David beforehand to face Goliath by first letting him learn to kill wild animals such as a lion and a bear, and so it has been with me. God taught me numerous lessons in smaller battles with His enemy in my day-to-day life, because He was preparing me to use these lessons in larger battles that were ahead.

God's boot camp did not turn me into an Amazon-like woman who was rebellious, overbearing, and dictatorial in dealings with others. It did not turn me into a woman who wore combat boots that were laced to my knees, so I could stomp men under my feet and stand tall in their face and dare them to try and control me. God's boot camp, it turns out, was actually a new-walking-shoes camp. In it, He helped me make the decision to take off my compliant, soft-soled, well-worn, "enabling" shoes and pay the costly price to make myself a pair of new, handcrafted, truth-lined ones, good for walking in victory every day. In this training camp, He helped me break in my new shoes. Slowly but surely, I learned to walk confidently with humility (my new definition of *bold)* always being thankful to God that He had given me the right to wear such shoes and to walk with Him in truth.

He also began to show me He wanted me to help other women do likewise. This realization came at a point in time well into my very difficult shoe making apprenticeship, when the Lord reminded me of the promise I had made to Him years before at the time my second son was born, when I told God that I would help His children who weren't breathing well if He would just let my son survive his life-threatening breathing problem. The memory of this promise to God, coming to me in the middle of a long and difficult time, helped me consider that what I was undergoing might not be simply for my benefit. It might be so that I could fulfill my vow to help God's children that were not breathing well—so that I could help them in the way He wanted.

Many years after that time, I stand assured that the costly shoes I wear today are not going to wear out on the path God has set before me. I bravely (yet still trembling at times) and boldly (confidently with humility) wear my new truth-lined shoes. They give me strong support for a truly submissive walk with God and man. They empower me to yield my preferences to others, to submit of my own free will to other believers, irrespective of their gender—as long as no moral principle is being violated, and to make peace righteously.

I feel greatly blessed to be able to stand strongly with humility and obey God. I have no desire to rule over or command or expect anyone to bow down to me or my thoughts, as some might like to suggest. My desire is to live in submission to God and be able to speak the truth in love when He shows me that I must. God isn't finished with me yet, but the new shoes He has given me thus far have made my feet beautiful. I have noticed that sometimes others also find them beautiful. Even some who don't believe in God have been curious and asked me about them.

I have also made another discovery. Satan doesn't like my new shoes one bit. The humble, yet strong, walk of a woman who is right with God by the blood of the Lamb and who is living by the power of Christ resting upon her (my definition of grace from 2nd Corinthians 12:9) is terrifying to him. Proverbs 28:1 says that the righteous are bold as a lion. I have found that when I am right with God, I can be bold like a lion when I must, and also, like this mighty and courageous beast, I don't have to retreat in battle or be stopped by the threats of the old enemy of God (well, not for long anyway), no matter who he uses to voice the threats (Prov. 30:30, NET). I have also discovered that in my new shoes I am able to bind the devil by prayer, and I do!

Is my life trouble-free today? No. The wonderful truth is, however, that I am not frightened by difficult circumstances because I have learned to a large degree how not to be controlled by the fear that outward things can produce. I have become a lover of truth. I love to speak truth and to listen to truth from others. If I am not walking in truth, I want to know it, even if it costs me. I have peace in my heart each day, knowing that for the joy that is set before me, I can go through whatever I must. What more could I want? Jesus, the one I have come to know through His faithful care and excellent instruction, is my present joy. I want Him. I want to walk with Him each day and be well-pleasing to Him. I want His smile. I want to do whatever He wants me to do, go wherever He wants me to go, and say whatever He wants me to say. Troubles will come, and troubles will go; but He will remain steadfastly with me as He promised.

My point is that Christian women who willingly give themselves to God to be trained and equipped by Him will be changed by Him for the better, from the inside out. They will become women of *chayil,* women whose presence on the earth makes a difference in the family of God, in human society, and in the unseen realm where spiritual warfare by prayer occurs. They will become women who can help captives find the way to freedom from sinful behavior. They will be able to help brethren who are walking in sin be cleansed and become warriors themselves who further the kingdom of God on the earth.

Katharine Bushnell wrote about women's responsibility to learn to follow Jesus and walk in truth:

"Thou shalt in any wise rebuke thy neighbor, and not suffer sin upon him," Leviticus 19:17, is the teaching even of the Old Testament. The words of Jesus Christ are even a more stern commandment: *"Take heed to yourselves: if thy brother trespass against thee, rebuke him; and if he repent, forgive him,"*—Luke 17:3. There is something most weak and unworthy in woman's acquiescence in man's pride and egotism, for the sake of not incurring man's displeasure. But at the same time let us see to it that when men vaunt themselves in our presence we do not add a wrong spirit to the wrong conduct on their part, and angrily speak otherwise than in kindness.

Above all, let us not "sin their sin" and be guilty of the same offense, by vaunting ourselves. We will be accused of this, at any rate, even if we should do no more than our duty and administer rebuke. (Bushnell, para. 386)

What I learned in God's new shoe camp helped me pass from childhood to "chayilhood"—from fear to fearlessness. It helped me gradually fill my little slingshot bag with devil-slaying stones from the Word of God, in particular, with eight smooth stones that once were lemons but now have been de-lemonized. All these Word stones in my little bag are weapons that protect me and others from the devil. They have the power to stop him dead in his tracks.

A Long Road of Learning

After leaving the abusive "church," where my husband and I spent twenty years of our young lives, we faced many difficulties. Once out of that environment, I was no longer under the thumb of abusive Christian men; however, because I had so deeply internalized their message and practice of the lemon verses, they still affected everything in my life, not the least of which was my marriage.

Our marriage was in bad shape, as were our children, but my husband and I were blind to this. I soon found myself in a big war in our family with wave after wave of battles that lasted more than five years. The devil reared his ugly head time and again as he sought to destroy our family relationships. God used that time for my learning as He brought about a turnaround in our marriage and also in our relationship with our younger son. Then, after that war ended, there was a long-term conflict with members of my family of origin. Alongside that came another multi-battle conflict that involved sexual sin being tolerated among believers. Then, another conflict began to emerge with our first son who was by that time a married adult. That battle ran simultaneously with a few other difficult situations with Christian brethren.

In all of this, I was a crumbling, often fearful, emotional wreck of a woman who was trying to walk with

God and found myself under attack. I had to fight through and learn how to do battle with evil forces behind the scenes, not with the flesh and blood that was in my face. I was driven to the Lord time after time and to his Word. Each time that I reached the end of my rope—my ability to cope—I would give up my efforts to save myself and cry out to Him for help, and every time His help would come through His Word and sovereign circumstances.

During these years, I did not experience long-term bad health or financial distress. My suffering was always in the psychological realm. Sometimes, the psychological pain was so great that I could hardly breathe. More than once I feared I was going to lose my mind. Once when I was praying desperately for mental relief, the Lord reminded me of a vow I had made to Him when I was in high school. I made that little vow after a long period of insomnia with its very unpleasant side effects. I had feared that I was going to die prematurely or lose my mind and end up in a mental institution. It was then I had promised the Lord that if He would save me from becoming mentally ill, I would help people who were mentally ill. In retrospect, I now see that God used my years of mental suffering to help me understand a lot about mental illness and its cause from a spiritual perspective. I learned that most psychological pain and mental difficulties come from seeds of wrong thinking that have grown unchecked. As long as they remain unchecked, they lead to bigger and bigger wrong thoughts. These will bear the fruit of irrational and evil actions in worse and worse degrees. Most importantly, I saw that the devil always plays a part in sowing wrong ways of thinking into people's minds, just as he did in Eden.

I found my way to freedom from psychological pain time and again when I finally told God, frankly and openly without holding back, all of my thoughts, even the ugliest ones, and then asked Him to change them to His thoughts. As I read the Bible, my thinking and my resultant behavior began to change and so did my psychological pain. That led to my learning how to use

God's Word, which is truth, to negate the devil's input and inroads into my thinking.

Throughout all the painful learning times, God's wonderful love and care, and His perfect provision for all of mine and my family's material and practical needs, always amazed me. Most amazing was the fact that no matter what I went through, I always came out loving Him more, loving others more, having more inner peace, and trusting Him more, knowing that He was in perfect control—even when situations were not fully resolved. You might say that my way of thinking and behaving came under a long-term renovation (Rom. 12:1) by God—somewhat like a fixer-upper house is gutted of its old structure, stripped of broken things, cleansed from accumulated filth, and then completely restored and remodeled with new and beautiful things according to the vision of the remodeler. As God changed my heart, His new home, I began to find that whenever I got run over by the devil (he never quits trying) and left as a crumbling, floundering, discouraged mess, I was able to recover in a much shorter time. I could get right back up, dust off his dirt and lies, and begin to live and walk with God again.

My Biggest Hindrance

My enabling ways were the biggest hindrance to the work that God wanted to do in me and in the lives of those I loved. *Fallen woman is in bondage to the devil and doesn't know that enabling is probably the biggest reason why she is fearful and powerless.* Enabling is in fallen woman's blood; in the same way, blaming others and slandering God are in fallen man's blood. Before I began to make any real progress towards becoming a woman of *chayil,* I had to see for myself, and admit to myself and to God, that I was an enabler.

An enabler is someone who gives another person the ability or means to do or continue to do something. They empower, equip, permit, or make possible the actions of another. This would seem to be a good thing, but in its modern-day usage, it is a bad thing. An enabler is someone who gives bad help instead of good help. The problem is that the bad help looks like good help. Though well-meaning, an enabler actually helps another person stay on a bad path. The woman who covers her husband's alcoholism by calling his boss and saying her husband is home sick when he has a hangover, is an enabler. A mother who continues to give her son money when he asks for it, even though she knows he is using it to buy drugs, is an enabler. A wife who constantly makes excuses for her husband's abusive behavior is an enabler. The list of symptoms of enabling goes on and on. It may be a little harder to see this one, but a woman who constantly nags a difficult husband is also an enabler. Her nagging is like a hammer that drives a nail deeper and deeper into wood. Her nagging sets her husband's bad behavior firmly in place, enabling him to feel justified in digging in his heels and plugging his ears. The last example I will give is also very hard to see because of the messages of the lemon passages: A Christian wife who remains silent under sinful treatment by her Christian husband or who watches him repeatedly commit other sins and is silent, is an enabler.

So why does a Christian woman enable? The simple answer is unbelief.

Some Selected Lessons

The rest of this section contains some selected hard-to-learn lessons that God taught me over a long period of time. Most of these concern the ins and outs of Christian female enabling. These were not easy lessons at all, but they were very necessary.

Dance Lessons

As a very young teen, while taking my first (actually, only) dancing lessons, it became apparent that my biggest problem in learning to dance was relinquishing the lead to my dance partner. I would let him lead for a few steps, then I would take over again, making a mess of the dance. I was only trying to *help!* Of course, the real truth was that I was afraid that I wouldn't be able to follow well and would make a fool of myself. I wasn't willing to risk that, so I made a fool of myself by leading. That pretty much describes the problem that I had in learning to follow Jesus on life's dance floor, which was actually a minefield! The turning point in my life came when God finally got my attention after a major land mine explosion. He told me He knew how to dance and that He didn't need my help leading. It was then I began to learn the powerful secret of surrendering my way for my partner's, or maybe I should say for my King's way, and taking the risk of allowing Him to lead me.

The explosion was a big conflict with my husband. I found myself for the umpteenth time on my bed crying about how difficult life was with him. I tried to pray but couldn't. Finally, I blurted out something to this effect, "Lord, the truth is that I don't want to pray for him anymore! Why should I when You never answer! How many more times is this going to happen? His problems are just too hard for You to solve!" In that statement, for the first time, my deepest problem surfaced: unbelief. God had put His faithful spotlight on me, and He had finally unmasked my sin so I could see it.

Funny how that works: *I was crying about my husband's problems, and God talked to me about mine.* At the root of all my trying to *help* my husband was my own unbelief. I was able to believe that God could solve anyone else's problems—but not those of my husband. I subconsciously believed that his problems were too deep-seated for even God to handle. I really didn't believe God was up to the task. I couldn't risk waiting for God, because I didn't really trust Him. My unbelief produced fear of what might lie ahead; and, to allay that fear, I tried harder and harder to fix things. On that remarkable day, I saw my unbelief and my fear standing naked before me, and on that day, I repented.

My unbelief-based self-effort was the reason my prayers for my husband had gone unanswered. God needed me to put down my prescription pad and let the Great Physician do His job. He wanted me to pray, believe, and allow Him to work in my husband—in *His* way and *His* time. God's way was to help my husband from the inside out, something only He could do.

What God had shown me about myself was true. I asked Him to forgive me for taking over and trying to fix my husband. I begged Him to give me the faith I needed to be able to really trust Him. That was the day I began to believe that God could help my husband. That was the day I started learning to take the risk involved in not trying to fix him. I started learning to pray in faith and trying to listen to and follow Jesus whenever conflicts arose. That was the day I started believing that He would lead me and that He would, indeed, help my husband. That was the day I started the long process of learning to follow God's lead rather than trying to drag Him along as I did things my way.

Jesus' corrective words had turned me around completely. He and I had lots more conversations on life's dance floor. I made many missteps and many, many requests for His help. I had to renew that day's repentance many times, because my take-over-the-dance problem clung to me tenaciously. My ungodly, deeply grooved, trying-to-fix-husband habit was always lurking, ready to take over when I let my guard down. But thankfully, my determination not to be an enabler and my new habit of repenting gave me the way to quickly transfer control back to Him. He consistently displayed His gracious and amazing ability to lead me. Today, I am a much better dancer—a much more dependent one. I continue to wear my costly new dance shoes and let Him keep improving my steps.

Hello, My Name Is Jane, and I Am an Enabler

Helping others in our own self-motivated and self-directed ways doesn't work. What people really need is God's help. They need to know His very real presence in their lives and His abiding and oh-so-capable ability to love them. They need to understand that His heart is always for their very best, which includes the discipline of a father toward his children. The only way we can truly help others is to ask God to help them and trust that He will. Then we cannot interfere with our own self-concocted ways, even if restraining ourselves feels like a woman trying not to push when she is in labor.

When we feel fear at the thought that God might not help the one we love, we have to boldly risk that possibility and move forward in faith, remembering that God's ways are not our ways. We have to wait for His clear direction, which He will give us if He wants us to do something in particular. He, unlike us, is patient and longsuffering and will allow others to suffer the consequences of their wrong behavior until they decide they want to change. He is in perfect control at all times, regardless of how things look. The consequences that He lets people face are designed by Him to wake them up and persuade them to change their minds. Our self-generated "help" interferes with God-arranged consequences. It keeps people from finding God's very real help. Christ is always interceding for them; and, in that, we may readily join Him.

Only God knows the heart of every human being, and it is in the heart where that ugly little root of every problem is: inordinate self-love. I say *inordinate* because there is such a thing as a measure of healthy self-love that each human being must have if they are to survive emotionally and psychologically, as well as physically. Inordinate self-love refers to love that is beyond reasonable limits in amount—it is self-love gone out of control. Only God knows how to truly help someone whose self-love has consumed them. Both enablers and the enabled are guilty of such self love. An enabler's help makes it possible for the enabled to stay on a bad path, or it drives that person to a worse one.

It was very hard to see myself as an enabler because my behavior didn't look bad to me—it looked good! Also, as I said, my enabling ways didn't change easily. Just when I would think that I was free from them, they would suddenly appear and order me back into their service. As an enabler, I am a longtime, official member of EA (Enablers Anonymous), and I will be a member as long as I am on this earth. Maybe I should greet people with an EA confession, "Hello, my name is Jane, and I am an enabler." Eve, the first enabler, founded the organization, and the number of its members has grown exponentially over the centuries!

My enabling ways didn't begin to end until I saw that my motivation was selfish. I wanted to help that other person because their behavior was making me hurt. I just *had* to do something to make things better *for me.* I needed to do something because if I didn't, no one else would, and I would be left hurting or annoyed or irritated. I went to great lengths to help, even when my efforts repeatedly met with failure. My true motivation was the need to stop my own hurting. Until Jesus showed me this, I truly believed that I was helping other persons for their sakes, because I loved them. (After all, God told us that, as a Christian, we are to love others and do good works, right?)

Did I say that probably the most important lesson I have learned is that a woman of *chayil* is not an enabler? Conversely, an enabler is not a woman of *chayil.* Let me restate the definition of a female enabler: She is a God-ordained female helper gone bad. She helps with her own ability, not that which God gives, and in her own way, not God's way. Driven by self-love, she helps others so she can feel better.

Blackbeard and the Word of God

I do not want to give you the impression that surrendering to God and stopping enabling means passivity. After God unmasked my unbelief and brought me to surrender my enabling ways, He didn't leave me dormant, sitting still in a corner while He danced on without me. There was no big, magical God-change in my husband. Rather, I began to learn a new way of being. I learned to pray for my husband and to watch and wait for direction from God whenever there was a situation that needed help. One of the first things God gave this new EA member was a very big lesson about the importance of the Bible as His means of communicating with me. He taught me this in an ugly situation between my husband and me.

Whenever my husband (who was at that time a somewhat backslidden and very frustrated Christian), would become angry, he would change from a calm, conservative, white-collar professional into a swarthy pirate sailing under the skull and crossbones flag on the high seas and would let his vocabulary rip with the best of 'em. I hated this. Being a Christian, he didn't like his sudden metamorphoses, either, but couldn't seem to stop the inevitable outburst when something went wrong or was not to his liking. I had begged him to stop, reasoned with him, tried to put the fear of God into him, nagged him, condemned him, been silent and said nothing, walked away and stayed away from him for a while. I had done everything I could think of, and more, to help him stop his terrible habit ... all to no avail.

One day, while praying for him about this and while feeling very discouraged and worn down by it, the Lord brought this verse to mind, "Let no corrupt communication proceed out of your mouth" (Eph. 4:29). I had the thought that whenever I heard him cut loose with his pirate verbiage, I should simply quote this verse. I asked, "Is that you telling me this, Lord? Aren't you supposed to take care of his problem? And doesn't the Bible say the husband is to be won without a word from the wife?" When I couldn't shake the thought that this was a word from the Lord in answer to my prayer, I decided just to move forward and see what happened. I was a little afraid, because I knew it would make my husband angry, but the next time Captain Blackbeard appeared, I was bold enough to cautiously quote my verse, "Let no corrupt communication proceed out of your mouth."

Captain Blackbeard immediately retorted, "@#!*@! Don't preach at me!" I surprised myself as I calmly responded, "If you can say those things in my presence, then I can quote the Word of God in yours."

Thus began a pattern: Every time, without exception, that I heard Blackbeard's words, Blackbeard heard a simple statement of God's words from me, "Let no corrupt communication proceed out of your mouth." Over a relatively short period of time, Blackbeard stopped appearing. Many months later, I was with my husband in a car going somewhere when a driver upset him and out came Blackbeard. I said nothing. He immediately turned to me and said, "Well?" I said, "Well, what?" He said, "Aren't you going to say your verse?" I responded, "I don't need to, you already heard it."

From that time to the present, old man Blackbeard (the old man that was crucified with Christ) is held in prison where he belongs with Christ's death sentence over him. There have been some times when Blackbeard has made a mad dash out of a momentarily unlocked prison door; but, my husband, who immediately hears God speak directly to him through that little verse, with a quick repentance, stops the old pirate in his tracks and throws him back into the brig. My husband has also been known to help me with that same little verse when I have had a Blackbeard word unexpectedly pop out of my mouth!

My point is that God will work with us in amazing and unexpected ways to answer our prayers when we start trusting Him to work in His way. Sometimes He involves us in the answer, as in the story of Blackbeard and me. Other times He takes care of things without our involvement. (Knowing my propensity to lead on the dance floor, I always have to remember to wait for clear direction from Him.)

As in the story of Blackbeard, I have seen the power of God's living Word over and over again in my life. I have seen the benefit of risking things and trusting Him to take care of them, which is just another way of saying denying myself and taking up my cross and following Him. I have grown to love reading the Bible so I can become familiar with God's thought, be able to hear His timely words to me, and speak them when He tells me to do so.

> 12 For the word of God [is] quick, and powerful, and sharper than any two-edged sword, piercing even to the dividing asunder of soul and spirit, and of the joints and marrow, and [is] a discerner of the thoughts and intents of the heart. 13 Neither is there any creature that is not manifest in his sight: but all things are naked and opened unto the eyes of him with whom we have to do (Heb. 4:12–13, KJV).

The point of the Blackbeard story is that praying for help or deliverance for ourselves or others doesn't put us into a cop-out or a do-nothing-at-all mode. Rather, it puts us into a watching-for-God mode, a dying-to-myself mode, and a following-His-lead mode. Such daily life experiences have been mine on the way to becoming a woman of *chayil,* a woman who can be used by God to help others, in particular the men in my family.

Even though the journey has been very difficult at times, if I had it to do over, I would take no other way. I have been truly loved by God, not coddled, but disciplined by Him as needed and brought closer to the wholeness that will be mine for eternity. I do not get discouraged any more when I find myself starting to behave again like an enabling mess-maker. As soon as I can admit to myself that I have come under the control of my fears and become focused on myself again, instead of on Him, I repent and start over again.

Today, when I consider the baggage that both my husband and I brought into our marriage from our families of origin, and also the distorted, family-unfriendly church environment that we were immersed in for almost twenty years of our marriage, it is both a miracle and God's mercy that we are happily married today and that our children have become strong, mature, faith-filled, God-loving people.

> But without faith [it is] impossible to please [him]: for he that cometh to God must believe that he is, and [that] He is a rewarder of them that diligently seek him. (Heb. 11:6, KJV)

The Three-legged Stool and Me

Midway through the previously mentioned five-year period of conflict with our twenty-something year-old son, we sought help from a professional counselor. After the counselor met with each of us alone (my husband, my son, and me), and after she spent a weekend reading all of my journal accounts that showed our bad family dynamic, she told me that her counseling focus was going to be on our son. She told me that I was not the cause of his current problem, as my son believed. She said that my husband and I had done all we could do to clear up any responsibility we might have for his condition. He now had to own his problem and find the way through it for himself, or not. We had to accept that. As for me, she told me that I had to continue on the path I was already on of learning not to enable his sometimes stormy behavior. Other than that, all I could do was pray. She wanted me to continue meeting with her, however, so that my son would not be hindered in making progress by feeling that he was her only focus. She said that in our meeting times that she and I could visit and become friends.

At my first appointment with her, after talking for a while, she asked me if I had anything I wanted to ask her. I told her I had a question about what it meant to practically experience the cross. I explained that for most of my life, my basic way of survival as a Christian woman—who was supposed to be silent in the church and was supposed to be submissive and quiet in my marriage, etc.—had been just to take all the hard things that happened to me as "my cross" and bear them. I asked her what she thought of my practice and my understanding of the cross. Although it helped me cope, it did not work that well as far as solving problems or finding true peace.

The counselor told me that my approach was like using a one legged stool as a seat. It could do nothing but topple over and leave me sprawled on the floor. She then told me that my Christian-stool needed three legs. She referred to each leg by a letter: H-I-S, an acronym for belonging to Jesus. The three letters stood for Honesty, Initiative, Sovereignty.

Regarding the Honesty leg, she told me that I needed to learn to face every difficult situation by first evaluating it in the light of the truth of the Bible. I needed to objectively determine what was true and false, right and wrong, according to God's view of the situation. Based on that, I should take the next step, Initiative. This meant to do all that I could to make the situation right. If my own sin was the cause, then I should repent. If it was the sin of another, I should do whatever I could to make things right with that person. If my actions changed nothing, then it was time for the third leg. The Sovereignty leg was the way of the cross. I should accept the difficulty as God's sovereignty in my life and bear my cross until God did something to change things, even if it was not until the next life.

As I considered what she told me, I realized that many times I had actually practiced the honesty leg and the initiative leg, but I had always felt guilty about doing so because I was under the strong influence of the lemon passages which did not allow for such behavior. On that wonderful day, my Christian walk-stool got three legs that continue to serve me well. That conversation was a very important one for me on my journey to becoming a woman of *chayil*. It set the stage for God bringing Katharine Bushnell's book into my hands and His beginning to give me light on the lemon passages.

God confirmed what this counselor told me with several passages of Scripture that were about the seriousness of having unresolved problems with other believers and about the importance of solving such problems (reconciling) according to the way God prescribed. Two of those passages were Matthew 5:21–25 and Matthew 18:15–17. From these, I learned that it was sin for there to be offenses among believers and for the involved parties to do nothing about them but silently "bear the cross" or "pray."

These passages supported the counselor's explanation that a person had to be able to recognize and name an offense and then had to take proper initiative to correct it. They confirmed that this was important to God. God's subsequent training to help me put the two missing legs on my stool included numerous lessons with respect to these passages. Most of the lessons involved my having to clear up long-term problems that existed because I had not obeyed these verses when the problems had begun.

For example, when I was fifty-six years old, I had to go and repent to one of my two sisters for not properly handling her mistreatment of me over a period of many years. God showed me that I had never obeyed His commands in Matthew 18. If I had, I would have gone to talk to her after she treated me cruelly or when she sometimes physically assaulted me. She had never apologized to me for such incidents. He showed me that I had enabled her bad behavior by silently forgiving her in my heart and moving on instead of obeying the Bible's directive to go to her about her offensive behavior. My way had been to manage the ongoing problem by avoiding her as much possible. She had interpreted my avoidance as not loving her, which had brought on more attacks. When God sent me to ask for her forgiveness for not properly reconciling with her in the past, she literally laughed in my face. She insisted that she had never hurt me and that I was the one who had hurt her. However, the next day, she came back to me and said she had thought more about this and realized that maybe she had hurt me; and, for the first time in our life, she said she was sorry.

My stool has three solid legs today. Gone forever is the one-legged, falling-over stool that told me that everything that happened to me was "the cross" at work in my life and that it was wrong for me to speak up or to do anything to try and make things right.

He Meant It When He Said To Have No Fear

Fear is the most common driver of women's enabling behavior. We are afraid of what will become of us if this, that, or the other thing was to happen, and we don't want those things to happen, so we do everything we can to prevent them. We run ahead of God to do whatever we think will help. The biggest reason that we enable, that we do for others what we should not do, is that we are afraid of what will happen if we don't. Unfortunately, fear and disobedience go together, and our fear-responses usually result in our disobeying God's Word, even though unintentionally.

As a child, I had learned the song, "Jesus loves me," but I was still afraid. What did that really mean? Did it mean Jesus cared about what I wanted, and that He also understood that there were things I didn't want? What if He did not want for me what I wanted for me? What if He wanted to withhold from me what I wanted? One day in my young adult life, after seeing how God had taken care of every detail in a certain situation, I came to a somewhat sudden realization. God had done far more for me in that situation than I would have ever done for myself. That was the first time it occurred to me that

Jesus loved me more than I loved me. Just think about this a little bit: Jesus loves you more than you love you. Now, off the top of my head, I'm pretty sure that's a whole lot. This also means that Jesus also loves those that you enable more than you love them.

In the Garden of Eden, Satan's argument was basically that God was not trustworthy, that He was holding back something that was good for Adam and Eve. In essence, his argument was that God loved Himself more than He loved these two beings, so they needed to take action on their own behalf and take care of their own interests. On the cross, Jesus corrected that slanderous representation of the devil with an act of love so great that we cannot begin to comprehend it. The cross of Christ declares two things: (1) God loves us more than He loves Himself, and (2) God's character is just and righteous, and He always does what is just and right, no matter how high the price He must pay. That means He is trustworthy and dependable. He will always, without one exception, do what is best for us. Whatever God says, He will do. Whatever He asks of us, He will give us the strength to do. He loves us, and nothing can ever separate us from His love. When He works on our behalf, in His time and His way, He always does far more than we expect and usually does so in ways that we don't expect. That is just who He is.

We don't have to be afraid to stop our interfering, enabling, self-protective ways. We must learn to stop them, because they hinder God's best for us and for those we love. He is waiting for us boldly to obey His Word and take the risk of handing all consequences over to Him. We cannot fix in another person's life what only God can fix. When we end our self-customized enabling and take care of our own obedience to Him and His Word, even if it seems like a risk-filled path, our wonderful Lord Jesus will come to help us. He will open another door, one that He will come through to work on our behalf and on behalf of those we love. It may take more time than we like, but He will do His good work; and, as He does, He will lead us in paths we would never have found by ourselves. He will help us do what we never could have done without Him.

A New Creation in Christ

There is another very important lesson that I would like to highlight because I think it was a really big one. The first time I remember the Lord speaking to me about my husband was after we had been married for about three years. I was putting the key into the lock of our apartment door when I heard God's still small voice in my heart. I was right in the middle of some serious thinking about how forgetful John was—how he could even forget to do something that was right in front of him. On my drive home that day, because of a recent incident of such forgetfulness, I had been mulling over similar events in the past. I remembered when I had asked John to run to the little 7-11 store near our first apartment and get a tomato that I needed for dinner preparation. He had come back with some other things, but no tomato. Another time, after we had bought a few groceries, I walked ahead of him out the grocery store door to our car. When we reached the car, I realized that he had walked off and left the two bags of groceries sitting on the end of the checker's counter. I had assumed he would carry them.

His absent-minded, forgetful episodes had accumulated over the first few years of our marriage to the point that they were really on my nerves. He didn't seem to be able to improve no matter how much I pointed out his problem. As I put the key in the door, I was midstream in a thought that went something like, "Whatever is wrong with him? Why is he so forgetful! Why can't he remember things?" That was when I heard in my heart, "If you continue to think and speak this way about him, he will get worse and worse. John is a new creation in Christ." I was stopped in my tracks by this clear thought and suddenly realized I had been listening to the devil speak poorly to me about my husband. Even though the devil's whispers were based in apparent fact, they were still lies; because the truth was that, according to the Bible, when John received Christ (shortly before we married), he became a new creation in Christ.

That may have been the first time that I used the sword of the Word of God to shut the devil's mouth. I said something to this effect: "Get behind me Satan. Don't talk to me about my husband anymore. He is not forgetful; He is a new man in Christ. I see that by faith; and, one day I will see it with my eyes, and so will you!" To the best of my memory, from that day forward, I stopped accepting whispers about John being forgetful. Interestingly, after that, John's problem of "forgetfulness" seemed just to fade away. Unfortunately, it took more time for me to learn that this wonderful sword of truth applied to more things than forgetfulness.

That little lesson is a really big one that applies to all areas of our thinking. Whatever God's Word says is true, even though we don't see evidence of it with our eyes. We can shut the devil's mouth by proclaiming the truth of the Word of God.

Oneness in Marriage

God began to heal the unhealthy dynamic between my husband, my sons, and myself as I learned to stop enabling it. The following account is from the late 1990s and is taken from my journal. This took place not long after God had begun working on my enabling ways. We were in a period of time in which our marriage was in very bad shape. Things were so serious that for the first time in my life, I had gone so far as to think through what steps I would have to take in order to leave him and be able to survive.

At the root of our marriage crisis was my husband's belief that we did not have to present a united front before our children. His perspective was that I was the problem; and, that if I would just let things go, all would work out. Though I begged him time and again not to correct me in front of the children, he would not stop. If I told him that the boys had lied to me, I would find myself in a lineup with them as he questioned all of us about what had happened. I came out on the losing end so many times that it's a wonder that my face did not erode away from all the salt water that ran down it. It took me a long time to learn that my husband had not been disciplined as a child and, therefore, had no idea of how important discipline of his sons was or of how to discipline in oneness with his wife. If my sons talked back to me or refused to obey me, it was always my fault for making an issue over something, never theirs.

Whenever I tried to tell John his approach was wrong and that we were supposed to present a united front to the children, he would not accept this. I would end up feeling guilty because he was my husband, and according to the Bible, I was supposed to submit to him and not teach him. I would work hard to avoid conflict with the children, but when they needed discipline from him and he refused to carry it out, I would either jump in and do it, or I would push him until he lost his temper and disciplined them in anger saying things to me like, "I hope you are happy now." My behavior was just as wrong as his, but I couldn't see it.

This kind of struggle had gone on for many years. Things had become so bad between us that our older son, who was married by then, had asked us to promise that we would attend a Family Life marriage conference. We agreed to do so. Here is an excerpt from my journal about that time:

> During the week before we were scheduled to attend the conference, our younger son became angry with me over a business issue and would not stop speaking to me in an ugly manner. I called John for help. I stood there in amazement as once again, John corrected me in front of him and began trying to arbitrate and reason. I begged him to remember how many times we had been here before, but again he said I could prevent this kind of incident if I wanted to. I took a downward dive. As the week progressed, John and I had several more altercations over issues with him. The last one was the night before we were to leave for the conference. I was so upset that I couldn't stop crying the whole time I packed. I tried to remind him of his promise after the last South Carolina disaster, and he acted like he didn't know what I was talking about. I finally told him I was not going to the conference with him.

I didn't want to be tormented at the conference by hearing how marriage was supposed to be, while knowing it was never going to be that way for me. It seemed best for me to work on accepting the way things were rather than looking at how they weren't. John insisted we should go because of our promise to our other son and his wife, so I finally agreed.

We didn't speak during most of the drive there. Friday night dinner was a nightmare. My swollen eyes made me look like death warmed over. John was trying to be nice to me, and I was disgusted by his attempts. I kept wishing that I had stayed home. During the first conference meeting, everything they said upset me more. As they described the upcoming weekend events, I cringed. Saturday evening was supposed to be a romantic time alone with your spouse. I could hardly wait. Before that, on Saturday morning, we were supposed to write a letter to our spouse about why we loved them. (Our other son had told us that we might have to write something to each other, so I had brought a copy of part of my December 1995 letter to John that told him what I appreciated about him. I was glad that I wouldn't have to write anything from scratch.) We were given an assignment to complete after each meeting—usually to answer some questions in our workbook and discuss certain topics with our spouse. I was not cooperative. I was a mess. I didn't even care that I was a mess.

By the time of our mandated Saturday night *romantic date,* we were set up perfectly for disaster. It was pouring down rain, and we couldn't find a restaurant or a parking place. We drove around town several times looking and finally parked across from a restaurant named Uno. (We later realized that the name of the restaurant meant "one." What a joke that was.) All of the messages had been about oneness in marriage. At dinner, John began to tell me that he had really been seeing something about oneness. I had not been responding at other times during the weekend, but felt like risking a question, "What have you seen?" He answered, "That we are one." I asked, "So, what is that going to mean practically?" John became furious. He asked me why I always had to pressure him. I clammed up and quit eating. He let me have it and told me I was being totally uncooperative and he was not going to try to communicate anymore. He said we would leave the first thing in the morning. I said, "Fine." John was mad all the way back to the hotel. I didn't really care.

When we got to the hotel, I started to get ready for bed. John tried to initiate conversation again. This time, I tried a little harder to explain (for the first time since our initial fight earlier in the week) what was wrong with me. I told him that I needed more than an apology. I needed verbal reassurance that it wouldn't happen again. I needed to be persuaded that he really intended to be different regarding how he let our son talk to me. He told me this was wrong to ask of him; an apology should be enough. I said the only way I could explain how I felt was with an example. If a husband was unfaithful to his wife, repented, was forgiven, was unfaithful, repented, was forgiven, over and over again, the day would come, probably sooner than later, that a repentance alone wouldn't help the wife. She would need a lot of continual reassurance. John did not like the illustration, but I told him that was how I felt. The thing with our son had been repeated so many times I couldn't count them. John was upset by this and got mad saying that I just enjoyed grinding him into the ground. I got mad also and decided I was leaving. I packed up my things. John laughed and said, "Where do you think you are going?" I told him that I was going to call my friend to come and pick me up. I picked up the phone to call her when John had a major change of attitude and begged me to talk with him again. Somehow, after that, we seemed to start communicating. I can only say that once again the Lord managed to rescue us by his grace, and I reached the point that I realized I could try again.

We went to bed and went to sleep. I woke up during the middle of the night with a song in my heart, "Grace, grace, God's grace, Grace that is greater than all our sin!" I knew the Lord was promising me that His grace was greater than my need and that He would do for me what I couldn't do. Then I remembered the ring that John had given me for our anniversary with thirty small diamonds, one for each year of our marriage. It occurred to me that, in numerology, the number 30 was the result of 3 times 10. I knew that the number 3 was for God, and the number 10 was for a complete period of testing, trial, and suffering. Then, all of a sudden, I knew in my heart that the Lord was telling me that this was our thirtieth year of marriage and that I was at the end of a thirty-year long, God-allowed period of suffering in my life regarding John. I had had a similar experience in my twenties when the Lord had told me that my fourteen years of sleep difficulties were over, and they were. I knew this was true, and I started crying and thanking the Lord. The next morning, I was a different person.

John saw the reality of our oneness before God at that conference, and things were never the same after that. What a wonder it was that we had come full circle in our marriage in conjunction with Campus Crusade for Christ ministries. The beginning of our marriage had been John's salvation at Campus Crusade in Arrowhead Springs, and this time of healing thirty years later had also come through a time at a Campus Crusade sponsored conference. He was truly different. For the first time, he saw the truth of marriage oneness. He talked about it all the way home, telling me what a revelation it was. He kept saying, "I know you've tried to tell me, but now I see it for myself."

I knew it wouldn't matter if he failed or not (his performance) after this, because I knew he probably would fail; but the difference for me was in what he saw and believed. In the past, he always told me he didn't believe we were supposed to be one in practical situations. That was the hardest of all for me. I was certain he would never say that again. Thanks to the experience he had at the Family Life conference, he was able to believe what the Bible teaches. I don't know if this makes sense, but what he believed was what made a world of difference to me. For the first time in thirty years, we had the same belief concerning marriage oneness.

During the next week John said, "I may not be able to explain what happened last weekend, but one thing I know: It was reality." The atmosphere in our home was very different. Our son appeared to be affected, even though he had not heard details about what happened to us. A spiritual victory was won. Jesus prevailed. Truth prevailed. We signed a marriage covenant that we had been given at the conference. John asked him to also sign the covenant as a witness. We framed and hung the covenant in our living room.

I do not blame John for the problems we had. Our situation was the result of the loss of biblically-based marriage and family relationships. John was the product of a broken home, a home without Christ and without truth. He was also a product of many years in a church where there was no healthy teaching about marriage and family relationships, and there were unhealthy practices regarding the same. I brought my own set of problems to our marriage from another messed up home and added to it my bad experience with the leaders in the church. Regardless of our problems, the prevailing truth was that God had saved both of us and, in His sovereignty, had put us together for our mutual benefit and for His glory.

In this account, you can see me as a conflicted and struggling woman who was dealing with a Christian husband that did not believe or practice what the Bible taught about parenting. God helped me through various means, including the recommendation by a son that we should go to a marriage conference for help. Although I did not behave well at all through most of that experience, when it was over, God had won a major victory. I learned that it was important to hold to God's truth and not give in to an unrighteous situation just because it seemed hopeless. We did have some difficult practical situations after that, but what God had shown John about his responsibility to present a united front with our children remained firmly in place. Whenever he failed, he was quick to see it and repent. It did not take long for our new way of relating to our children to become the norm.

Over many years, I have been privileged to see the love and power of God working in my husband's life (and mine), changing him (and me) from an old man into a new man in Christ. This kind of change hasn't happened with an overnight miracle, but it has happened. Where we are today seems miraculous to me. I have watched my husband, from my very close-up vantage point for almost five decades, as God has been at work changing him into the new creation in Christ that he became on the day he believed in Christ. I have seen Him change more than any other human being I know.

Today, I can say that my husband, who once lived, even as a born-again Christian, like a fallen, proud, lost man, has become a godly, loving, humble man (well, most of the time humble)—a new man in Christ. He knows how to say, "I'm sorry," better than anyone else I know. He has seen and acknowledged his failures as a husband and father and is actively doing things to make up for those shortcomings with me and our grown children. He prays for his children and grandchildren. He prays for me. He treats me with love and respect (well, the great majority of the time).

In 2007, when I was in the process of reading Bushnell's book, John became curious one day about my reading material. I had not mentioned it to him and had actually gone to some lengths to keep him from seeing it, not wanting to become engaged in some kind of discussion about women and their roles. I just wanted to read Bushnell for myself and see what she had to say. John pressed me to tell him about the book; and, when I did, he said he wanted to read it. I told him it was difficult reading and, if he was really interested in the topic, that he should first read Jesse Penn-Lewis' book, *The Magna Charta of Woman*. He read that book, and then he read Bushnell's book. He was profoundly affected by what he learned and was grateful for it. It explained something that he had always known in his heart to be true. He had suffered a lot during the twenty years we spent in the woman-subduing church, because his wife did not fit, or fall in line with, the stereotypical good Christian woman model that was expected there. It was a great relief to him to realize that there was biblical evidence that I was not abnormal, but normal, and that his desire to let me be free was not only normal, it was right and was biblically supportable. He subsequently wrote a paper to men entitled "Woman 101—What Every Christian Man Needs To Know," explaining what he had learned from Penn-Lewis and Bushnell.

We truly have become joint-heirs together of the grace of life and have seen God work mightily in answer to our prayers. Thankfully, our prayers are no longer hindered by a fallen, improper male-female dynamic in our relationship.

The King and I

Next, I'm going to share with you an inspiring story about another woman of *chayil*, Anna Leonowens, who was a contemporary of Kathryn Bushnell. To begin, I had no idea that a movie I always loved, "The King and I" (with Yul Brenner and Deborah Kerr), was based on a true story until I happened upon an autobiographical account of the time that Anna Leonowens spent in Siam. Anna, who lived in the late 1800s, was the real-life "I" of *The King and I*. I found the story of this brave, bold, and strong woman of *chayil* to be very enlightening and encouraging. It brought clarity to some of the things I was learning at the time I read it. Anna was a praying

Christian woman. I found her to be a woman after my own heart, that is, one driven to God and to prayer by all the hard things around her in real life. For example, after the death of her young husband, she was left with two small children and no support. She sent her daughter to live with relatives in England and took her young son with her to the far away country of Siam, where she had been offered a teaching position. She wrote the following in her journal shortly after she and her son arrived there:

> When at last I found myself alone, I would have sought the sleep I so much needed, but the strange scenes of the day chased each other in agitating confusion through my brain. Then I quitted the side of my sleeping boy, triumphant in his dreamless innocence, and sat defeated by the window, to crave counsel and help from the ever-present Friend; and as I waited I sank into a tumultuous slumber, from which at last I started to find the long-tarrying dawn climbing over a low wall and creeping through a half-open shutter.
>
> I started up, arranged my dress, and smoothed my hair; though no water nor any after-touches could remove the shadow that night of gloom and loneliness had left upon my face. But my boy awoke with eager, questioning eyes, his smile bright and his hair lustrous. As we knelt together by the window at the feet of "Our Father," I could not but ask in the darkness of my trouble, did it need so bitter a baptism as ours to purify so young a soul? (Leonowens)

Anna's difficulty in Siam was mostly with a strong-minded, proud, self-made man (her employer) in a culture that had very little regard for women. The King of Siam, in his quest for western knowledge, let down his cultural guard enough to allow a foreign woman to teach his many children (and many wives). Anna was a strong woman and, in my opinion, a fearless one, to go where she went and do what she did, and to do so alone. Also, she did it over 150 years ago (1862), during a time when English women were expected to be dependent wives and mothers, not independent members of the secular work force. Because of their gender, women had very few rights and very little ability to independently provide for themselves.

This modern day woman of *chayil* was a strong and capable woman of God who took on the daunting task of presenting truth to the king of a male-dominated, heathen culture. Even though it caused her a lot of suffering, she boldly, with respect and a measure of humility, displayed for him the freedom as a fellow human being that she had been given by her Maker, much to the king's chagrin.

I found the Brenner and Kerr movie version of her story to be fundamentally true to her autobiographical account, with the exceptions being some Hollywood embellishments and the hint of Anna's romance with the king. In spite of these embellishments, a wonderful message for women comes through in the movie. In it, the king constantly struggles with Anna, seeking to subdue her, to prove he is smarter than her, that she is only a lowly woman, etc. Anna never flinches. She calmly and sometimes emphatically holds her ground, every inch of it. She is submissive to his demands as much as possible, as long as they do not violate principle.

After a time, it becomes evident that the king is being greatly influenced by her—her character, her strength, her morality, and her Bible. At the point that he is about to beat a young female servant, in front of others, Anna calls his hand on his barbaric behavior. He rants and raves, insisting that he most certainly will do what he had set out to do. When he cannot bring himself to swing his whip at the cowering girl while Anna is standing there watching him, he throws the whip down and runs from the room. The next scene shows him on his death bed, broken by what was, to his way of thinking, a terrible failure and shame. He has lost what he considered to be real manhood. Realizing he has been bettered and subdued by the boldness, strength, and values of a free "woman," he has fallen sick. In the final scenes of this story, he dies, and his firstborn son takes his place as king. The new king gives his first speech, and the role that Anna's teaching and way of living have played in molding the new, young king into a new kind of man with a new set of values is evident.

In light of the Bible's teaching about the old man and the new man (Rom. 6:6; Eph. 2:15; 4:22, 24; Col. 3:9–10), I couldn't help but see the symbolism in this story. The King of Siam's way of life matched that of the old man with the fallen, Adamic nature that is self-assertive, independent, proud, and capable of abusively ruling over others, especially women. I also couldn't help but see that Anna, a living example and voice of truth to him day after day as she taught his family, was symbolic of the role and influence that a spiritual, godly, loving, moral, truth-speaking, properly-submissive, and praying woman fulfills in such a man's life. The king's death pictured the death of the old, Adamic man, and the king's son, taking his place as the new king, pictured the regenerated, transformed new man that reigns in place of the old fallen one. Most women have a King of Siam in their life. If you find it hard, as I did, to believe God can help your King of Siam, remember Anna's story.

You might also call to mind the wonderful scene (my favorite) in the movie of Anna's story where she dances with the king round and round the palace ballroom to the song, "Shall We Dance." Put yourself in that scene as Anna and think about this: The real King wants you to follow His lead on your life's dance floor. Can't you hear Him asking you each day, "Shall we dance?"

From a Wimp to a Warrior

God knows how to change suffering, voiceless women into women of *chayil.* Or maybe I should say God knows how to turn wimps into warriors, because that is what He did for me. I will be eternally grateful that He patiently trained me in my very own customized boot camp. I will always remember how He showed me the armor that He had provided for me when I became a Christian (Eph. 6), and how He taught me to put it on and start using it. I didn't go forward alone. I took His hand, entered that first battle, risked an outcome I might not have liked, and began to see Christ's victory over the devil in my husband's life. I have a lifetime now of learning to use the built-in enmity (extreme hostility) that God put between woman and the serpent in the Garden of Eden. Today, to those in the "seen" world, I may look like your average grandmother; but, to those in the "unseen," I think I look a little more like Joan of Arc.

Important: Sin Renders Christians Ineffective

Sin in our life as a Christian renders us powerless before God's enemy. It opens the door to defeating attacks by him. In this book, I have been talking about a big sin in the body of Christ with respect to the relationships between men and women. It is big both in its degree and its time span. Righting this wrong involves a spiritual battle of epic proportions. This battle cannot be won and the powers of darkness stopped if the Christians who stand up to call for repentance are not cleansed from their own relationship sins. In other words, to enter this large-scale battle and be effective, we, as individual women of *chayil,* must be cleansed of *all relationship sins* in our own lives. Only then can we be effective in pointing out such sins in others. This does not mean only gender-based relationships in our life; it means *all* wrong relationships. If we are serious about walking with the Lord and being spiritual warriors, we have to ask God to shine His laser light of truth on our lives and expose any and all relationship problems in which we are involved. Then, we have to take steps to correct what He shows us. This is what it means to repent!

When God began this work in my life, mostly He used these passages: Matthew 5:21–25 and Matthew 18:15–17. After uncovering my problem relationships, He used these verses to show me what I had to do to attempt to make these wrong relationships right. This was difficult! I have written more about that in my book on the Lord's Prayer. In brief, as He taught me to apply these passages of Scripture, I learned many other valuable lessons. For one, I learned the difference between judging sin and judging the sinner. The first we must do, the last we must not do. We can judge sins or evil deeds, because we can see them and name them. We then must do our biblically mandated part to help remove them. We cannot, however, pass judgment on the person who committed the sins by saying such things as "that good-for-nothing" or by holding them in contempt in our thoughts and actions or by despising them in our hearts or by rejecting them with our tongues. This is sin. Only God fully knows a person; and, therefore, only God has the position to render righteous judgment on everything about a person. According to the Bible, however, in certain situations, we have to make a judgment about believers who are committing evil deeds. If a sinning believer has been properly warned and has refused to stop habitual sinning, the Bible refers to this kind of person as "such a one" and requires other believers not to associate with them:

> But actually, I wrote to you not to associate with any so-called brother if he is an immoral person, or covetous, or an idolater, or a reviler, or a drunkard, or a swindler—not even to eat with such a one. (1 Cor. 5:11, NASB)

We should, however, continue to pray for that believer.

Most of the examples I have given in this chapter were related to relationship sins in my life. God was faithful to help me see my sins and do something about them because I loved the truth of God's word and had committed myself to walk in it. As women of *chayil* who are serious about walking in the light with Him, we must ask God to always bring to our attention any sins in our lives concerning our relationships with others. Then, we should give due diligence to obey the Matthew 5 and 18 passages.

The Cross Is the Power of God

I hope that what I have shared in this chapter has succeeded in shedding a little light on what a modern-day Christian woman of *chayil* is like and also on how God stands ready to help Christian women become women of *chayil*. His main help is to teach us in practical ways about the most fundamental Bible truth: the cross of Christ. To us who are saved, it is the power of God (1 Cor. 1:18). The cross is the place where we see ourselves, see our sin, and bow and repent. It is the place where we choose to yield all to Him. It is the place where we stop and He begins. He takes us by the hand, and we begin to learn to follow Him. It is the place where He begins to help us see others as He sees them, and to change us from the inside out so that we can love as He loves. The cross is where we learn that sometimes He asks us to suffer on behalf of others.

Hanging on a wall in my home, I have a tall rectangular picture of a long straight path that runs from the bottom edge of the picture to near the top edge. Along both sides of the narrow path are the edges of a flower-filled field. On the path there is a line of sheep of various sizes following each other, appearing to move, if you will, from the bottom of the picture to the top. All you can see of these sheep is their backsides. I have always loved this picture. It reminds me that, like sheep, we must follow the shepherd on the pathway of the cross. We can learn from other sheep who have gone before us on this path and from those who are traveling with us on it now.

The lessons of the cross are exemplified in the lives of all the Bible's women of *chayil*. They, too, were inducted into God's army and attended His new-shoe basic training camp. Sarah and Zipporah had to stop enabling. Abigail had to risk her own life in order to save others. Eve had to show the way back to God for all women who would come after her. Her pathway was one of great loss and suffering. Millions of women have faced similar suffering. They have lived with self-loving, wife-blaming, God-slandering, fallen husbands who naturally rule over them. They have worn themselves out trying to please and take care of such husbands. They have watched them hurt their children through neglect, cruelty, or pride. They have found their husbands uncommunicative. They have seen them, like great, great, great ... granddad Adam, hiding their sin (Job 31:33), saying as little as possible lest they be exposed as failures. Women have spent themselves weeping, thinking, struggling, and hoping that one day, they would find an answer to their difficult relationships with their husbands.

Eve's story shows them that they can learn to have absolute trust in God and depend upon Him in all their down-to-earth, practical, real-life family situations, problems, and needs. They can learn as she did how to turn fully to God so that He can use them to produce godly families. Family by family, God will win, and Satan will lose. The truth that frightens the devil is that women who turn *fully* back to God, making Him their number one, have the power to transform fallen society, one family at a time, starting with their own. It probably won't happen overnight, just as the first family did not change overnight, but it will happen.

I have learned, and continue to learn, from Eve's good example. God has worked a change in my family, turning it into a godly one. Some facet of Eve's good example comes to mind frequently: We do not have to wait until a crisis comes like the one Eve faced before we turn ourselves completely back to God. We can turn now. We can fall on Him now in brokenness and seek His help. We don't have to wait until some horrible event falls on us and breaks us (Matt. 21:44, Luke 20:18).

When we moved to our current home a few years ago, I decided that my greatly-loved sheep picture was a bit too "country" for my new décor, so I put it away in a closet. I recently pulled it out and re-hung it. Now, each time that I see that long path on the wall before me, I usually take note of two small sheep near the bottom of the picture. I think of those little sheep as today's women of *chayil* who are following a long train of faithful women of *chayil*. I am one of those followers. I believe that, on the day God put Katharine Bushnell's book in my hand years ago, He planted my feet solidly on that path in the line of many women who have gone before. I hope that God will use this book to bring more women onto that path, the path of victory over the devil.

As we follow in the footsteps of our brave female forbears, we will see the fulfillment of Isaiah 61:11:

> For as the earth brings forth her bud, and the garden causes the things that are sown in it to spring forth, so the Lord God will cause

righteousness and praise to spring forth before all the nations. (Isa. 61:11, AKJV)

God has a purpose for each of us that is bigger than our own small world of difficulties. As Christian women learning to follow Jesus, our training to be brave and bold in small matters is really about learning to fight the enemy bravely and boldly on the big warfront of the earth. Actually, all our small spiritual victories in daily life are part of that big battle. Our experiences have a cumulative effect in the unseen spiritual world. Just like small stones piled on one side of a balance scale eventually tip the scale, our accumulated small victories will have a tipping effect in the spiritual realm. David first killed a lion and a bear before God had him face and kill the giant, Goliath, and free Israel from the attacking Philistines. The skills we learn as we take the sword of the Spirit, the Word of God, and learn to wield it in our small battles, will be likewise used, in God's time, in bigger battles, to fell our old enemy and free God's people and all of the earth from his darkness.

Humbly Brave and Bold

Godly courage and boldness is born of a desire to stand one with God and to stand against the devil for the benefit of others. It is not the angry, in-your-face boldness seen in some proactive women in today's feminist movement. The right way for Christian women to be bold and do what God is asking of them is seen in the cross of Christ.

The way that Jesus took to victory over the devil was the way of the cross. The cross that He bore no one but Him could bear; however, He told us that we were to take up our own crosses and follow Him. Paul told us that it was right for us to fill up that which was lacking in the sufferings of Christ for His body's sake, and he appealed to us to know the fellowship of Christ's sufferings. This means that if we follow Christ faithfully, we will have experiences that will resemble His on the cross. Our crosses, however, will be unique and particular to each of us, as He calls us to bear them for the benefit of others.

He is our pattern for the kind of boldness needed to obtain victory over the enemy today. When He came, He spoke the truth in love as He walked with and followed His Father in righteousness. He was willing to suffer for doing so, in whatever way His Father willed. The disciples eventually learned for themselves the way of the cross, as we can tell from Peter's and Paul's writings. They learned that suffering for well doing was well pleasing to God and it would be rewarded in God's time.

So, as women, we must learn by experience what it means to follow in the footsteps of Jesus and of those who learned the way of the cross from Him. Simply recognizing and vocalizing the age-old male-female problem and seeing its real cause will not solve it, nor will any fleshly method, be it passive or active. The only thing that women can do that will end this ancient problem is to learn to take up their crosses and follow Jesus. The way of the cross is the only way that brings victory over the devil and bears true and godly fruit. The devil can use any other approach to stop forward progress.

Some people believe that any kind of confrontation is in itself fleshly and ungodly and, therefore, wrong. Jesus showed us otherwise. He boldly confronted the hypocritical leaders of God's people with the truth of God's Word. They were involved with the devil and walking in disobedience, and He was bold to point this out to them. He did not sin in doing so. (If confrontation in itself was sin, then Jesus could not have died in our place as a sinless man because He was definitely confrontational.) When He confronted His own people with truth, He was doing what His Father showed Him to do, and trusting Him for the outcome. He was loving His Father's words and taking care of righteousness. His hope was in His Father alone and not in the outcome of His obedience.

Isn't that where we naturally are radically different from Him? Maybe I should just speak for myself: That is where I differ from Him. The outcome in any situation in which I involve myself on behalf of righteousness can quickly become my focus. If the outcome is suffering, looking bad to others, being spoken about poorly, I easily melt into a pile of tears and retreat. (Truthfully, I no longer melt so often or so easily, but I have melted many, many times; and, I know that at any moment, without His emboldening help, I still can.)

Desire To Please Him

To walk in right and devil-defeating ways as women, we must desire one thing above all else: to be well pleasing to Him first and foremost. Paul desired only to know Christ and Him crucified. He wanted to know experientially the power of His resurrection and the fellowship of His sufferings. He wasn't controlled by temporary outcomes. This lesson, in my opinion, is the hardest lesson for a Christian to learn. As human beings, we thrive on approval from others; and, when instead, we receive rejection, we nose-dive into despair. If we do not guard against it, we will end up letting the approval or disapproval that comes from fellow human beings control us. This will render us useless to God. Faithful followers of Jesus thrive when they know that God is pleased and is smiling on them, regardless of what others are saying about them or doing to them. This way of living is easy to talk about, but absolutely is not easy to practice.

I do not yet classify myself as courageously brave and bold, but I think I am now among the tremblingly brave and bold. God is still at work teaching me to calm my heart when it starts to quake. One time, when I was first beginning to give voice to some of what I was learning about women in the Bible, I had occasion to be with a small group of Christian women in a discussion. I ventured to share a little about my burden for women, because it seemed to fit in well in the discussion. One woman, in response to what I said, offered a gentle word of correction that made me realize she had misunderstood what I shared.

That night, going to bed, I was thinking about this and told the Lord how much I hated being misunderstood and how hard it was for me to risk being misunderstood. It was dawning on me that, if I began to share things He had been showing me for the past six years about women, I was most likely going to find myself on the path of being misunderstood. I wondered if I was reading Him right. Did He want me to write about this or not? I awoke the next morning still feeling heavy in my heart. I opened my email to find a *Jesus Calling* installment sent out by a friend. I had not received one of these from her in months. My morning note from God said:

> You are walking along the path I have chosen for you. It is both a privileged and a perilous way; experiencing My glorious Presence and heralding that reality to others. Sometimes you feel presumptuous to be carrying out such an assignment. Do not worry about what other people think of you. The work I am doing in you is hidden at first, but eventually blossoms will burst forth, and abundant fruit will be borne. Stay on the path of Life with Me. Trust Me wholeheartedly, letting My Spirit fill you with Joy and Peace. (Young, 244)

That morning, at this surprising personalized word from my ever-present, loving King, my fears retreated and my "brave-and-bold-o-meter" moved a little higher. These words are to every Christian woman. He is at work. Do not worry about what other people think about you! Follow Him!

Chapter 11

The Bondwoman and the Bloody Husband; Free Women Speak

*For the time has come for judgment to begin at the house of God;
and if it begins with us first, what will be the end of those who do
not obey the gospel of God?*
(I Pet. 4:17, NKJV)

I F WE READ THE SIGNS OF THE TIMES in the light of the
Bible, we understand that the day of the Lord—a day
of God's judgment and wrath at the end of time—is
rapidly approaching. We learn from the Old Testament
that, before God moves His hand in judgment against His
people or worldly kingdoms, He always warns them by
confronting them with their sins so that they might
repent. The truth about women's freedom in Christ,
which has only begun to emerge in the last two centuries,
has shined a bright light on a huge, long-term cancer in
the body of Christ. It is time for the house of God to be
cleansed and healed by repentance.

This chapter focuses on our part, as women of *chayil*,
in the cleansing and healing. It provides some strong
biblical support for the difficult things that we must do.
Our job is to speak in love the unadulterated truth from
God's word and expose the cancer. We must do this
regardless of what it may cost us. We simply cannot be
silent. A statement that has been attributed to a well-
known, vocal Christian man who was in Nazi Germany is
profound:

> Silence in the face of evil is itself evil. God will not
> hold those who are silent guiltless. Not to speak
> is to speak. Not to act is to act" (Sojourners).

In the Bible, God does not silence women but
empowers them and uses them to proclaim His Word:

> The Lord gives the word [of power]; the women
> who bear *and* publish [the news] are a great host.
> (Psa. 68:11, AMPC) [see also Bushnell, para. 206]

And, lest we forget, the outpouring at Pentecost was on both men and women, and women also spoke:

> 16 but this is what was spoken of through the prophet Joel: 17 "AND IT SHALL BE IN THE LAST DAYS," GOD SAYS, "THAT I WILL POUR FORTH OF MY SPIRIT ON ALL MANKIND; AND YOUR SONS AND YOUR DAUGHTERS SHALL PROPHESY ...." (Acts 2:16–17, NASB) [see also Bushnell, para. 207]

The baton of the truth about God's view of women according to the Bible has passed to us. Seeing the truth of our freedom in Christ and recognizing the fierce war between the seed of woman and the seed of the serpent, we must stand up confidently and begin to live and proclaim the truth about this. We will be doing so for the sake of:

- A lost world
- Christian women whose gifts lie dormant because of errant teachings and beliefs about women
- Christian men who deny women the true freedom that God has given them in Christ and believe that they are obeying God when they do so
- Women who continue the age-old pattern of enabling and perpetuating this dark situation
- Most of all, Him who died for us—that we do not deny His work on the cross which set free all who believe, both male and female

With any who would want to hold us in silent subservience to their supposed authority over us just because they are males, we must respectfully disagree. We must explain to them that God has not set them over us because of their gender and that we are not bondwomen; we are free women. We must tell them that confronting this sin is very unpleasant to us, but we have no choice seeing the seriousness of their sinful position before God. No doubt, some, both men and women, will oppose us and try to silence us, but opposition to truth can never stop it. The only thing that can stop truth is silence. If we are not silent, truth will ultimately prevail (Isa. 59:14–21).

Christian Women Must Be the First ... To Repent

As Christian women, we bear a great measure of responsibility for the great logjam of gender-based sins in God's family that block the mighty river of God's blessing on the earth. We have quietly allowed Christian men to sin against us over and over again. We have obeyed unbiblical mandates from them. We have been afraid to do anything that looks like we are trying to teach them anything about God. We have trembled at the thought that we might be seen as trying to usurp their authority. We have not taken responsibility to study the Bible for ourselves and discover the truth about women in the Word of God.

There was a time when women were held back from seeking such truth because they were not afforded the benefit of having an education; however, that time has long passed, leaving us without excuse. This logjam will never be broken up and washed away until we, as women, see the role our passivity has played in its creation and its maintenance—*and we repent!* Some of us have even added our own logs to the jam by insisting, as good submissive Christian women, that our fellow sisters in Christ obey the Bible's lemon translations. I used to be one of these women.

If we want to end our pattern of enabling Christian men's sin, we need to repent, obey God's Word, and do what He requires of us. Jesus commanded:

15 "If your brother sins, go and show him his fault in private; if he listens to you, you have won your brother. 16 But if he does not listen [to you], take one or two more with you, so that BY THE MOUTH OF TWO OR THREE WITNESSES EVERY FACT MAY BE CONFIRMED. 17 If he refuses to listen to them, tell it to the church; and if he refuses to listen even to the church, let him be to you as a Gentile and a tax collector. 18 Truly I say to you, whatever you bind on earth shall have been bound in heaven; and whatever you loose on earth shall have been loosed in heaven.

19 "Again I say to you, that if two of you agree on earth about anything that they may ask, it shall be done for them by My Father who is in heaven. 20 For where two or three have gathered together in My name, I am there in their midst." (Matt. 18:15–20, NASB)

Jesus further commanded:

Take heed to yourselves: if thy brother trespass against thee, rebuke him; and if he repent, forgive him. (Luke 17:3, KJV)

In simplest terms, this means we have a biblical responsibility to repent for our enabling silence and begin a long overdue, straightforward, and very serious conversation with Christian men. We can't stay silent and be found faithful. Like it or not, this is the place in which we find ourselves at the close of the age. In his pure Word, God has shown His view of womankind.

Bushnell warns that women who remain silent are practicing what she calls a kind of "sham virtue." She believes that they bear responsibility "for the *lack* of gentleness, meekness, humility and chastity among men."

Woman was created as a help "meet," sufficient for man; and because it was "not good" for him to be alone. And later, by all he had lost *she* was left sole heir of a great inheritance,—to furnish the seed for a better race. She has fulfilled her call in part, by the virginal birth of Jesus Christ. Its complete fulfillment implies a large spiritual progeny growing out of the spiritual activity of woman. She must not sell her birthright (for it is the same one, except greater, that Esau sold), by a vicious self-effacement.

That is sham virtue in woman which lends a cloak or gives stimulus to vice in man. *"By their fruits ye shall know them."* That which begets virtue in others *is* virtue; that which begets vice *is* vice. A wifely self-immolation which encourages masculine sensuality is vice. A feminine "humility" which gives place for the growth of masculine egotism is vice. Women need to ponder these things, and their responsibility (as the mothers and trainers of the men of the world), for the *lack* of gentleness, meekness, humility and chastity among men. Women must train their sons in *all* these virtues. (Bushnell, paras. 411–412)

The Repentant Can Call for Repentance

Christian men who are in disobedience to God's Word with respect to women will one day face God's ultimate judgment for this; actually, in many ways, they already are under judgment. Christian women will face similar judgment for enabling such sin. As enlightened and repentant Christian women, we can do what is necessary to help save men, and ourselves, from such judgment. We can and must demonstrate their sin in no uncertain terms—like Sarah did when she told Abraham to cast out the bondwoman and her son, and like Zipporah did when she cut off the foreskin of her son and threw it at Moses' feet calling him a "bloody husband." Confronting Christian men's sin will be as difficult and distasteful for us as it was for these Old Testament women, but we must do it! We must help them see their as yet unrecognized sin, so they can remove it by repentance.

There is an unusual verse about women found in the Psalms:

The Lord announces the word, and the women who proclaim it are a mighty throng [or "great host"]. (Psa. 68:11, NIV)

There does not appear to be a time in history where a great host or a mighty throng of women has proclaimed the Word of God, so it stands to reason that Psalm 68:11 is a prophecy of something that has not yet come. I submit to you that there is a very great possibility that this throng will be made up of today's Christian women of *chayil.* Bushnell believed the Lord's second coming would be heralded by such women. She pointed out two passages in the Bible that caused her to believe that a great company of women would prepare the way for

Christ's second coming. One of them was Psalm 68:11, which was newly and correctly translated in her day (in the Revised Version) to reflect that the great host mentioned in that verse is made up of women. She also believed that a sister passage, Isaiah 40:10–11, would one day be, likewise, correctly translated to reflect that women would herald the second coming of Christ. She wrote:

> The Prophet Isaiah saw the day of the Lord's second coming, when scattered Israel would be gathered together, and led back to their own land, by the hand of Jehovah (Isa. 40:10–11). The prophet represents God as calling: *"O thou [woman] that bringest good tidings to Zion, get thee up into the high mountain: O thou [woman] that bringest good tidings to Jerusalem, lift up thy voice with strength; lift it up, be not afraid; say unto the cities of Judah, Behold your God!"* (R. V.). There is precisely the same warrant, from the original Hebrew, for inserting "woman" in this passage in Isaiah, as there is for inserting "woman," as the Revision does in Psalm 68:11. The "woman" has received tardy justice in the latter passage [Psalm 68:11*] by the translators; and such will one day be the case in the former one [Isa. 40:10–11*] (see pars. 209, 773). (Bushnell, para. 826) [*references added for clarity]

I, too, believe that women will begin to prepare the way for the second coming of Christ, and it will be with a cry for repentance! The meat of their repentance message will be to Christians, to those in the church who need to repent for their suppression and oppression of women. It will also include a call for believers to repent for practicing all the things God hates. It will go something like this: "Repent, for the time of the manifestation of the kingdom of God and the revelation of the sons of God is at hand! Repent for defiling the house of God by being or by receiving unrepentant brethren who continue in all forms of sexual sin! Repent for untold numbers of broken, disharmonious relationships in the body of Christ! Repent for lording it over fellow believers! Repent for treating women as if they were inferior, second-class citizens in the kingdom of God and for suppressing their spiritual gifts! Repent for preaching forgiveness without repentance! Repent for not preaching the true message of the cross which is both love *and righteousness!* Repent for not calling sin "sin" and for not helping Christians *see* their sins and repent for them! Repent for lifting up the name of God in hypocrisy!"

The Bondwoman: Sarah Helped Abraham Do the Right Thing

We have a strong biblical role model in Sarah—one that we should keep in view as we press the conversation about the critical importance of woman's freedom and about God's way of fulfilling His promise through beings who are free. When Paul wrote to the Galatians, he reminded them that Sarah told Abraham to cast out the bondwoman and her son. He also explained the significance of this:

> 22 For it is written that Abraham had two sons, one by the bondwoman and one by the free woman. 23 But the son by the bondwoman was born according to the flesh, and the son by the free woman through the promise. 24 This is allegorically speaking, for these women are two covenants: one [proceeding] from Mount Sinai bearing children who are to be slaves; she is Hagar. 25 Now this Hagar is Mount Sinai in Arabia and corresponds to the present Jerusalem, for she is in slavery with her children. 26 But the Jerusalem above is free; she is our mother. 27 For it is written,
>
> "REJOICE, BARREN WOMAN WHO DOES NOT BEAR;
> BREAK FORTH AND SHOUT, YOU WHO ARE NOT IN LABOR;
> FOR MORE NUMEROUS ARE THE CHILDREN OF THE DESOLATE
> THAN OF THE ONE WHO HAS A HUSBAND."
>
> 28 And you brethren, like Isaac, are children of promise. 29 But as at that time he who was born

according to the flesh persecuted him [who was born] according to the Spirit, so it is now also. (Gal. 4:22–29, NASB)

Paul's point was that Hagar was a picture of those in Judaism who were still in bondage at the time of Paul's writing. They were bound, held under the law which God had given to keep them for Himself and to protect them from the enemy while they waited for their Messiah. Paul's point was also that Sarah was a picture of the free woman, "Jerusalem above." This was the church which was made up of both believing Jews and Gentiles, all who were free in Christ. The Gentiles had been desolate without a husband, but now, in Christ, they would have more children than the Jews—those who had been married to God. Everything had changed. Both Jews and Gentiles now had access to God and to freedom in Christ. Those in Judaism could only produce an Ishmael that was born of the work of the flesh, because they were not free. Those in Christ could produce an Isaac that was born of the Spirit, because they were free.

Today's Hagar and Ishmael

Paul further interpreted Ishmael's mocking of Isaac as the flesh persecuting the Spirit. He likened the Judaizers to Ishmael and the believers to Isaac. The Judaizers were being used by Satan to mock and persecute the believers and to teach them things that would rob them of their freedom. Paul's message still applies today because much of what we see today in Christendom is an Ishmael. I am bold to make this statement because:

- Today's situation is the product of many centuries of free Christian men using Christian women who were *not free, but were in bondage to male superiors, similar to Hagar being a slave to Abraham.* In general, Christian women have not been free to hear from Christ and give voice and feet to His direction in their lives. They have not been free to carry out specific purposes He had planned for them, because they were required, even forced, to silently submit to the governance of the spiritual leadings of their male superiors. That which has been produced by free men with bound women is Ishmael, and it is not the true heir of the kingdom of God.

- Just as Sarah facilitated the birth of Ishmael, Christian women have been promoters, supporters, and participants in this sad state of affairs for centuries. They have willingly followed the voice of Christian men instead of that of Jesus and have worked with them to build what is considered today by many to be God's house. Rather than following Christ first, as their personal and supreme Lord, they silently allowed Christian men to keep them in bondage under authoritarian mandates. They have helped male Christian leaders produce a church that is born of work based in man's self effort.

- Many new covenant women are entangled in a yoke of bondage to this day. New covenant men are responsible for this to this day. Such men have sinned; and, in so doing, have forfeited their own freedom.

The true heir, Isaac, will be like Christ in every way, and will come by promise and by the power and work of the Holy Spirit. That will happen when free Christian women and men work together in true harmony and mutual respect and submission to each other and to the Father, Son, and Holy Spirit.

Just as God used the words of the free woman, Sarah, to correct the Ishmael problem in the Old Testament, and just as Paul used Sarah's words to correct a similar situation in the New Testament, God will use the words of today's free women to correct today's situation.

Today's Ishmael Mocking Isaac

Throughout history in Christendom, we can find young Isaacs—the products of the Holy Spirit working through Christian men and women who recognized and practiced their God-given freedom together. Today, we can see such a young Isaac in Christendom in those men and women who are speaking and practicing the truth that men and women have the same freedom in Christ. Also today, this young Isaac's presence is provoking Ishmael to mock and persecute him.

In the following selected quotes taken from a message by a well-respected, present-day Christian teacher on the topic of Christian women and their roles, one can easily see Ishmael mocking Isaac. This leader's purpose was to speak out against the growing voice in the Christian community about what this leader refers to as "evangelical feminism." My purpose is to illustrate the Ishmael and Isaac principle in Christendom, not to single out a Christian leader for his prejudices. The following excerpts are taken from one of his sermons entitled, "The Subordination and Equality of Women":

> We are constantly hearing about the battle for women's rights. I'm sure if it goes far enough, we'll have a men's lib to try to gain back some of the ground that's been lost ...

> A woman, whether she is married or single, must recognize the fact that in general, as a woman, she must have a spirit of submission to all men....

> If I have [gave] you my opinion on the subject, I couldn't live with myself. I'd have to duck for the next six months. *(Laughter)* ...

> It's no different with the women's liberation movement. We now have Christian feminists— whatever that might be—Christian feminists who are advocating the fact that there is only in Christ equality. They wave the flag of Galatians 3:28, that in Christ there is neither male nor female. On the basis of that and on the basis of 1 Peter 3:7, that a husband and a wife are heirs together of the grace of life, they postulate the fact that there is no such thing as authority and submission between men and women either in marriage, in the church, in business, in education, or in any other dimension.

In fact, there are many people who definitely and strongly feel that Paul was nothing but a male chauvinist....

There are many churches now that are battling the issue of should we or should we not have female elders? People ask me, "What do you think about women pastors?" I always give the same answer, "I never think about them."...

These books are coming out, written by women and in some cases by men, saying that whenever the Bible says this, it's either cultural, it's either Paul repeating his opinion, it isn't inspired by God or we're misinterpreting it.

Those who listen to such writers are going to be confused....

In other words, eventually they must deny revelation. Once you've done that, you have really let the cat out of the bag. Then they become the judges of which part of Paul is inspired and which is not. Of course, that's a deadly attack.

A woman is to be in subjection. A man is to be in authority....

Women are not to teach, they are to learn. They are not to take authority in the church and rule over men. That's very, very simple. It's very, very clear. Couldn't confuse anybody....

The woman is the submissive one by creation and by virtual [sic] of her weakness in the Fall that confirms her submissive role....

What law? The law of God. It is not just creation, it is God's Old Testament law that women are to be submissive. This is God's New Testament standard as well....

But what apparently happened in Corinthians was sort of an abuse of Christian liberty. Some of the women, feeling they were free in Christ, began to throw away their veils. It wasn't burn your bra, it was burn your veil. *(Laughter)*

Whenever you see a woman today who doesn't wear a bra or dressed in that manner, that woman is not a submissive woman. That woman is not radiating a dependence on a man. She is announcing something to everybody who sees her, and that something is, 'Look at me. I'm interested in something other than what I've got.' At least flirting with it....

Every time I see—there used to be a big deal on this—unisex. They used to have stores where you could buy unisex clothes. I just recognize that it's difficult—in fact, as I thought about this over and over again, I had a hard time trying to figure out a modern illustration, because we don't have much difference anymore. You can't tell from the back anymore because of the hair. You can't tell the kind of—It's hard to tell. One good thing today is beards. *(Laughter)* I've been thinking about growing a beard just so there wouldn't be any confusion. *(Laughter)* Next thing you know is, all the men get beards, women will go out and buy artificial beards."...

The man must recognize that God has given him authority, and he has to accept that and take it and rule for God. The woman must realize in any relationship that she has been given the place of submission.

This isn't wrong. This is the way God made it. This is the way He designed it. You don't play golf with a fishing pole, and you don't go fishing with a golf club. God has made people in the same sense to do a certain thing. That's the way they're made, and that's the way they function, and that's the way they're fulfilled. "Man has authority over woman."...

That's why I say the whole idea is ludicrous. There's not even an argument Biblically. They're making much ado about nothing. "Full of sound and fury," said Shakespeare, "signifying nothing."...

There are places where she will speak and proclaim the Gospel to unsaved friends and neighbors and to other women and whatever, but the one place where she will not preach, where she will not lead, is in the church. In the assembly of the church, when it comes together in its corporate meetings, she is not permitted, because there God wants to establish the male as the authority, carry out His pattern....

Women may have the gift of prophesy. I'll tell you who did. Phillip had four daughters with the gift of prophesy. Did you know that? It's in Acts 21:8-9. He had four daughters with the gift of prophecy. You say, "Where did they prophesy?" I don't know where, but I'll tell you one place they didn't prophesy. Where? The churches. (MacArthur)

Today's Sarah

Today's Christian women of *chayil* need to inform men who speak in the preceding manner that God is not pleased with what they have produced with the help of bound women. The only fruit that is pleasing to God comes from free beings, male and female, as were Abraham and Sarah. There is definitely a young Isaac in the church today—where women's freedom in Christ is recognized—but it is overshadowed by the older, stronger, and often-taunting Ishmael. When Ishmael is named for what it is—the non-heir—and is cast out, the whole earth will be blessed through Isaac. Isaac will be the heir—one that is produced by the Holy Spirit working through men and women who are both free! Christian men and women alike must endeavor to stand fast in the freedom for which Christ set them free and not be entangled in the yoke of bondage.

In light of Paul's words in Galatians, it should go without saying that men should not subjugate women, but should help them walk in their freedom. Christ will come a second time to new covenant men and women, all of whom are free to choose to follow and submit to Jesus as their Lord and also to one another, irrespective of gender, and none of whom are lording it over another.

Freedom and authority working together properly look like this: free beings submitting to God first and then to one another. Freedom and authority together *do not* look like this: a subset of beings (males) asserting their authority over another subset of beings (females), and expecting the second subset to be subservient because of their gender. The latter is what we see in the previous quotes from a modern-day Christian teacher. For anyone who has been set free by Christ's death on the cross to assert, or to impose, his authority over another free being is something ugly. It is the modus operandi of the devil's counterfeit authority.

God, the supreme authority, wants us, His created beings, to decide to willingly yield to Him because this is in our best interest. His way is to persuade us to make this choice. He does not pontificate from His throne about how He has set things up in a certain order and then demand that we must bow, whether we want to or not. That is not the gospel. Rather, He persuades us through the gospel that it is a good thing, even the best thing, for us to bow our knees to Him—to the one who humbled Himself, left His throne, willingly submitted to His Father's will, and laid down His life for us. He demonstrated what true authority in action looks like. True authority sets people free. It does not enslave them or taunt them or shame them into servile submission.

If authority works as described by the Christian leader in the previous quotes and if, as his message suggests, the important issue is who is in authority, then this leader must bow to the Word of God and acknowledge that through a free woman named Sarah, God set a precedent for women to be able to assert authority over men and for men to have to obey them!

The issue, however, is not authority, nor is it which human beings are in authority over which other human beings. The issue is freedom in Christ: All believers are free to follow the Lord and choose to submit to Him and to one another so Isaac can come into being. Both men and women have been given this freedom, and neither has the right to claim to have absolute authority over another being that they wish to control.

Today's Sarah needs to tell today's Abraham to cast out the bondwoman and her son. Today's Abraham needs to listen and obey as Abraham did, acknowledging that Christian women can be used to speak for God. Instead of a mocking Ishmael, the church will become a wonderful Isaac, the house of the living God filled with believers, male and female, standing in the freedom they have because Christ has set them free. It will be the house of the living God, the pillar and base of the truth, filled with His presence and power. God will hear her prayers, and things on this earth will change.

The Bloody Husband: Zipporah Did What Moses Failed To Do

We also have a strong role model in Zipporah, Moses' wife. She is not a well known Bible character, and I would guess there have not been many sermons given about her. However, if it were not for her, Moses' calling would have come to an end in death; because, when he was traveling back to Egypt to deliver the children of Israel, God sought to kill him. It appears that Zipporah came to understand why Moses' life was in jeopardy, because she took a sharp stone, circumcised their son, and threw the foreskin at Moses' feet and called him a "bloody husband" (Exo. 4:24–25).

This strange account is very significant. Moses' uncircumcised son was evidence of Moses' disobedience. He had not kept God's requirement and circumcised his son when he was eight days old. This disobedience might not seem that serious to us, but it was serious enough to God that, rather than let Moses carry out his God-given mission while he was in a state of disobedience, He would kill Moses. Moses, it appears, was dull to the seriousness of his sin. Maybe the reason that God judged Moses in front of Zipporah was because she had played a role in his disobedience, possibly having not wanted her new baby to be hurt by circumcision. At any rate, she was the one who had to step up and do something to save Moses.

She appears to have understood the reason for God's judgment coming upon him. We can see that circumcising her son with a sharp stone was extremely difficult and distasteful for her, because she threw the foreskin at Moses' feet and told him he was a bloody husband to her.

Understanding the Significance of Circumcision

Before I can say how we can apply Zipporah's experience to our own, I need to make a little detour and discuss circumcision. Although circumcision is not a very appealing topic, we can learn something profound from what the Bible has to say about it.

According to Paul, the need for circumcision ended when Christ died on the cross. Circumcision was a very, very big thing to the Jews, so it was a hard pill for the Jews to swallow when Paul said that God no longer required it. The uncircumcised Gentile Christians were being troubled by the Jewish Christians who were promoting circumcision. Paul explained to the Gentile Christians:

> 11 Therefore remember that formerly you, the Gentiles in the flesh, who are called "Uncircumcision" by the so-called "Circumcision," [which is] performed in the flesh by human hands— 12 [remember] that you were at that time separate from Christ, excluded from the commonwealth of Israel, and strangers to the covenants of promise, having no hope and without God in the world. 13 But now in Christ Jesus you who formerly were far off have been brought near by the blood of Christ. 14 For He Himself is our peace, who made both [groups into] one and broke down the barrier of the dividing wall, 15 by abolishing in His flesh the enmity, [which is] the Law of commandments [contained] in ordinances, so that in Himself He might make the two into one new man, [thus] establishing peace, 16 and might reconcile them both in one body to God through the cross, by it

having put to death the enmity. (Eph. 2:11–16, NASB)

I have always found this passage to be a head-scratcher, in particular this part:

> who made both groups into one and broke down the barrier of the dividing wall, by abolishing in His flesh the enmity, which is the Law of commandments contained in ordinances.

What does this mean? Why did Paul equate "the enmity" with the "law of commandments contained in ordinances"? Why did he say that Christ broke down the wall between the Jews and the Gentiles by removing these things? While working on this book, for the first time, this troublesome phrase began to make sense to me in light of the fact that "the enmity" was something that began at the time of the Fall.

In the beginning, God put enmity in place between the woman and the serpent and the seed of the woman and the seed of the serpent (Gen. 3:15). This enmity is the reason for the war between the holy seed, those in the line of Seth, and the seed of the serpent, the Gentiles. Satan understood that if he could keep God's people in an unholy state, they could not subdue and conquer the earth, so he used his seed, the Gentiles, over and over again to tempt God's people into idolatry and sexual sin.

When God told Abraham that he and all his male offspring had to be circumcised, He was establishing a sign in man's flesh, his reproductive part, in order to mark or distinguish His people as different from the Gentiles. Circumcision was a sign of separation between those who belonged to God and those who belonged to the devil. It was intended to serve as a protective wall between them. Thus, the Bible refers to the Gentiles as the Uncircumcision and to God's people as the Circumcision.

Paul knew the real significance of circumcision from verses in the Old Testament (Deut. 10:16, 30:6; Jer. 4:4). In Romans, he explains this significance:

> 28 For he is not a [real] Jew who is only one outwardly *and* publicly, nor is [true] circumcision

something external and physical. 29 But he is a Jew who is one inwardly, and [true] circumcision is of the heart, a spiritual and not a literal [matter]. His praise is not from men but from God. (Rom. 2:28–29, AMPC)

So, in addition to being a sign in the flesh that separated the Jews from the Gentiles, the Bible also tells us that outward physical circumcision was a sign of man's inward problem—a heart problem due to man's fall. Out of man's fleshly, fallen heart came all kinds of wickedness. (In the days of Noah, the condition of man's heart was so bad that every thought was continually only evil [Gen. 6:5]. This was the reason that God flooded the earth and killed everyone except the few righteous people that remained—Noah and his family.)

Centuries after Abraham's time, God gave the children of Israel the Law, the Ten Commandments, through Moses. At that time, God became their husband. Moses also gave them many related ritual laws, or ordinances, that they had to keep in order to remain holy and be able to appear before God. These ordinances mainly involved making offerings for sin. No one but God's chosen people had access to Him, and their access was through keeping the law and its ordinances. Thus, these ordinances also functioned as a barrier, a dividing wall between them and the Gentiles.

Although this arrangement was a deterrent to sin, it could not solve the problem of man's wicked heart, so sin continued to abound, and God's people continued to find themselves in bondage to the devil. When Christ, the once-for-all, perfect sacrifice for sin, came and shed His sinless blood, He opened the way for all men, both Jews and Gentiles, to come to God. Both Jews and Gentiles were given access to God by faith in Christ's redemptive work.

This is why Paul wrote that Christ's death removed the protective barrier of the dividing wall. It was no longer necessary to separate the Jews and the Gentiles because Christ had won the ancient war, once and for all on Calvary. His death had paid in full the price for the sin of all mankind, including the Gentiles. His death and His resurrection destroyed the devil and broke the power of sin's hold over man. His victory on Calvary removed the enmity that was set in place by God at the time of the Fall. Through Christ's death and resurrection, God created one new man made of both Jews and Gentiles, and thus made peace on the earth.

In the new creation, which Jews and Gentiles become by faith in Christ, there is zero enmity. This is an amazing fact. The first Adam began the enmity, and the last Adam, Christ, ended it forever. (The last Adam, Christ, also showed us what God intended the first Adam to be like!)

To summarize, the Jews (God's people, seed of woman) had access to God by blood offerings; the Gentiles (the devil's people, seed of the serpent) had no access. Circumcision was the sign in the Jews' flesh of the separation that God had established. Christ's death on the cross gave Gentiles access to God and removed the barrier of the requirement of circumcision and also of the biblical ceremonial ordinances related to having access to God, both of which God had set in place. The wall's purpose had been to separate holy from unholy in order to keep out the devil and his polluting evil spirits. When Christ shed His blood, the wall of enmity was abolished and both Jews and Gentiles could become holy and have access to God by the blood of Christ.

These are glorious, irrefutable, and unchangeable facts. We see them by faith when we see Jesus by faith. Today, as believers, we do not yet see the manifestation of all that Christ accomplished on the cross, including the removal of the ancient enmity. We do not yet see with our eyes that all things have been put beneath His feet, but we do see Jesus! Following Him, we are participants by faith in the final outworking on the earth of the reality of all He accomplished on the cross, including the way of peace He opened. The time is coming when all things will visibly come under the rule of Christ in the kingdom of God (1 Cor. 15:24). His peace will fill the earth. Until that day, we remain in a war, learning to experience now by faith all that Christ has already accomplished for us. With these realizations about circumcision, let's come back to Zipporah.

Today's Circumcision and Uncircumcision

Moses was himself outwardly circumcised; but, inwardly, his heart was not circumcised. He was living in a state of disobedience as evidenced by the fact that he had not circumcised his son. He was in this condition when he responded to God's call and was on his way to deliver the children of Israel. Today, many Christian men are in similar disobedience. Like Moses, they are in the process of carrying out God-given missions in God's holy name, while at the same time they are in disobedience and have uncircumcised hearts. One such blatant disobedience is evidenced by their lording it over female believers.

Zipporah had to do something to demonstrate and correct Moses' disobedience, to save his life, and to make it possible for God to use him to deliver the children of Israel. What she did benefited all the children of Israel, because Moses lived to carry out his mission. Today's women, upon seeing the plight of Christian men, need to take steps maybe as drastic as Zipporah to help these men end a very serious disobedience that sooner or later will bring God's judgment upon them. In particular, they need to help them end their suppression of Christian women.

In light of what we have seen about circumcision, let's also take one more look at Abraham. Abraham was not circumcised when he and Hagar conceived Ishmael. However, before Abraham and Sarah conceived Isaac, God required that Abraham be circumcised. Abraham was ninety-nine years old when his old flesh was cut off. No doubt, that was a painful experience. Even after Isaac was born, Abraham still continued to love Ishmael and treat him as his heir. This shows that even though he was circumcised outwardly, his heart still was not circumcised. Sarah had to help him circumcise his heart by telling him that Ishmael had to go. When God told Abraham to obey her, he did. At this point, his heart, which naturally loved Ishmael, was circumcised. Having to cast out a son he loved, but whom God had rejected, was painful but necessary.

Those whose hearts have not been circumcised can only produce a spiritual Ishmael. A spiritual Isaac can only be produced by free beings who have circumcised hearts. God accepts what comes from His people when they do not trust in themselves and act from themselves, but trust in Him fully and receive from His hand what He has promised them by the power of His Spirit.

The Free Woman: God's Way

Today's complementarians are like Abraham in that they love and want to preserve Ishmael. They want the status quo concerning women to continue as it has for centuries. They want women to stay in a state of subservience to men. They are willing to make a few concessions, here and there, concerning things women can be allowed to do, but they will not budge on their belief about women's submission in the church. They do not realize how serious it is to God that their beloved Ishmael's mother is a bondwoman.

Today's egalitarians, on the other hand, want to change the status quo. Their focus is on Christian women having the same rights as Christian men—the same freedoms, if you will. However, they too love Ishmael. Their love is seen in the way they address the problem. Instead of casting out the bondwoman and her son, they are fighting for women's right to participate equally in today's Ishmael.

God's way is neither of these. His way is for the bondwoman and her son to be cast out so that He can freely fulfill His promise through His people that are free together in Christ. The true church is a free woman. She is made up of free men and free women. God's way is to bless by the power of the Holy Spirit and produce an Isaac—something which far surpasses anything man can do for God. Ishmael is man's creation. Isaac is God's. Ishmael cannot be "improved" by committees or councils who decide to let some women teach, or do other things, under certain conditions. These are hypocritical band-aids, not cures.

Isaac comes by the Spirit in coordination with free beings whose hearts have been circumcised. Isaac comes when God's people, male and female, repent and begin to walk in mutual love, respect, and submission one to another—when they have true oneness and harmony like the Father, Son, and Holy Spirit. Isaac comes when all God's people, both male and female, are free to follow Him. What God wants and what He accepts is Isaac. When Isaac comes, there is no need for men to drum up plans to stimulate new church membership or to find new gimmicks to spread the gospel. All their energies will be required to take care of the influx of new converts and old backsliders who will be drawn to God by the powerful work of the Holy Spirit. I suggest that many of the revivals recorded throughout Christian history are the appearance of Isaacs—movements born of the Spirit in coordination with free beings.

Free Christian Women and Goliath

Woman was instrumental in man's fall. God decreed that she would be instrumental in his restoration. Just as David slew Goliath with a single stone from a pouch of five stones, free Christian women have eight de-lemonized stones with which to slay their modern day Goliath: one from the Old Testament and seven from the New. Today's Goliath is Bible translations and understandings that misrepresent the truth concerning Christian women. Christian women must set these de-lemonized verses on the table before modern-day translators (Christian academics, professors, and clerics) and tell them that it is time for bondage-producing lemon translations to go.

Bible translators must look into the lemon passages in the context of the whole Bible. They should read existing scholarly findings and arguments from women (and men), and also study the history of womankind in Judaism and Christianity. In this way, they will uncover for themselves the subtle work of the devil in mistranslating God's words that pertain to women. Then they will be able to produce grape translations of these passages. Such translations will be the sword of truth that takes the head off of Goliath.

God will reward an honest search for the truth about woman. Ask and it shall be given. Seek and ye shall find.

Knock and it shall be opened unto you. The truth will open and show the way to transform Bible lemons into the grapes that they really are! Healing in the body of Christ will begin. Evil in the home and society at large will be thwarted by woman-uplifting, freeing, and protecting, as well as accurate, translations of the Word of God.

Such transformative truth has the potential to release women from the bondage of the devil's lies and to change them from the subdued to the subduer (of the devil)! When lemons turn to grapes, Isaiah's words can be spoken and experienced with great joy by many women:

> 1 The Spirit of the Lord GOD [is] upon me; because the LORD hath anointed me to preach good tidings unto the meek; he hath sent me to bind up the brokenhearted, to proclaim liberty to the captives, and the opening of the prison to [them that are] bound; 2 To proclaim the acceptable year of the LORD, and the day of vengeance of our God; to comfort all that mourn; 3 To appoint unto them that mourn in Zion, to give unto them beauty for ashes, the oil of joy for mourning, the garment of praise for the spirit of heaviness; that they might be called trees of righteousness, the planting of the LORD, that he might be glorified. 4 And they shall build the old wastes, they shall raise up the former desolations, and they shall repair the waste cities, the desolations of many generations. 5 And strangers shall stand and feed your flocks, and the sons of the alien [shall be] your plowmen and your vinedressers. 6 But ye shall be named the Priests of the LORD: [men] shall call you the Ministers of our God: ye shall eat the riches of the Gentiles, and in their glory shall ye boast yourselves. 7 For your shame [ye shall have] double; and [for] confusion they shall rejoice in their portion: therefore in their land they shall possess the double: everlasting joy shall be unto them. 8 For I the LORD love judgment, I hate robbery for burnt offering; and I will direct their work in truth, and I will make an everlasting

covenant with them. 9 And their seed shall be known among the Gentiles, and their offspring among the people: all that see them shall acknowledge them, that they [are] the seed [which] the LORD hath blessed.

10 I will greatly rejoice in the LORD, my soul shall be joyful in my God; for he hath clothed me with the garments of salvation, he hath covered me with the robe of righteousness, as a bridegroom decketh [himself] with ornaments, and as a bride adorneth [herself] with her jewels. 11 For as the earth bringeth forth her bud, and as the garden causeth the things that are sown in it to spring forth; so the Lord GOD will cause righteousness and praise to spring forth before all the nations. (Isa. 61:1–11, KJV)

When Christian Men Listen

Satan is terrified that Christian men will listen to Christian women. He fears that men will stand up and repent for their own sins and the sins of prior generations of Christian men against women. He knows that when men:

- Are bold and brave enough to reconcile with women by admitting that there have been centuries of unjust treatment and suppression of them in the name of God;

- Give feet to this admission by repenting to the women in their own lives, be they mothers, sisters, wives, or daughters;

- Stop blaming women and learn to sacrifice themselves on women's behalf;

- Begin to show honor (great respect) to the weaker female vessels (1 Pet. 3:7); and

- Remove Satan's carefully crafted lemons from the Bible;

Then the prayers of God's people will be wonderfully answered, and Satan's final expulsion will be eminent.

Such righteous men will appear as the standard God promised to lift up against his enemy when he came in like a flood. Surely it is time for such a standard against a flood of evil men spreading darkness and terror over all the earth.

Some might minimize the importance of discovering and declaring the truth about God's view of women by claiming that not all Christian men oppress women. My response would be that as long as there remains even one woman-suppressing Christian man, it is incumbent upon men who are not oppressors to join the conversation in hopes of persuading that one last man to repent.

Bone to His Bone

In Ezekiel 37, the Spirit asked Ezekiel, "Son of man, can these bones live?" The answer: Yes, they can. When the dry bones scattered in the valley heard the Word of the Lord, they came together, bone to his bone. After the dead, dry bones had reconnected, then the Spirit of God came into them as breath and they stood up on their feet, an exceeding great army. I always thought that the "bone to his bone" imagery in Ezekiel was analogous to bones coming back together as in a human skeleton.

Another meaning presents itself when considering Adam's comment regarding his wife, Eve: "This is bone of my bone and flesh of my flesh." This statement points to the unique bond between a man and his wife. God told Ezekiel that the bones in his vision were the children of Israel. God was their husband, so we could say He regarded them as bone of His bone. Adam's close relationship with Eve was broken at the time of the Fall. God's close relationship with the children of Israel was broken by the time of Ezekiel's vision, as evidenced by the dead, dry, and scattered bones in the valley.

To my knowledge, the prophecy in Ezekiel 37 has not yet been fulfilled. Isn't it possible that, at the close of the age, the coming together of Christian men and women through repentance to stand as one body rightly connected bone to his bone would be a fulfillment of Ezekiel 37? When these dry bones come together and are reconnected to each other, will not God's breath enter them and make them a great army, the victorious bride of Christ?

In the Old Testament, when the children of Israel heard about the sins of their fathers and were convicted, they wept and prayed and repented. They went to extreme measures to correct their sins (Ezra 9–10). It is time for Christian men and women to do likewise. When women turn back to God and stop enabling fallen men, and when men likewise repent for their proud, women-blaming ways and put on their new creation life in Christ, the result most certainly will be a fresh outpouring of the Spirit upon the body of Christ. The whole creation will be set free from the bondage of corruption into the glorious freedom of the sons of God (Rom. 8:19–23).

The Greatest Story

You might wonder why God didn't just spell out plainly the truth about the devil, man, and woman at the opening of the Bible in the Genesis account. Why only now at the close of the age does this light begin to dawn?

A really good story opens with just enough mystery about its characters and plot to capture people's attention and draw them into the quest to discover the truth of the whole story and solve its mystery. Furthermore, a really good story has life lessons that are applicable to those who hear it. The best and most engaging stories are complex ones with many twists, turns, sub-plots, and clues that are woven together along the way, ever moving a reader forward to the time that all the pieces fit perfectly together and the plot resolves. At that point, the story leaves the deposit of a life-changing message in the hearer's heart.

The Bible contains the greatest story ever told with the greatest message ever presented to mankind. It is produced and directed by the best storyteller of all time, using many human storytellers to join with Him in its development. Their segments fit together across a long period of time creating a work of perfection that shows forth the beauty and glory of the true author and finisher—not only of the story—but of everything.

Ultimately, each person must hear and be persuaded in his or her own mind to do the right thing with the Bible's message. The right thing is to believe it, to say so, and to inherit the eternal blessing that faith brings. It makes sense that the opening of the Bible only sets the stage and gives some small clues that will become keys as the story unfolds. God is both the beginning and the ending of this greatest story ever told. Its climatic and pivotal point came in the birth, life, death, resurrection, and enthronement of Jesus Christ. The rest of the story is what is still playing out today.

The Final Act

We are in the time of the final act, the grand finale. All the characters have been fully developed and an expanded, worldwide stage has been set. There is a universal audience. The devil and his minions are sitting in the front row of the theater. They are eating bags of popcorn, laughing, and applauding themselves for the tremendous mess they have succeeded in creating on earth's stage.

The curtain opens, and some small, seemingly insignificant, female heroines appear. These women are holding baskets filled with grapes from God's vineyard. They are armed with the Word of God; and, in particular, they are carrying eight smooth yellow stones. A throng of valiant men also appears on the stage. They are holding de-lemonized Bibles high in the air and proclaiming, "The victory is won. The accuser of our brethren is cast down which accused them before our God day and night. And they overcame him by the blood of the Lamb and by the word of their testimony, and they loved not their soul lives unto the death."

With hands halfway to their mouths, the front row spectators are suddenly frozen with fear. Their evil eyes are glued on the large throng of *free,* godly women and men standing on the stage before them—all singing a victory song and twirling on their feet with great joy like a victorious, dancing army. They are clothed with breastplates of righteousness, belts of truth, gospel shoes, and helmets of salvation. In that instant, the front row creeps realize that their lemon-fueled stealth weapon, which they have successfully used against women and men for two millennia, has been rendered useless.

Their final doom appears to be imminent. In unison, they drop their popcorn boxes, jump from their seats, knock over their sodas, and frantically begin to look for the exits. Something has gone terribly wrong. This looks all too familiar. They have a flashback of God turning the tables on them when Christ walked out of the grave two thousand years before. Before they can escape, the yellow stones and the de-lemonized Bibles have hit them solidly in their foreheads. Down to the ground they and their evil leader fall, like Goliath at the feet of God's little David.

I don't know about you, but I want to be among those female heroines in this final act. I want to see the men in my life among those male heroes who are holding high de-lemonized Bibles.

While thinking about the transformative effect on people that can come from turning lemons into grapes, I drew a little sketch. It surprised me that I could reduce the whole message of this book to a simple, childlike picture which shows: When lemons become grapes, then caterpillars can become butterflies, and frogs can become princes.

When

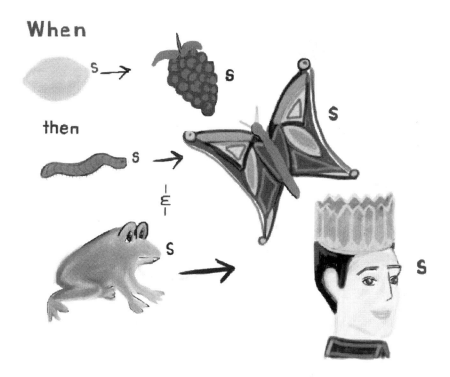

then

This picture fits this book because it is primarily written to help women become butterflies so they can help their frogs become princes. However, it occurs to me that I should draw another sketch that illustrates something else that is true: When lemons become grapes, then frogs can become princes, and caterpillars can become butterflies. In other words, a Christian man who learns the truth about woman from de-lemonized Bible passages, or from his butterfly mother, and practices it, will become a prince. He then can help any caterpillars or cocooned Christian women in his life become butterflies! One example of this comes to mind: Dave Meyer, husband of the well-known female Bible teacher, Joyce Meyer, was a prince when he met caterpillar Joyce. He told Joyce that before he met her (paraphrased from my memory) that he had asked the Lord to give him a wife who needed help so he could help her! Now that is the prayer of a prince! His prayer was answered; and, today, Joyce is a beautiful butterfly—a woman of *chayil!*

The victorious throng on earth's stage at the end of time is God's glorious butterfly. She is a woman of *chayil,* who is made up of both men and women. Earth's story closes with this awesome, beautiful, exceedingly-capable, powerful, and victorious, yet humble, woman who has been freed from earth's cocoon and exalted to reign with her King in His beautiful, holy, and righteous kingdom. She is the bride of Christ, the Lamb's wife (Rev. 21). The Bible has a very, very, very happy ending. At the climax of this greatest story ever told, the rest of the heavenly audience will resound with wave after wave of joyful praise, giving blessing and honor and glory to Him who sits on the throne and to the Lamb.

An Open Letter to Bible Publishers and Translators

In the near future, I, along with some others, will be writing an open letter to Bible publishers and translators. We will post that letter on our website. Our open letter will make a strong appeal for de-lemonization of the lemon verses.

We are adding our voice to the voice of others who are crying in the wilderness concerning the truth about women. We believe that God will bless every attempt to further the conversation about women and Bible translations. If you are persuaded that translations must be revisited and corrected, I encourage you to write and send your own letter. If you like, you may use parts of our letter. Or, you may duplicate and send our entire letter with the signatures of concerned people you know who wish to participate in this appeal (see www.TheThreadOfGold.com).

Chapter 12
The Beautiful Butterfly: God's Beloved Song of Songs Woman

I am my beloved's and my beloved is mine ...
(Song 6:3, KJV)

THERE IS A BEAUTIFUL PICTURE that is hidden prominently in the middle of the Bible in a very small book: the Song of Solomon, also known as the Song of Songs. The woman in the Song of Songs is a beautiful creation of God's making, who by the end of the book emerges like a butterfly out of a cocoon. She has become fully His, and He has become fully hers. She is a beloved, betrothed, and blessed woman!

In this wonderful book of the Bible, the Spirit of God uses inspired poetic writing to capture the symbolic story of love between Solomon and a woman. It is commonly accepted that Solomon symbolizes Christ. Some say that the woman symbolizes the church. Some say she symbolizes an individual believer. I believe there is merit to both of these symbolic interpretations of the woman. However, I also believe there is a third thing that the woman in Song of Songs symbolizes: all godly women throughout time.

In my book, *The Song of Songs Woman: A Dance of Two Armies,* I show how this small book of the Bible symbolizes the interactions between God and godly women, individually, collectively, and historically, from the time in the Garden of Eden to the second coming of Christ. The beautiful butterfly that emerges at the end of the story portrays woman in a way that redefines our traditionally held views of womankind, and it does so for the better. This woman matches the character, capability, and beauty of the woman that emerges at the end of the Bible, the bride of Christ.

From beginning to end, the story paints a picture of the pathway that believers travel to become God's woman of *chayil*. It also exemplifies the truth that all (and women in particular) who live godly in Christ Jesus will suffer persecution (2 Tim. 3:12); and, that all those who suffer such tribulation will, after a little while, be perfected, established, settled, strengthened, and ultimately presented to Jesus by God the Father as His spotless, holy, and victorious bride (2 Pet. 5:10).

The simple fact of the existence in the Bible of the book, Song of Songs, is testimony to the tender, kind, and loving heart of God toward all His seeking believers and toward women in particular. Its content reveals, in particular, His keen awareness of what women have suffered at the hands of God's enemy because of his hatred for them, and it shows God's faithfulness to bring them from oppression and bondage to a place of freedom, peace, victory, joy, prosperity, effectiveness, and, most of all, blessing to others.

A Glimpse of God's Ways

While I was writing *The Song of Songs Woman*, God showed me a refreshing, exciting, revelatory, and powerful picture of the destiny of both males and females who have received Christ Jesus as their Lord and Savior. He also showed me something wonderful about His ways, which the Bible tells us are not our ways. God knew that Satan would use the men that women loved—fathers, sons, and husbands—to afflict them. He told Eve what she would face when she turned away from Him to Adam, and He warned her that she would have multiplied sorrow and sighing as she bore male children. He also warned her that her husband would rule over her. He knew, when He promised that her seed would crush the serpent, and when He placed hatred between the devil and her, that she and all godly women after her would suffer because of that hatred.

Women have, indeed, experienced the suffering that God spoke about in the Garden of Eden. He could have saved them from centuries of being oppressed by the seed of the serpent, but He didn't. He could have saved Adam and Eve from the Fall, Abel from being murdered by Cain, Israel from rejecting God, and Christ from dying on the cross, but He didn't. He also could have saved you and me from the difficult paths we have traveled down in our own lives. He could have saved us from those who stole our inheritance and from those who would not help us find Christ, when that was their job. He could have saved us from those who "beat" us when we were seeking truth. He could have saved us from all such difficult experiences, but He didn't.

The simple fact is that God's ways are not our ways. Nevertheless, His ways are wonderful. Christ, who is the Way, showed us God's way on the cross. Although the way of the cross looks foolish to the world, it is the wisdom of God. Through it, He shows us that life comes out of death; light comes out of darkness; peace comes out of pain; victory comes out of defeat; joy comes out of sorrow. As one line of a hymn says, "After long agony, rapture of bliss, right was the pathway leading to this" (Frances Havergal). "This" refers to knowing Him intimately, loving Him, and letting Him make His home in the gardens of our hearts. This is what human life is really about. As we come to see the wonder of who He is, we will find Him using us to help others see the same.

Just as Solomon's love for the Song of Songs woman didn't fail, God's love for us will never fail; and, just as the Song of Songs woman came to a point in her journey where the sky cleared and all the inward and outward attacks ended, so will we. Just as she became a woman of *chayil* made ready for her bridegroom, so will we.

And one day, after all of our trials are over, we will see that all we have passed through has made us into women whose price is *far above rubies!* We will dance around our enemies like two victorious armies (Song 6:13). We will hear Him say as Solomon did:

Many daughters have done well [*chayil,* adverb],
but You excel them all. (Pro. 31:29, NKJV)

We know by faith that Satan has already been dealt the crushing blow on the cross by Christ, the male seed of woman; yet, as the Bible teaches and our experience shows, Christ is still waiting for all of His enemies to be made a footstool for his feet (Heb. 2:8–9). The birth of the conquering man child (literally male-child) of Revelation

12 has not yet happened. After that birth, Satan will be cast out of the heavens and Christ will come the second time to set up His kingdom on earth (Bushnell, paras. 810–828).

As Christians, we are in the time of birth pangs, along with the whole creation, which is groaning and travailing, waiting for the manifestation of the sons of God. We are part of the woman represented by the sign in Revelation 12, spiritually laboring to bring forth what is possibly the last and biggest wave of godly men on this earth (the man child), who will finish the job of making God's enemies a footstool for the feet of Christ. We have this joy set before us!

Out of My Cocoon

While sitting at His feet writing this and other books, God has surprised me with the answer to some of my lifelong questions. Why did God let me:

- Have a cold, mean, verbally, and sometimes physically abusive father?

- Marry a man who was un-fathered and didn't know how to be a husband or a father?

- Have two sons who beat my female soul as they modeled the behavior they saw in their father?

- Follow, respect, learn from, serve, and submit to male Christian leaders who one day turned on me and beat me to a pulp, spiritually speaking?

I have known women who have kind, loving, God-honoring fathers, husbands, and sons, and were taught by faithful, humble Christian leaders. I have silently wondered why God withheld these things from me. Was I such a difficult case that God needed to give me intense, circumstantial discipline and psychological hardship to get through to me? Was I being punished? Also, why had He put me through many difficult life circumstances and taught me to practice Christ's words in Matthew 5:22-25 and Matthew 18:15–17. Why had He even required me to apply the instruction in these verses to situations of unresolved relationship problems that were in my distant past?

Considering the great, tender, and patient love of God for womankind that came into my view while writing about women in the Bible, I heard the Lord in my heart saying in essence, "There have been no accidents in your life, Jane Carole Anderson; I allowed all of the hard situations in your life that left you shut inside an ugly cocoon. It was because I had a purpose for you, and there were things that I needed you to see and understand— things that you could not have seen or understood without choosing to follow Me through these difficult experiences. You may have looked like an ugly worm to yourself and to others, but I saw you as a butterfly."

I knew instantly that this was true. Jesus had been with me every step of the way as I learned to invite Him into the circumstance at hand and let Him do His work both in me and in it. I would not know Him as I do today without all these difficulties. My cocoon is where the person that I am today was formed. My cocoon time has helped transform this little worm into one of God's little butterflies. It made me into someone who cares about women who are oppressed by the seed of the serpent; someone who wants to help oppressed women find the freedom they have in Jesus and discover the purpose to which He has called them; someone who also cares about men, in particular, those who oppress women in the name of God; someone who prays for such men to become the godly men Christ made them in His new creation; and someone who prays for God's kingdom to come on earth as it is in heaven. It has made me into a woman warrior—a woman of *chayil*.

God's Woman of Chayil Out of Her Cocoon

God's woman of *chayil*, the bride of Christ, is described in her full battle attire in Ephesians chapter six. There can be no question that she is a warrior. (The previous chapters of Ephesians describe how she became one who is right in her relationship with God and her relationships with others.) This is her description:

- *She wears a breastplate of righteousness:* She has put it on by choice. All of her life is right with God.

- *She has her loins girdled with truth:* She knows the truth of God's Word and walks in it. She loves truth and pursues it in all matters so that the enemy cannot deceive her or others.

- *She has her feet shod with the preparation of the gospel of peace:* She understands and proclaims the truth that the ancient enmity between woman and the serpent ended on the cross of Christ. She declares that the first truly godly man, Christ, the seed of woman, who had no sin whatsoever, was God manifest in the flesh. She proclaims that Jesus was the firstborn (Heb. 1:6) of many such sons of God and that sinners now have access to God. She invites them to take the free gift of His salvation and become sons of the living God.

- *She has taken up the shield of faith:* She holds it strongly before her. With it, she puts out every flaming thought-dart from God's enemy. She stands without fear before God, shielded by her faith in Christ.

- *She has upon her head the helmet of salvation:* She has been transformed by the renewing of her mind, and her thoughts are set on things above where Christ is seated at the right hand of His Father.

- *She has taken up the sword of the Spirit, which is the Word of God:* With it, she wins every battle, small or great. She puts to flight armies of evil spirits by allowing the Spirit of God to speak through her.

- *She is standing:* Having done all, she will stand, ready for the coming of her bridegroom and king and for His kingdom to be on earth as it is in heaven.

And the greatest wonder about this woman warrior is that she is a volunteer soldier, not a conscript! She wanted to be in God's army. She wanted to be clothed in white. Just like the butterfly fights its way to full freedom, she has fought her way by faith out of earth's dark cocoon. Her face is radiant, reflecting Him. She is a glorious sight to behold!

A Foretaste of the Spirit's Healing

While writing this last chapter, I remembered a very unusual experience that I had in 2006. When I mentioned this memory to my husband, he said, "That story belongs in your book." I instantly knew he was right. It was a fitting testimony for the end of this book. This 2006 experience involved some Christian men who, moved by the Holy Spirit, wept in my presence after I obeyed God in a way similar to Zipporah and Sarah. Interestingly, this experience happened *before* God introduced me to Katharine Bushnell's book. In 2008, I wrote about this unusual experience on an Internet discussion forum, and that post is still there today.

One Day with Four Weeping Christian Men

In January 2006, about three months after we published *The Thread of Gold,* I had a very, very unusual and unforgettable experience with the Lord. It gave me a very personal and real look at God's heart of love for us. One day, I was at home with no travel plans in mind, and three or four days later I was in Anaheim, California, on a whirlwind visit of four days. I felt like I had been picked up by the Spirit and transported there. I won't share how this came about, but it had the handiwork of God stamped all over it, as did the whole trip. My thirty-three year old son, Matt, was with me. From the time our feet touched the ground in California until the time we departed, we were carried by the Spirit from one heaven-made appointment to the next. The Lord set the agenda as the days unfolded, and we hardly had time to eat, sleep, or change clothes.

My unusual experience took place on two days of that trip. It involved four different Christian men at four different times.

The First Christian Man

I had met the first Christian man and his wife thirty-five years before when my husband and I and our three-month-old son stayed in their home during a church conference. I had not spoken with him since that time. After he read *The Thread of Gold,* he called my husband and me and made us promise we would call him if we were ever going to be in Anaheim. Matt and I met him and two others in a restaurant on a Sunday morning. During our fellowship, the Lord was so awesomely present that even the waitress and people nearby were listening to our conversation.

Afterwards, Matt and I went with this Christian man to a very dry, dull, and dead Christian meeting. After that meeting, he stopped me and said, "Jane, before you get away, I have to say something." Tears welled up in his eyes and started to run down his face, "What happened at that restaurant was ... *incredible!"* I said, "Yes, it was!" We both knew the Lord had been there. (And, we also both knew that the meeting we had just suffered through had the Lord nowhere in sight.) He continued to shake his head tearfully. He said a little more, the essence of which was that the experience in the restaurant had been a reminder of what it was like to have the Lord present in fellowship. It had moved him to tears.

He wanted me to try and tell another man (a leader among them) what had happened at the restaurant, so he called him over to where we were sitting. I said a few things but soon realized this leader had no interest. He was clearly pre-occupied with his own religious things and service to God and hurried away. The tearful man wanted this leader to know that he had just been with Jesus in a way reminiscent of their past together, but the leader simply had no ears to hear.

The Second Christian Man

After lunch that day, another Christian man came and introduced himself to me. He was a well-known former leader from another city that I had heard speak at conferences but had never met. He said a few things to me, left, returned, said a few more things, left, returned, and said more things. Each time he returned, he was becoming more emotional. By the third time, we were both standing there crying. (Remember, we had never met before!)

He told me that someone had given him and his wife a copy of *The Thread of Gold* and he had been trying to read it, but it was very hard for him. By the third return, he had managed to tell me that he had been hurt by all the very bold and strong women in his life. He thought that the fact that I had written a book meant I was probably just another such woman. This was the reason he was having a hard time reading it. He explained how much it had helped him to see how I had behaved in the meeting that morning. He had been sitting behind us and seen how my son had to pull me up out of my chair to get me to respond to an invitation for visitors to stand. That had taken away his thought about me being too bold and strong. As he was explaining all this, he began to cry. I did also. The Lord's presence was very strong as we stood there talking and crying. I still have that picture in my mind as clearly as if it happened yesterday, and I recall the wonderful sense of wholeness, cleanness, and comfort I felt. I had never experienced anything like that before. Again, this was with someone I had never met before.

Here was a man, a Christian man, who had been deeply wounded by women during his lifetime (both by his relatives and other Christian women), standing before me, a Christian woman, who had been deeply wounded by men in my life (both by my relatives and other Christian men). We were crying together about this, and the Spirit was palpably there, crying with us. In those few moments, I had the thought that we were being given a foretaste of the powerful work of the Spirit to heal every wound and to wash away every hurt, and even to remove the memories of all the harm people had inflicted on one another. It was like a miniature of the whole body of Christ, with men and women being washed and made whole and restored to one another by the Spirit. I just don't have the words for it, but I knew the Lord was showing me something of His work to come. Remember, I had this experience *before* God used Katharine Bushnell's book to set the woman-topic in front of me.

The Third Christian Man

After this, my son and I went to the home of a Christian man and his wife who had invited us to come for a visit with them. I had never met either of them before but had only heard of the man by name in the past. They had received a copy of *The Thread of Gold* and had read it. We had some small talk, mostly with us asking them questions about themselves. Then, the man turned the conversation to us. He said he had something he wanted to say. He opened his mouth to speak and couldn't. He looked at me and, much to my surprise, he burst into tears. His whole body shook as he wept. I was stunned, as was Matt. He wept a minute or so; then he finally spoke. "Sister, what they did to you! I want to tell you how very sorry I am!" He proceeded to vocalize his sorrow for my experience and continued to weep. He was not just crying, he was sobbing and weeping and shaking. I didn't know what to say or how to respond. I had never seen a man cry like this. I tried to comfort him, saying, "It's okay. I am okay. I am thankful for everything." He said, "No, I need to say it. It was terrible. I am so very, very sorry!" He shed more tears.

Afterwards, as I reflected on what had happened, the Lord showed me that He was using this very caring and tenderhearted Christian man to show me His own heart. This is how God feels about Christian women who are abused by Christian men. I will never, ever, ever forget that experience.

The Fourth Christian Man

The next day, Matt and I were invited to another Christian man's home. I had never met him before. He had contacted me via email after reading *The Thread of Gold*. As we sat in his living room and talked a little, all of a sudden, he stopped talking and began to weep just as the third man had done. He said something like, "What the brothers (referring to church leadership) have done to so many ... what they did to me ... they just don't know. The Lord's heart is so grieved and breaking." Matt and I began to cry with him. We prayed together for our Father to forgive those who had hurt others and to heal us all.

A Glimpse of God's Heart

I saw something about the heart of God through all these experiences:

- Like the first man, God is grieving for what we have lost that is rightfully ours: His prevailing and powerful presence among us.

- Like the second man, God wants to, and will, wash, heal, and restore us one to another, both male and female, as we communicate and confess our faults one to another.

- Like the third man, God is in agony of heart for all those who have been wounded and abused. He loves them deeply and has hurt with them. Even though they couldn't see it at the time, He was afflicted with them.

- Like the fourth man, God is full of sorrow over those of His children who have done such damage to their own Christian brothers and sisters.

The impression made on me during that trip by those godly Christian men who let me see the Lord in the deep feelings of their hearts has remained. Through them, I had a glimpse into the very heart of love of our longsuffering God. God has great sorrow over His wounded people. In the Bible, through Jeremiah, God let us see His tears for His people. At the same time, through Jeremiah, He also spoke very hard words to them, because He always rebukes and chastens those whom He loves when they are in error. His correction is motivated by His love. Its purpose is to show us mercy. Words of warning in the Bible that expose our idolatrous hearts should bring us to our knees with tears of repentance.

A Fifth Weeping Christian Man

On the day in 2008 that I wrote the post about the four weeping Christian men, I kept thinking that there had been five. I just couldn't remember the fifth one. I went ahead and posted my story about the four weeping men on the Internet. Then, about an hour later, I received a phone call from an older Christian man who many years before had been in the same church that I wrote about in *The Thread of Gold*. He had been out of that church for many years. I had my first conversation with him when he contacted me by phone after reading *The Thread of Gold*. He did not have an Internet connection and spent much of his time praying. He had no knowledge of my post.

When he called that day in 2008, he requested that I stand with him in prayer for a particular church leader whom we both knew. He had no idea that just before his phone call came, I had read an Internet post about this very church leader—one who had exercised unjust church discipline over me in 1977. The caller, of course, did not know about the post I had just read. He told me that this leader had been particularly on his heart that day. He began to pray for him over the phone. His prayer was very heartfelt and moving. As he prayed, he began to cry. I started crying, too. He stopped and asked me to pardon him. He said he couldn't help crying because he was having such intense feeling about this.

He also told me about a dream he had some months before that had caused him to begin praying for this leader and other such leaders. He said that the Lord had shown him that these leaders had been caught up in idolatry and had committed spiritual fornication. Yet, God still loved them intensely.

As he shared, I sat there thinking over and over, "How could this be happening?" On a day I decide to write about my experience with five weeping Christian men and I come up one man short, the Lord sends a fifth weeping Christian man via the phone. Through this last-minute appearance, God reminded me that He does not sleep. He is very much present and involved in all we do, even posting on an Internet forum. God used this fifth man's tearful prayer to show me that He always has some watchman on the walls who are interceding for all His children--especially for those who have become bound by sin.

Insights from Hindsight

The following sentences which I wrote about my experience with the second weeping man in my original Internet post stand out to me now:

> I felt like we were being given a foretaste of the powerful work of the Spirit to heal every wound and to wash away every hurt and even to remove the memories of all the harm people had inflicted on one another. It was like a miniature of the whole body of Christ with men and women being washed and made whole and restored to one another by the Spirit. I just don't have the words for it, but I knew the Lord was showing me something of His work to come.

It is astounding to me that I had this experience that spoke to me about the Spirit bringing healing between men and women a year or more before God put Katharine Bushnell's book in my hands. It is also amazing to me that, while praying about how to end this book, God surfaced this ten-year old, tucked-away memory for me to use, hopefully, for the benefit of many others.

My experiences with these five Christian men, men who were weeping over particular situations, were to me, when taken as a whole, like a small-scale, spiritual foretaste of what will come in the body of Christ when women and men get into right relationship with one another through genuine repentance. It was a taste of what can happen when women break silence and speak the truth in love. (Truth had come to them when they read of my church experiences in *The Thread of Gold.*)

I took my timely remembrance of this experience as a confirmation that God was indeed behind the writing of *A Woman of Chayil,* and its message was of Him. Repentance, reconnection, and healing by God's Spirit, like that which occurred with these five men, is what is needed today on a large scale between Christian men and women in the body of Christ.

In 1977, when I was judged unrighteously and, spiritually speaking, was thrown into a pit, God brought this verse to mind, "As a sheep before its shearers is dumb, so he opened not his mouth." At the time, I understood that to mean that I should not try to defend myself. He could have given me Luke 17:3, "If your brother sins, rebuke him," but He didn't. If He had, I would not have been able to accept that as being from God because I believed, as Christian men and the King James Bible had taught me, that it would be sin for me to challenge or try to correct men, no matter how egregious their behavior was. I now can see God's wisdom in telling me to suffer that mistreatment in silence. He allowed that suffering for His purposes. His ways are not our ways, and His thoughts are not our thoughts. At that time, through the words of an old hymn, "... the tangled skein will shine at last, a masterpiece of skill untold," He promised me that one day in the future He would make sense for me of all that had happened.

It was in 2005, almost twenty-eight years after that unrighteous judgment, before I finally finished doing what the Bible makes plain I should have done in 1977 (Matt. 18:15–17). These Christian men had hurt me; but, I had also hurt them by my silence, because it enabled their bad behavior. Repentance and obedience began my journey out of that darkness. The first step out was in 1990 and 1991, when my husband and I wrote letters to the leader who was responsible for what happened to us in 1977. We involved a few others who could help us try to communicate with him. That effort failed. Then in 2005, with the publication of *The Thread of Gold*, we, in effect, told the church. We had practiced the Matthew 18 directive, but only in hindsight do we now see this clearly. Also, I now realize this: When I wrote *The Thread of Gold*, as a woman who had been sinned against by Christian men, I was actually doing what I have advocated in this book, *A Woman of Chayil*.

The Thread of Gold was my final step of obedience in my repentance for having silently, in ignorance, enabled these Christian leaders' sin against me. Blessing followed the publication of that book in many ways; but, the unique experiences that God gave me with the weeping men three months after the book was published served to capture and encapsulate a taste of that blessed time for future discovery. Revisiting it now, I can see that any blessing on *The Thread of Gold* was due to the repentance in my life that was behind it, because repentance is God's secret weapon against His enemy.

I still marvel at the large number of Christian men, including some leaders, who contacted me after reading *The Thread of Gold.* They thanked me for having the courage as a woman to write my story, and they told me how much it helped them. A good number expressed their sorrow for what had taken place. One of them, a leader in the offending church organization, told me that my testimony had helped him return to a personal walk with Jesus—something that he had lost in the authoritarian church environment of which he was still a part. I had assumed that *The Thread of Gold* would mainly help other Christian women who had experienced similar mistreatment. It still astounds me that what I wrote impacted Christian men as it did. I have no doubt this was the work of the Holy Spirit.

A distinctive aspect of my experience with the weeping Christian men is that the fourth and fifth men *were weeping for other men.* The fourth man was weeping for other men he knew in this particular situation who had been hurt by authoritarian church leaders as he had been. The fifth man was weeping for those very offending church leaders. I hope that I will live to see the day when Christian men on a broad scale in the body of Christ are so convicted and repentant for their misuse of authority that they will weep for other men, will pray for them, and will help them repent.

Lastly, a few more things now stand out to me about the experience with the third Christian man. He is the one that had been deeply hurt by strong Christian women in his life. In *A Woman of Chayil,* I have mainly described as enablers those Christian women who mean well and are truly trying to help. I believe that such women are in the majority; however, as this man's words showed, there are some Christian women who, though they may be in the minority, enable men and damage them in more patently self-centered ways.

Some of these enabling Christian women may push, control, or dominate their husbands, saying they are only trying to help them, when the truth is they are getting their husbands to do what pleases them. Others, with the outward appearance of being good and helpful wives, use their husbands for their own ends. They benefit by supporting and encouraging behavior in their husbands that is offensive to God. For example, a wife may promote her husband's greed, social position, or prestige for her own sake, making him more prideful and offensive to God. Jezebel was such a woman. There are other Christian women who, by being what they consider to be good, faithful, and helpful wives, remain happily married to unbelievers. They depend on their husbands to meet their needs and never share the gospel with them, not wanting to risk disrupting their marriage relationship and negatively impacting their way of living. I think that these kinds of female enablers hurt men in worse ways than well-meaning enablers do. Regardless of the kind of enabler, all need to repent of their enabling ways.

There are also some Christian men who enable their wives in all the aforementioned ways. A Christian man may support his wife's sins in the name of loving and protecting her. However, if he shields her from correction when she sins rather than helping her repent, he is part of the problem. He is a male enabler. If he claims this is his Christian duty as a husband, he is deceived. Men enablers also need to repent. Enabling comes in many shapes and sizes, but it always hurts people and does not help them find God.

No, There Were Six

Beginning in 2006, after the publication of *The Thread of Gold*, every autumn except for one, I have held a four-day women's retreat. On the last morning of the 2016 retreat, we read together the account of the five weeping men. When we finished, one of the women said, "Jane, there is another weeping man you forgot. Remember the weeping leader in your book, *The Thread of Gold?* He was actually the first man to weep."

This Christian leader she was referring to had begun weeping while I was talking to three church leaders, of whom he was one. A few others were present to witness this. While I was speaking, this leader had unexpectedly leaned forward, put his head in his hands, and begun to weep. He hadn't shed just a few tears—he had sobbed. We all had become very quiet and waited, not knowing what to think. I had just said that I felt that we had lost the blessing we had been experiencing for a number of years prior to this time. I had mentioned some ongoing "sin in the camp" of which I was aware and had suggested that possibly this, or some other sin, was the reason. While weeping, this leader said something to the effect that he felt that he was the one responsible for the lack of blessing among us. He ended our time together saying that he and the other two leaders would get back with us regarding the things we had talked about; however, they never did.

Instead, a regional leader, who learned about this leader's emotional breakdown, took steps to see that he was relocated and basically demoted. Apparently, the regional leader and the other leaders present in our meeting did not talk to him about why he had wept or why he had suspected that he was the problem. Sometime later, the relocated leader was discovered to have been committing ongoing sexual sin. At that time, his fellow leaders simply whisked him away and concealed his sin instead of exposing it as the Bible mandates (1 Tim. 5:19–20). Later, his seduction of another leader's wife resulted in two families breaking up. That sin spread like leprosy, eventually causing a long-term split between fellow believers over whether or not he had ever repented for stealing his brother's wife.

So, this scenario was actually my first experience of the Spirit strongly convicting a sinning man when I, for the first time, ended my enabling silence. Another thing stands out about this experience: The other leaders should have wept with him and for him, and should have helped him as the Bible requires. They chose instead to conceal his sin and protect the outward appearance of their organization and the ministry they supported.

In earlier chapters, I charged Christian women to stand up fearlessly and speak the truth in love to a broader audience. When I made such a charge, I had no thought that this was what I had done when I wrote *The Thread of Gold*. God surprised me with this understanding as I wrote this chapter. I hope that my experience with six weeping Christian men will encourage Christian women to overcome their fears and obey God with respect to sinning Christian men in their lives. The Spirit will begin to work! He will convict such men and bring about repentance and blessing.

Without Fear

Right before we published *The Thread of Gold*, I almost gave in to fear. After spending over a year to write that book—when it was time to take the final step and publish it—fear came knocking with a vengeance in the form of a middle-of-the-night panic attack. I woke up with an overwhelming feeling of dread and terror at the thought of putting myself in the line of fire once more before the same Christian men who had so deeply wounded me years before. These men, by that time, had advanced to top leadership positions in the Christian organization whose practices were exposed by my book. This organization had become very litigious over the years. They had sued, or threatened to sue, people who wrote unfavorable things about them. I was panicked by the thought that they might sue me and take me to court! They might damage the final years of my life even more than they had damaged the early ones!

That night, I decided that I could *not* go forward with the book. I said, "I'm sorry, Lord, but I can't! I have finally recovered from what they did those many years ago. I don't want to give them opportunity to hurt me again! I can't go through that or put my family through that!" Afterwards, as I lay there awake in the dark feeling sad and discouraged, part of a verse slipped into my mind, "No weapon formed against you shall prosper ..." What? Where was that verse? I turned on the laptop which was beside my bed, opened my brand new electronic Bible software, and searched for it. I read Isaiah 54:17 in its entirety:

> No weapon formed against you shall prosper,
> And every tongue [which] rises against you in
> judgment
> You shall condemn.

This [is] the heritage of the servants of the LORD,
And their righteousness [is] from Me,"
Says the Lord. (Isa. 54:17, NKJV)

My eyes fell on a commentary that was open in a window just to the right of the Bible verse. It said that the words, "every tongue which rises against you in judgment," in Isaiah 54:17 refer to someone rising up against someone else in a court of law. What? I read the comment again. I was dumbfounded. This simply could not be coincidence. I said, "How do You do this, Lord? Here I am, terrified of being taken to court in a lawsuit, and You whisper to me through a Bible verse and a commentary that all who might rise up against me *in a court of law,* I will condemn! ... Alright, Lord ... I believe You, and ... I will go forward." At that moment, I was filled with incredible peace. We did go forward, and I never again experienced even a moment of fear regarding the publication of *The Thread of Gold.*

When we decide to obey Jesus, He will meet every need and empower us to do whatever He asks of us. He will also give us peace that passes understanding.

The Wisdom and Knowledge of God

I did not write the book, *A Woman of Chayil,* seeking some kind of restitution for all that women have suffered. Nor did I write it with the hope of extracting some kind of cowed admission and repentance from men who have hurt women.

I wrote it to help both men and women alike turn their eyes upon Jesus and see Him as He really is: See Him on the cross, dying to save us and set us free from sin and death; see Him resurrected in the garden, testifying that God's love for us is stronger than death; see Him interceding for us on the throne, praying that God's will be done in our lives; see Him patiently coming to us by His Spirit, again and again, seeking to draw us back to Himself.

I wrote it with the hope that the Spirit might use it to reprove men and women alike of sin and righteousness and judgment (John 16:8), especially with respect to their relationships with each other in the body of Christ. Repentance by both men and women will open the way for a fresh outpouring of the Spirit on earth. God will work among people in power until His kingdom comes in fullness, and the knowledge of Him covers the earth as the waters cover the sea (Hab. 2:14).

In eternity's brilliant light—where all things will be finished, where everything will be manifest and seen as it really is, where there will be no darkness at all—we will rejoice forever in Him! If I sound a bit too joyful this side of that glorious day, how can I be otherwise? Faithful is He who began a good work in us that He will surely finish! In that day, we will utter these words with full understanding and with exceedingly great joy:

> 33 Oh, the depth of the riches both of the wisdom and knowledge of God! How unsearchable are His judgments and unfathomable His ways! 34 FOR WHO HAS KNOWN THE MIND OF THE LORD, OR WHO BECAME HIS COUNSELOR? 35 OR WHO HAS FIRST GIVEN TO HIM THAT IT MIGHT BE PAID BACK TO HIM AGAIN? 36 For from Him and through Him and to Him are all things. To Him [be] the glory forever. Amen. (Rom. 11:33–36, NASB)

Appendix A—An Open Letter to Bible Publishers

We intend, in the near future, to post a copy of an open letter to Bible publishers and translators on our website: www.TheThreadOfGold.com.

Appendix B— More About Katharine Bushnell

A sixteen-page autobiography of a 19th century woman of *chayil* entitled, "Dr. Katharine C. Bushnell, A Brief Sketch of Her Life and Work," is available at http://godswordtowomen.org/bushnell_brief_sketch.pdf. The following is a short biographical sketch of Bushnell found in Susan Hyatt's book:

> After a time as a Methodist Episcopal medical missionary in China, she had a medical practice in Denver. Then in 1885, Francis Willard persuaded Dr. Bushnell to become the National Evangelist of the WCTU's Department for the Advancement of Social Purity. This meant giving up her medical practice, but she "had not studied medicine for its own sake, but as a help in Christian work." She sensed God calling her to this important new work, and from that time forward, she worked relentlessly for women. One of her first efforts involved risking her life exposing the "white slave trade" of prostitutes and the horrific abuse of girls and women in the lumber camps of Michigan and Wisconsin. Her crusades against this cruelty to and degradation of women extended around the world to England, India, China, Hong Kong, and San Francisco.

As Hardwick points out in her recent biography of Bushnell, her final crusade came through the power of the pen. While a doctor in China, she had begun to see how culturally-biased translations of the Bible intensified female bondage. Because she knew that the true gospel heals and liberates, she devoted the last forty years of her life in diligent language study, biblical translation, and writing. Among her voluminous writings is the treasure chest for women's Bible study, *God's Word to Women.*

Hardwick notes that Bushnell "saw the task of educated women as twofold." She believed, "They must spread to all women in all places the full gospel message of the same freedom and equality as men have in Christ Jesus." And she believed, "Educated women must attack the 'false teachings as to the place of women in God's economy' and break ... the 'tyranny'" of biased, erroneous biblical translation and commentaries." [footnote numbers have been omitted]

Katharine Bushnell, by passing on the truth she learned about woman in the Bible, has unwound the grave clothes of many women and men and set them free. Her book, rediscovered years after it went out of print, shows that in God's new creation (which came into being through Christ's death and resurrection), Christian women are seen by God in the same way that He sees Christian men. Women are under direct submission to the Lord Jesus, just as Christian men are. Women are not in a different class of persons who must submit to men in place of direct submission to Christ. As the Bible says, "You cannot serve two masters" (Matt. 6:24, Luke 16:13). As believers, we each have one master, Christ. Bushnell's solid and substantial work on behalf of women shines like a clear beacon of light into today's Christian situation.

Appendix C—Lemons and Grapes Comparison Chart

The following table shows the lemon translations next to suggested amended grape translations for easy comparison. Also included are suggested footnotes to be added to translations. (For a detailed explanation about how the grape translations were produced, please refer to chapters 3 and 7.)

OT Lemon (Gen. 3:16)	OT Grape (Gen. 3:16)
3 Unto the woman he saith, "I will greatly multiply thy sorrow and thy conception; in sorrow thou shalt bring forth children; and thy desire shall be to thy husband and he shall rule over thee."	Unto the woman He said, "A snare has increased thy sorrow and thy sighing. In sorrow thou shalt bring forth children. Thou art turning away to thy husband and he will rule over thee."

NT Lemon #1 (1st Cor. 11:1–16)	NT Grape #1 (1st Cor. 11:1–16)
1 Be ye followers of me, even as I also am of Christ.	1 Be ye followers of me, even as I also am of Christ.
2 Now I praise you, brethren, that ye remember me in all things, and keep the ordinances, as I delivered them to you.	2 Now I praise you, brethren, that ye remember me in all things, and keep the ordinances, as I delivered them to you.
3 But I would have you know, that the head of every man is Christ; and the head of the woman is the man; and the head of Christ is God.	3 But would I have you know that, "the head of every man is Christ and the head of the woman is the man and the head of Christ is God;
4 Every man praying or prophesying, having his head covered, dishonoureth his head.	4 every man praying or prophesying, having his head covered, dishonoureth his head,
5 But every woman that prayeth or prophesieth with her head uncovered dishonoureth her head: for that is even all one as if she were shaven.	5 but every woman that prayeth or prophesieth with her head uncovered dishonoureth her head, for that is even all one as if she were shaven;
6 For if the woman be not covered, let her also be shorn: but if it be a shame for a woman to be shorn or shaven, let her be covered.	6 if the woman be not covered, let her also be shorn, but if it be a shame for a woman to be shorn or shaven, let her be covered"?
7 For a man indeed ought not to cover his head, forasmuch as he is	7 For a man indeed ought not to cover his head, forasmuch as he is

the image and glory of God: but the woman is the glory of the man.	the image and glory of God: and the woman is the glory of the man.
8 For the man is not of the woman; but the woman of the man.	8 For the man is not of the woman; but the woman of the man.
9 Neither was the man created for the woman; but the woman for the man.	9 Neither was the man created on account of the woman; but the woman on account of the man.
10 For this cause ought the woman to have power on her head because of the angels.	10 For this cause ought the woman to have authority over her head because of the angels.
11 Nevertheless neither is the man without the woman, neither the woman without the man, in the Lord.	11 Nevertheless, neither is the man without the woman, nor the woman without the man, in the Lord.
12 For as the woman is of the man, even so is the man also by the woman; but all things of God.	12 For as the woman is of the man, even so is the man also by the woman; but all things of God.
13 Judge in yourselves: is it comely that a woman pray unto God uncovered?	13 Judge in yourselves: it is comely that a woman pray unto God uncovered.
14 Doth not even nature itself teach you, that, if a man have long hair, it is a shame unto him?	14 Even nature itself does not teach you that "if a man have long hair, it is a shame unto him,
15 But if a woman have long hair, it is a glory to her: for her hair is given her for a covering.	15 but if a woman have long hair, it is a glory to her: for her hair is given her for a covering."
16 But if any man seem to be contentious, we have no such custom, neither the churches of God.	16 But if any man seem to be fond of dominating we have no such custom, neither the churches of God.

NT Lemon #2 (1st Cor. 14:29–40)	**NT Grape #2 (1st Cor. 14:29–40)**
29 Let the prophets speak two or three, and let the other judge.	29 Let the prophets speak two or three, and let the other judge.
30 If any thing be revealed to another that sitteth by, let the first hold his peace.	30 If any thing be revealed to another that sitteth by, let the first hold his peace.
31 For ye may all prophesy one by one, that all may learn, and all may be comforted.	31 For ye may all prophesy one by one, that all may learn, and all may be comforted.
32 And the spirits of the prophets are subject to the prophets. 33 For God is not the author of confusion, but of peace, as in all churches of the saints.	32 And the spirits of the prophets are subject to the prophets. 33 For God is not the author of confusion, but of peace, as in all churches of the saints.
34 Let your women keep silence in the churches: for it is not permitted unto them to speak; but they are	34 "Let your women keep silence in the churches: for it is not permitted unto them to speak; but they are

commanded to be under obedience, as also saith the law.	commanded to be under obedience, as also saith the law.
35 And if they will learn any thing, let them ask their husbands at home: for it is a shame for women to speak in the church.	35 And if they will learn any thing, let them ask their husbands at home: for it is a shame for women to speak in the church."
36 What? came the word of God out from you? or came it unto you only?	36 What? came the word of God out from you? or came it unto you only?
37 If any man think himself to be a prophet, or spiritual, let him acknowledge that the things that I write unto you are the commandments of the Lord.	37 If any man think himself to be a prophet, or spiritual, let him acknowledge that the things that I write unto you are the commandments of the Lord.
38 But if any man be ignorant, let him be ignorant.	38 But if any man be ignorant, let him be ignorant.
39 Wherefore, brethren, covet to prophesy, and forbid not to speak with tongues.	39 Wherefore, brethren, covet to prophesy, and forbid not to speak with tongues.
40 Let all things be done decently and in order.	40 Let all things be done decently and in order.

NT Lemon #3 (Eph. 5:22–24)	**NT Grape #3 (Eph. 5:21–24)**
21 and be subject to one another in the fear of Christ.	21 … willingly submitting yourselves one to another in the fear of God.
22 Wives, [be subject] to your own husbands, as to the Lord.	22 Wives to your own husbands, as to the Lord.
23 For the husband is the head of the wife, as Christ also is the head of the church, He Himself [being] the Savior of the body.	23 For the husband is the head of the wife, as Christ also is the head of the church, He Himself [being] the Savior of the body.
24 But as the church is subject to Christ, so also the wives [ought to be] to their husbands in everything.	24 Therefore as the church is willingly submitted to Christ, so let the wives willingly submit to their own husbands in everything.
	Note: This passage could benefit from a footnote in translations similar to the following:
	These verses are used as the main support in the New Testament for the belief that wives are to be under the headship of their husbands and that they need to submit or be subject (understood to mean "obey") in everything. The verb translated "to subject" is from two Greek words: *hupo,* meaning "next after" or "under" and *tasso,* meaning

"arrange." The sense of this word in a Christian context can be defined as yielding one's preferences to another, where no principle is involved, rather than asserting one's rights. Paul used this word to express how we should comport ourselves with one another in Ephesians 5:21, and Peter used it likewise in 1st Peter 5:5. If Paul had intended to convey the meaning "obey," he could have used the Greek word, *hupakouo,* which means "to obey," such as he did in Colossians 3:22 and Ephesians 6:1.

Christ demonstrated how husbands should love their wives and how they could make it possible for their wives to respect them: by loving them to the extent of willingly laying down themselves for them. Christ, as the "head," did not demand submission, but won it by His self-sacrificing love. As a new creation, as a new man in Christ, according to Paul, man is to love his wife in the same way Christ did when He laid down his life for the church (Eph. 5:25).

NT Lemon #4 (Col. 3:18)	NT Grape #4 (Col. 3:18)
18 Wives, be subject to your own husbands, as it is fitting in the Lord.	18 Wives, be subject to your own husbands, as it is fitting in the Lord. **Note:** No change to the translation is necessary except possibly a footnote referencing Ephesians 5:22–24.

NT Lemon #5 (1st Tim. 2:8–15)	NT Grape #5 (1st Tim. 2:8–15)
8 I will therefore that men pray every where, lifting up holy hands, without wrath and doubting. 9 In like manner also, that women adorn themselves in modest apparel, with shamefacedness and sobriety; not with broided hair, or gold, or pearls, or costly array; 10 But (which becometh women professing godliness) with good	8 I will therefore that men pray every where, lifting up holy hands, without wrath and doubting. 9 In like manner also, that women adorn themselves in modest apparel, with shamefacedness and sobriety; not with broided hair, or gold, or pearls, or costly array; 10 But (which becometh women professing godliness) with good

works.

11 Let the woman learn in silence with all subjection.

12 But I suffer not a woman to teach, nor to usurp authority over the man, but to be in silence.

13 For Adam was first formed, then Eve.

14 And Adam was not deceived, but the woman being deceived was in the transgression.

15 Notwithstanding she shall be saved in childbearing, if they continue in faith and charity and holiness with sobriety.

works.

11 Let the woman learn in silence with all subjection.

12 But I suffer not a woman to teach, nor to usurp authority over the man, but to be in silence.

13 For Adam was first formed, then Eve.

14 And Adam was not deceived, but the woman being deceived was in the transgression.

15 Notwithstanding she shall be saved in childbearing, if they continue in faith and charity and holiness with sobriety.

Note: No change to the translation is necessary; however, the addition of a footnote similar to the following would be very helpful:

All of these instructions were written by Paul to Timothy because of a situation in the church that was due to the Ephesian culture. Ephesians were greatly under the influence of the worship of the Roman goddess Diana (same as the Greek goddess, Artemis). Every sentence that Paul wrote concerning women (and men) in this lemon passage can be understood in light of certain temple practices in that worship (Ephesian men lifted up hands in prayer to Diana for victory in battle; women wore fine jewelry and clothing and hairdos to worship Diana; women who worshipped Diana believed in female superiority and their right to dominate men; women believed they would die in childbirth if they offended the goddess). There were newly converted women in the church in Ephesus who were still very much under the influence of their old idolatrous worship of Diana. Paul was telling Timothy how to educate them in Christian truth.

In verses 11–14, Paul was telling Timothy to warn a particular woman who had been converted from the

	worship of Diana, that, just as the young Eve in the garden was deceived, she too, as a new convert, could be deceived. She should learn from others in Christ, even males, who were older in the Lord than her, like Adam was older than Eve. She needed to set aside her old cultic belief in female superiority and learn, even from males.
NT Lemon #6 (Tit. 2:3–5) 3 The aged women likewise, that they be in behaviour as becometh holiness, not false accusers, not given to much wine, teachers of good things; 4 That they may teach the young women to be sober, to love their husbands, to love their children, 5 To be discreet, chaste, keepers at home, good, obedient to their own husbands, that the word of God be not blasphemed.	**NT Grape #6 (Tit. 2:3–5)** 3 The aged women likewise, that they be in behaviour as becometh holiness, not false accusers, not given to much wine, teachers of good things; 4 That they may teach the young women to be sober, to love their husbands, to love their children, 5 To be discreet, chaste, keepers at home, good, obedient to their own husbands, that the word of God be not blasphemed. **Note:** No change to the translation is necessary; however, the addition of a footnote similar to the 1st Peter 3 note would be very helpful.
NT Lemon #7 (1st Pet. 3:1–6) 1 Likewise, ye wives, [be] in subjection to your own husbands; that, if any obey not the word, they also may without the word be won by the conversation of the wives; 2 While they behold your chaste conversation [coupled] with fear. 3 Whose adorning let it not be that outward [adorning]of plaiting the hair, and of wearing of gold, or of putting on of apparel; 4 But [let it be] the hidden man of the heart, in that which is not corruptible, [even the ornament] of a meek and quiet spirit, which is in the sight of God of great price. 5 For after this manner in the old	**NT Grape #7 (1st Pet. 3:1–6)** 1 Likewise, ye wives, in subjection to your own husbands, that if any obey not the word, without the word they also may be won by the behavior of the wives 2 While they behold with fear your holy conduct. 3 Whose adorning let it not be that outward [adorning] of plaiting the hair, and of wearing of gold, or of putting on of apparel; 4 But [let it be] the hidden man of the heart, in that which is not corruptible, [even the ornament] of a meek and quiet spirit, which is in the sight of God of great price. 5 For after this manner in the old

time the holy women also, who trusted in God, adorned themselves, being in subjection unto their own husbands:

6 Even as Sara obeyed Abraham, calling him lord: whose daughters ye are, as long as ye do well, and are not afraid with any amazement.

---

time the holy women also, who trusted in God, adorned themselves, being in subjection unto their own husbands:

6 Even as Sarah obeyed Abraham, calling him lord: whose daughters ye are, as long as ye do well, and are not afraid with any amazement.

Note: Verses 1 and 2 could benefit from a footnote in translations similar to the following:

These verses do not mean that a woman must submit to her husband absolutely and never say a word. They mean, instead, that a woman should live out, or demonstrate, the truth of the Word of God before her husband. This means she will submit to him willingly, unless for conscience' sake she cannot. If he asks her to do something that violates the Word of God and His holiness, she will not submit to him, but to Christ. She can certainly speak about her faith in Christ to her husband. She will follow Christ and live righteously in the hope of awakening her husband's proper fear of God and helping him be won to Christ. If she suffers for this, this is well-pleasing to God.

Verses 3 to 6 could also benefit from a reference to the footnote on Ephesians 5:21–24 about the meaning of *hupotasso* (regarding subjection). Also, a note could be added about Abraham submitting to Sarah in the matter of Ishmael, showing mutual submission in their marriage relationship.

Bibliography

Bio. "Susan B. Anthony Biography." Say Media, Inc., 2016.
http://www.biography.com/people/susan-b-anthony-
194905/videos/susan-b-anthony-the-quaker-belief-2080101528
(accessed September 5, 2016).

Bristow, John T. "What Paul Really Said About Women: The Apostle's
Liberating Views on Equality in Marriage, Leadership, and Love."
San Francisco: Harper & Row, 1988.
http://www.beliefnet.com/faiths/christianity/2003/07/what-paul-
really-said-about-women.aspx (accessed June 30, 2016).

Burleson, Wade. "Artemis and the End of Us: Evangelical Errors
Regarding Women." Istoria Ministries Blog. February 22, 2013.
http://www.wadeburleson.org/2013/02/artemus-and-end-of-us-
evangelical.html (accessed September 14, 2016).

Bushnell, Katharine C. *God's Word to Women: One Hundred Bible
Studies on Woman's Place in the Church and Home.*
Minneapolis: Christians for Biblical Equality, 2003. (The original
book is available at: www.godswordtowomen.org. A condensed
version is available on Amazon Kindle under the title, God's Word
to Women. The original is recommended.)

Encarta Dictionary. In Microsoft Office Word 2010. Microsoft
Corporation, 2010 (software program).

ESV Permanent Text Edition. Crossway: 2016.
http://www.esv.org/about/pt-changes/ (accessed September 18,
2016).

Foh, Susan T. "What is the Woman's Desire?" Westminister
Theological Seminary: The Westminster Theological Journal 37
(1974/75) 376-83.
https://faculty.gordon.edu/hu/bi/ted_hildebrandt/otesources/01-
genesis/text/articles-books/foh-womansdesire-wtj.pdf (accessed
August 30, 2016).

Greek Interlinear Bible. Scripture4All Publishing. 2010.
http://www.scripture4all.org/OnlineInterlinear/NTpdf/1co11.pdf
(accessed September 2, 2016).

"Greek Texts." From Bible Hub, Greek Text Analysis. 2016.
http://biblehub.com (accessed September 19, 2016).

Horn, Wade. "Of Elephants and Men." Fatherhood Today. From
Gordon MacRae. "In the Absence of Fathers: A Story of
Elephants and Men." June 20, 2012.
http://thesestonewalls.com/gordon-macrae/in-the-absence-of-

fathers-a-story-of-elephants-and-men/ (accessed September 5, 2016).

Hyatt, Susan. *10 Things Jesus Taught About Women—And a Few Things He Didn't Teach.* Grapevine: International Christian Women's History Project & Hall of Fame, 2009.

Hyatt, Susan. *In the Spirit We're Equal: The Spirit, The Bible, and Women—A Revival Perspective.* Grapevine: Hyatt Press, 1998.

KJV Exhaustive Concordance Greek Dictionary. Cedar Rapids: Thomas Nelson. In Laridian (software program).

Lane, Bo. "How Many Pastors Are Addicted to Porn? The Stats are Surprising." http://www.expastors.com/how-many-pastors-are-addicted-to-porn-the-stats-are-surprising (accessed August 25, 2016).

Leonowens, Anna H. *The English Governess at the Siamese Court.* Boston: Fields, Osgood, & Co., 1870.

MacArthur, John. "The Subordination and Equality of Women." From "Grace to You" sermon, April 25, 1976. http://www.gty.org/resources/sermons/1844/the-subordination-and-equality-of-women#top (accessed August 31, 2016).

Nestle, Eberhard. *Η ΚΑΙΝΗ ΔΙΑΘΗΚΗ.* Text with Critical Apparatus. British and Foreign Bible Society, 1904. From Bible Hub. http://biblehub.com/interlinear (accessed August 31, 2016).

Penn-Lewis, Jesse. *The Magna Charta of Woman.* Minneapolis: Bethany Fellowship, 1975.

"Resources for Learning New Testament Greek." http://www.ntgreek.org/learn_nt_greek/verbs1.htm (accessed August 21, 2016).

Senior, Jennifer. "In Conversation: Antonin Scalia." New York News and Politics. 2013. http://nymag.com/news/features/antonin-scalia-2013-10/index3.html (accessed September 23, 2016).

Sojourners. "Bonhoeffer Quotes to Remember: A Pastor Who Resisted Evil Unto Death." https://sojo.net/articles/11-bonhoeffer-quotes-remember-pastor-who-resisted-evil-unto-death (accessed August 31, 2016).

Trombley, Charles. *Who Said Women Can't Teach?* NJ: Bridge Publishing, Inc., 1985.

Thayer, Joseph H. Thayer's Greek-English Lexicon of the New Testament. HELPS Word-studies, 2011 by Helps Ministries, Inc. (accessed via Bible Hub July 3, 2016).

Vine, W. E., Merrill F. Unger, and William White, Jr. *Vine's Complete Expository Dictionary of Old and New Testament Words.* Thomas Nelson, 1996.

Wijngaards Institute for Catholic Research. "Greek Philosophy on the Inferiority of Women." quoted from Aristotle, Politica, ed. Loeb Classical Library, 1254 b 10–14. http://www.womenpriests.org/traditio/infe_gre.asp (accessed October 16, 2016).

Wikipedia. "First Great Awakening." 2016. https://en.wikipedia.org/wiki/First_Great_Awakening (accessed August 31, 2016).

Wiles, James. "Zechariah and Elizabeth: A Silence Broken," Biblical Illustrator, Winter 2007–08.

Young, Sarah. Jesus Calling. Nashville: Thomas Nelson, 2004.

Websites Used for Bible Verses

BibleGateway. https://www.biblegateway.com.

Bible Hub. http://biblehub.com.

Bible in Basic English. http://www.biblestudytools.com/bbe.

Blue Letter Bible. https://www.blueletterbible.org.

77577674R00206

Made in the USA
Lexington, KY
29 December 2017